W9-BNM-639

Are You Old Enough to Read This Book?

Reflections on Midlife

Are You Old Enough to Read This Book?

Reflections on Midlife

Edited by Deborah H. DeFord

Introduction by Linda Ellerbee

The Reader's Digest Association, Inc.
Pleasantville, N.Y./Montreal

With many thanks to David Sendler, editor-in-chief of New Choices *magazine, and his staff, especially Gail Harlow, executive editor, Jane Healey, research editor, and Jo Ann Tomback, administrative assistant, without whom this book would not have been possible.*

—Deborah DeFord

PROJECT ART EDITOR:
Jane Wilson

All the material in this book, except for the introduction, has appeared previously in *New Choices* magazine.
For dates of first publication, see page 192.

Library of Congress Cataloging in Publication Data

Are you old enough to read this book : reflections on midlife/ introduction by Linda Ellerbee : edited by Deborah DeFord.
p. cm.
ISBN 0-89577-978-1
1. Midlife age—United States. 2. Aging—Social aspects—United States. I. DeFord, Deborah H.
HQ1059.5.U5A74 1997 97-14158
305.244—dc21

Printed in the United States of America

… it does happen.
One morning you wake up
and your age begins with the number five.

— Linda Ellerbee

TABLE OF CONTENTS

ON MARRIAGE

ON PARENTS & CHILDREN

TABLE OF CONTENTS

ON FRIENDS & LOVERS

ON WORK & NEW CHALLENGES

ON VALUES

THE DAY IT HAPPENS

by Linda Ellerbee

Unless you die first, it does happen.

One morning you wake up and your age begins with the number five.

Personally, I blame the moon. If a year were 16 months long, you would be only 37. I remember 37. Hair down to there, breasts up to here. Horizons still unlimited. Possibilities still infinite. Okay, maybe not infinite. At 37, I did begin to understand that I might not become a brain surgeon, a possibility, no matter how impractical, to which I had clung for years. It could happen, I would say to myself. It could.

At 50, I finally knew it couldn't.

I am not going to become a brain surgeon. I am not going to play third base for the Yankees. I am probably never going to live in France. It's highly unlikely that I shall ever stop the show on a Broadway stage. Choices have been made. At 50, to quote the great 20th-century philosopher Popeye, "I yam what I yam."

The good news is that I'm not what my parents were. Few baby boomers are. Our parents, at 50, were old. Settled. Sedentary. Set in their ways. They watched television. They played bridge. Some played golf. They did not go rock climbing. They never heard of a StairMaster. Take a look at Goldie Hawn. Did your mother look like that at 50? How about Mick Jagger? Was your father doing that at 50?

So here we are, the baby boomers, this huge lump of population, this basketball moving through the snake, doing our best to redefine what it means to get older. What can we do to change the process? How can we age, if age we must, in ways different from our parents? Can we hang on to our looks, our energy — our jobs? Can we compete with 30-year-olds? Can we learn new tricks? Can we still change the world?

We are a generation that believes we can have it our way, mainly because we so often have. Most of us do not face this age thing gracefully. We fight. Some harder than others. Some of us go into heavy denial. What do you mean — the horizon is no longer too far away to see?

Ah, but tomorrow has always seemed such an important word to us, and such a long one.

Then we learn the truth.

We can exercise ourselves to the skin and bone. We can eat nothing but broccoli. We can pay the plastic surgeon, dye our hair, date (and/or marry) much younger men and women, boogie the night away, quit old careers, start new businesses, make new friends and change old habits, but we cannot stop time. We cannot go back and be who we were. Those people are gone. We must, eventually, accept what is. Fact doesn't stop being fact just because you don't like it.

It's that simple, but simple never was the same as easy. So many of us are, at 50, megastressed. And for cause. Many waited to become parents until we were in our late 30s, or even our 40s. Few have had the luxury of not having to work for a living. Most of us are tired a lot. We're taking on twice what our parents did while flailing about with modern conveniences like cell phones, computers, and remote controls that are supposed to save us time —but in the end, mine don't. Do yours?

And we worry. We worry about breast cancer, prostate cancer —and wonder why we seem to know so many people with cancer. Did our parents, when they were 50, see their friends dying of cancer, or AIDS? We worry that Social Security won't be there for us. We worry about insurance, debt, and money in general. We worry about our kids. Some of them are grown and still living at home. These are the people who are going to take care of us in our old age? Gimme a break.

Mostly, the reason we worry about getting old is because, when you get down to the truth of the matter, it means you have less time left. They say time goes, but they are wrong. Time stays. We go.

They also say that 40 is the old age of youth and 50 is the youth of old age—and they ought to be shot for saying it, for I have come to believe that what being 50 really means is that we are at last, like it or not, grown-ups.

It's not so bad, really. It just takes a little getting used to. So what if the guy flying the plane seems so young? So what if professional athletes begin to look like large children and that doctor looks as if he can't possibly be out of medical school yet and suddenly you begin to notice articles in *People* magazine about famous television stars you've never heard of? So what if you go to high school reunions and discover that people who look old are only your age?

So what if I don't look like Goldie Hawn or Jane Fonda. Hell, I didn't look like them when I was 25, either.

I am healthy, active, trying new things—my first white water rafting trip is scheduled for this spring—and when I look in the mirror I say to myself, "I can't believe you're 52! You look weeks younger!"

See, I laugh at myself better now, too. It's a gift that has come with age. With time. With—dare I say it?—a little wisdom.

Try to think of 50 as a trailhead. It's not, as the old way of thinking would have you believe, all downhill from here. It's the beginning of a new path up a new mountain. Perhaps this book can help smooth your way up this mountain. I hope so. I have been to the top. The view is good. The air is clear. And the horizon still seems a long way away.

NEW AT GETTING OLD

...and just learning what it takes to be a "neophyte codger"

By Roy Blount, Jr.

Since I turned 50 on October 4, 1991, I have rammed my canoe into a log with an alligator on it in the Okefenokee Swamp. I have taken up scuba diving, to the extent of going on two dives with people who actually lured sharks into our midst. (This was at first terrifying and then insulting—the sharks showed no interest in me at all.) I have drunk malt liquor for several hours in a juke joint in Clarksdale, Mississippi, in which I noticed a bullet on the floor next to my foot, and then retired to the room where Bessie Smith died. I have ridden a former rodeo horse for eight hours over roughish country in zero-with-the-windchill-factor weather. I have taken a batting lesson from Amos Otis, the former major leaguer. And I have sung "Wooly Bully" and "Louie Louie" with an authors' rock 'n' roll band on an eight-city bus tour.

On the other hand, I have not been getting any younger. In fact, do you know what Amos Otis said to me? "You've got some old habits." And the other day in the video-rental place, I complained about the volume at which the employees were listening to Paula Abdul in concert.

"Does it have to be so *loud*?" I asked the young woman at the counter. She looked at me uncomprehendingly.

"Does it *have* to be?" was all she said. She evidently couldn't associate having to be with being loud. I got the feeling that she associated having to be with . . . whatever I was, to her.

So, I'm trying to figure out some way that I can get younger. Or at least newer.

It makes no sense to me that I am older than I think of my father as being. He died when he was 60, but I always think of him as being roughly in his 40s. Now I'm in my 50s and trying to put that into perspective.

To my children, it's simple: I'm a lot older than they are. It used to be that I was primarily a lot bigger and more responsible. But now my son is markedly larger than I am, at least if you go by such crude measures as physical stature; and my daughter is married, whereas for me, six years is too soon after divorce to settle down.

My children are adults. That is, young adults. Adults with an asterisk. (I heard a couple of people their age *reminiscing* the other day. Talking about the old days. Give me a break.) But, still, adults. So I am a person who is a lot older than adults. I would rather not look at it like that.

Here's how I would rather look at it: I'm in my *early* 50s. I'm new at getting old.

Hey, yeah, toss in a Paula Abdul move; I'm getting into a fresh field. I'm a rookie old-timer, a fledgling gaffer, a tenderfoot duffer, a whipper-snapper as far as senescence goes, a raw AARP recruit.

This notion (as opposed to the look the young woman in the video store gave me) fits my self-image. See, I was born in October and started first grade a month before I was 6, so I was always younger than nearly everyone in my class. And I was a late bloomer physically. I was always among the last of my friends to ride a bike, to grow body hair, to go through the change of voice, to start going steady and to get a driver's license.

Trailing my peers was hard on me at the time, but now it's cool. Who wants to be in the forefront of a bunch of paunchy old guys?

Are you familiar with the term *neoteny*? It means the retention, due to slow maturation, of immature characteristics in the adult of a species.

For instance, grown-up ostriches retain the downy feathers of nestlings. Grown-up dogs still play with balls. And grown-up human beings have the following characteristics of newborns: proportionately large heads, relative hairlessness, natural defenselessness.

Humans remain protected babes-in-arms and spoon-fed tads and indulged adolescents much longer than other animals do. And in advancing human societies, each generation remains larval longer than the previous one. Accordingly, our brains grow larger and we develop technology and give a lot more thought to what we want to do in life. I grew up feeling underdeveloped. Now I feel neotenic.

Okay, I don't want to get *too* bright-eyed and bubbly, because those of you who have been getting old for years—all you *veteran* senior citizens, all you old maturity hands—will start giving me a hard time.

"Kid," you'll be telling me, "better take it easy. When you've been getting old for as long as we have, you'll realize it's a long season."

I can hear you saying those things because I have already heard myself saying similarly crusty things to these so-called young adults and felt myself enjoying it. I was talking to a friend the other day who is older than I am by, I don't know, 10 or 12 years—who's counting?—maybe 13 or 14 years. He hunched down in his chair, twisted his face into a magnificent look of crabbiness and declared himself a prime example of *geezerismo*.

Fine. I can get into that. But no matter how old and cranky you become, there's always somebody who's older and crankier. Someone who'll say, "Where do you get off acting old? You're barely in diapers." I don't want to look back all the time—I want to look forward. Rather than run the risk that somebody downright ancient will come along and make me feel callow, I am going to make a *point* of my relative inexperience.

What I am is a neophyte codger, an upstart oldster, a fossil in short pants, a greenhorn graybeard, a Methuselah-come-lately, a 52-year-old wonder who remains a bit damp behind the ears. Not only is most of my living-in-the-past still ahead of me, but I'm gathering even more past while I may. At the millennium I want to be able to lean back in my chair and say, "Ah, the 1990s. Those were the days. When I was just *getting* old. And I was *really* getting it, too, back then. But I'm not resting on my

Proving that middle age is a great time to try new things, Blount joined a camel safari in Kenya.

laurels. As soon as I catch my breath, I'm going to go out and get even older. I'm 59 *already*. No telling how old I'll be tomorrow."

But I'm getting ahead of myself. Right now I want to stress apprenticeship. Maybe I don't ever have to think of age as catching up to me if I think of myself as learning to get old. Think what a great moper and grumbler I'll be when I'm 80! Then, too, what if I don't make it to 80? Well, maybe in my 70s I'll set aside an hour or so every week to grumble into a tape recorder, so I can leave something behind that will give people an idea of what might have been. Then, too, what if I don't make it to 70? Well, I'll worry about that in my 60s.

What I intend to do now, in my 50s, is develop a whole new concept of *old*.

In fact, I might discard old altogether and replace it with ol'. As in any ol' time. I was comfortable with the concept of ol' long before I gave any thought to getting old: You ol' scamp; look at that cute little ol' puppy there; I'm gonna get me a big ol' chocolate cone; we'll have ourselves a fine ol' time; hooray, here comes good ol' Roy Rogers.

As a matter of fact, my first name goes well with ol'. There is an Ol' Roy brand of dog food. I bet I could get so thoroughly into being ol' that people would say of me, "Ol' Roy, he's come through to the other side of ol': Lo! Ol' Roy put the L-O in mellow."

One thing about being new at something, you can be a little obnoxious about it, and people will say, "Well, give him time. He'll outgrow this, too."

And if I do, I'll try being new at being *ancient*. ■

Roy Blount, Jr., is a contributing editor to The Atlantic Monthly.

Be Dependable, Live Longer

By Myrna Lewis

Nice guys may finish last, but they also live longer. A recent study has found that conscientious and dependable men and women are 30 percent less likely to die in any given year of adulthood than their less prudent peers.

The study, conducted by Howard S. Friedman, Ph.D., a psychologist at the University of California at Riverside, interprets data amassed from research on 1,178 California boys and girls that began in the early 1920s and lasted through the 1980s, when most of the subjects were past age 70. "We found that conscientious people live, on average, about two to three years longer than other people, though we don't know exactly why," Friedman says.

The presumption is that if someone is dependable and orderly, he or she will lead a healthier life. But can a person learn how to be conscientious in midlife or later? Friedman says yes. "You can strive to make your actions more conscious and deliberate. Develop a list of goals to reinforce a positive habit you are trying to develop. Take an active rather than passive role in dealing with your problems." Others who have a tough time meeting responsibilities might consider some form of counseling to help them understand and modify their behavior.

Finally, Friedman says, conscientious people deserve more respect than they usually get. "Don't write off such a person as a nerd," he counsels. "Nice guys—and women—are also nice folks to be around."

So Your Body and Mind Won't Let You Down

By Nissa Simon

Fresh notions have turned upside down the melancholy view that aging inevitably goes hand in hand with deterioration and decrepitude. Today, a man of 50 can expect to blow out the candles on 27 more birthday cakes, and a woman of 50 will probably hear 32 more choruses of "Happy Birthday to You." Best of all, those years can be healthy, vigorous and productive.

Put Breakfast Back on the Schedule

"To help ward off disease and stay healthy, there's no question that you've got to eat at least five servings of fruits and vegetables a day. And if you don't start your day with breakfast, you're not going to make that quota," says Paul Lachance, Ph.D. "I'm a fan of the classic breakfast. Orange juice, hash browns, an egg and whole wheat toast sounds good to me."

According to Lachance, professor of food science and nutrition at Rutgers, the State University of New Jersey in New Brunswick, many people tend to grab a cup of coffee and a vitamin pill for breakfast and skip lunch. Then, because they haven't had enough food during the day, they eat too much heavy food at night. The ideal? A good breakfast, a main meal at lunch and a light supper.

Keep Moving for Better Health—and Better Sex

Exercise may not be the fountain of youth, but it's probably the closest we'll get. Exercise increases cardiovascular endurance, keeps cholesterol levels in check, raises levels of "good" HDL cholesterol, builds bone and revs up metabolism to help burn extra calories, thus protecting against creeping weight gain.

Such activities as brisk walking, cross-country skiing, cycling and swimming will help you keep in shape. But don't forget resistance training. Thirty minutes with weights or machines a couple of times a week will help guard against age-related loss of muscle.

The added payoff turns out to be a satisfying sex life. "Sexual response for both men and women depends on adequate blood flow," says Irwin Goldstein, M.D., professor of urology at Boston University School of Medicine. "And if you want good blood flow, you must avoid conditions associated with artery blockage."

The same factors that contribute to the risk of a heart attack—hypertension, diabetes, high cholesterol and obesity—also interfere with a gratifying sex life, says Goldstein. So it follows that exercise, which helps your heart, also helps your sex life.

Use Your Brain

Add mental activity to physical activity, and you can help protect yourself against the effects that researchers otherwise see in the aging brain. "Put lightly, it comes down to 'use it or lose it,'" says Larry Squire, Ph.D., of the University of California, San Diego. Remain interested in the world around you, stretch your mind and continue to work. Although small declines in some functions can be detected from the third decade of life onward, the brain continues to adapt by forming new connections. "It retains a lot of flexibility and capacity for growth and change well into old age."

"When it comes to mental health, 50 is the prime of life," adds Ron Kessler, Ph.D., a professor at the University of Michigan's Institute for Social Research. "Rates of anxiety are at their lowest, and the incidence of depression is also quite low."

Myths about the midlife crisis abound, notes Kessler, but, compared with people at any other time of life, men and women now reaching their 50s are in better shape. Research suggests that these men and women remain in good health, have done away with the anxieties of youth, have seen their children leave the nest and have probably paid off the mortgage. "This will be a golden decade," promises Kessler, "so enjoy it."

DO YOU THINK YOUNG—OR OLD?

A quiz that may give you the answer

By Lawrence Eisenberg

In the early 1980s, a roller-skating craze hit the country. Reporting on it for a magazine, I visited New York's hottest skating club, where I quickly became a roller whiz. A year later, my enthusiasm unspent, I ordered custom-made skates and decided to try them out on the street. Strapping on knee and elbow protectors, I zoomed through the doorway of my apartment building. I was used to skating on level, polyurethaned wood floors, but I was now headed rapidly down a city sidewalk that was rough, uneven and sloped toward the corner. Seconds later, I crashed. Two 60-ish women walking past stared down at me, and one commented, "No shame!"

If this were an incident out of your life, who would you be? The mature but flexible person who chooses to take a chance, possibly a foolish one, on roller skates? The more conservative, sensible citizen, motivated by the physical limitations and behavioral proprieties of middle age? Or somewhere in between?

The following quiz may give you a clue. Taking it with you are four experts: Bob Arnot, M.D., a health and medical correspondent for CBS News and author of *Dr. Bob Arnot's Guide to Turning Back the Clock* (Little, Brown); David G. Folks, M.D., professor of psychiatry at Creighton University and the University of Nebraska; Myrna Lewis, assistant professor at Mount Sinai School of Medicine and *New Choices* columnist; and sex therapist Ruth Westheimer, Ed.D., author of *Heavenly Sex* (NYU Press) and other books. After taking the quiz, check the scoring instructions and compare your answers with our experts'.

1. Your doctor has just said that your blood pressure and cholesterol are high and you're 22 pounds overweight. Running to catch the bus home, you get so winded that you collapse into your seat. Your reaction is:

a. I'm going down the tubes, so I might as well update my will.

b. Tomorrow I'll cut down on the chocolate bars and hot dogs.

c. As soon as I get off this bus, I'm checking out every avenue of exercise and diet to see how I can salvage myself.

2. Your sex life is:

a. A pleasant memory, but it's a relief not to be in the arena anymore.

b. Substantially curtailed, but sometimes surprisingly exciting.

c. A constant, uninhibited challenge to find new ways to please and be pleased, and I don't care who knows it.

3. You've just watched a TV magazine program reviewing the Oklahoma City bombing and the rising statistics on illegal assault weapons and teenage pregnancies. The program's host says, "Whatever happened to the 'good old days'?" and you think:

a. They're gone forever, and all we have left are rudeness, violence and no respect for age.

b. I miss the gentleness and simplicity of those days and wish they were more adaptable to today's fast lane.

c. Were they so good? I don't remember a year without natural disasters, violent crime and at least one war somewhere.

4. Every Friday night:

a. My spouse and I play bridge with our two closest and oldest friends.

b. We go to dinner with an alternating group of pals.

c. We try to do something different from what we did the previous week, even if it turns out to be a disappointment.

5. Arriving at the multiplex cinema, you discover that *The Bridges of Madison County* is sold out. Your other options are *Braveheart* and *Die Hard with a Vengeance*. You will:

a. Go home and watch your video of *It's a Wonderful Life*.

b. Toss a coin to decide which film to see.

c. See *Die Hard* . . .

6. When you hear young people using expressions such as "cave" (for capitulate), "lame" (bad), "chill" (calm down) and "wiped" (exhausted), what's your reaction?

a. They're ridiculous and typical of the rampant illiteracy in their generation.

b. They're a bit silly, but they'll get over it just as we got over "sharp" and "groovy" and "hepcat."

c. They're cool.

7. You're about to be forcibly retired by your longtime employer. Your reaction is:

a. Hooray, now I can spend the rest of my life golfing and being a couch potato.

b. Who do they think they're pushing around? I'm going to contact my lawyer.

c. My lawyer's on the case, and in the meantime, I'll investigate other opportunities in my field or consider trying something new.

8. If you were to read tabloid reports that Brad Pitt rarely showers, your reaction would be:

a. Brad who?

b. That's too much information.

c. It's his life, and the smell-o-vision concept never made it into theaters.

9. How do you feel about revealing your age?

a. It's nobody's business.

b. I'm proud of it.

c. You show me your driver's license and I'll show you mine.

10. If someone calls you a prig, you:

a. Feel flattered because it indicates that you have moral standards.

b. Spend a little time on self-examination.

c. Assume that he's mispronouncing some other word.

SCORING

Give yourself 10 points for each *a* answer; 5 points for *b*; 0 points for *c*. A total score of 55–100 suggests that, like some ancient Egyptians, you may be too tightly wrapped. 30–50 means you're middle of the road, with possibilities. 0–25 rates you flexible, young at heart and open to new experiences.

Here's how the experts voted:

QUESTION 1:
Arnot, Folks and Lewis picked *c*.
Arnot: "I'm going to rip all the fat out of my coronary arteries, expand my lungs, build bigger muscles and bike to work."
Folks: "Anyone who votes *a* needs some rehabilitation."
Lewis: "I would consider it slowly suicidal not to take action, especially since I know what action to take. An *a* vote is a very passive and depressive approach."

Westheimer chose *b*: "It's realistic that people say, 'Not today but tomorrow.' But this is more a medical question and has to be discussed with a health professional."

QUESTION 2:
Arnot and Westheimer voted *c*.
Arnot: "Because it's the perfect answer."
Westheimer: "Anything that has to do with sexual activity should be like a surprise, should be kept interesting. Anybody who picks *c* would get from me an A-plus."

Lewis says she would fall between *b* and *c*. "Those who vote *c* are the people I love, who have the true spirit, who have the gift of life, but I don't think many are that wildly sexual in later life. I am not totally uninhibited, and I do care a little bit about who knows it. A *b* vote doesn't mean that your sex life has to be curtailed. But it also doesn't mean hanging from the chandelier, which *c* implies."

Folks picked *b*: "I just happen to know that as people get older, their frequency of sexual encounters decreases, but that doesn't change the excitement or pleasure that goes with it."

QUESTION 3:
The entire quartet voted *c*.
Arnot: "It's a great answer."
Folks: "The media coming into your living room has a lot to do with the increased awareness of natural and other disasters. In different centuries, I'm sure people didn't have any awareness of what was going on 100 miles away from them."

Lewis offers a qualification: "I do feel that there's a special problem with gun proliferation. But I think we can figure out what to do about the incidence of teenage pregnancies if we can muster the will to do so."
Westheimer: "It's not true that the good old days were all so good."

QUESTION 4:
Arnot, Folks and Lewis voted *c*.
Arnot: "I think you have to see how much further you can go. Try flying a high-performance jet fighter—you can do that now as a civilian. I've flown an F-16. Another suggestion is to see how much closer you can come to the surface of a local river when you bungee jump off the bridge."
Folks: "Variety is the spice of life, and it's a good thing not to get into a rut."
Lewis: "I like to see my friends, but not that often. A vote for *a* sounds like a very secure way to live your life, but it doesn't allow enough high adventure for me."

Westheimer saw value in all three choices: "There is something very comforting about once a week playing with the same people. Keep the Friday night for your best friends, so they don't look for another couple to play with. Thursday night, do something different."

QUESTION 5:
Arnot and Folks voted *c*.
Arnot: "Put down your money for *Die Hard* to see if Bruce Willis could really keep up with you at the gym."
Folks: "I saw the reviews on *Die Hard*, and they looked much more exciting than *Braveheart*. I really admire Bruce Willis because he has a tough job—he's married to someone [Demi Moore] who's much better at acting than he is."

Westheimer chose *a*. "*Die Hard* is violent? Go home and put a good video on your VCR. I don't know what *A Wonderful Life* is. If it's a romantic movie, like nostalgia, okay."

Lewis: "None of the above. I would rather look around town for some interesting new film or go to a cabaret or a jazz club with somebody wonderful. Or I'd call up a friend and have an evening of conversation."

QUESTION 6:

Arnot, Lewis and Westheimer voted *c*.

Arnot: "Those expressions are cool; and for more, just ask the young people what kind of surfboard they're riding."

Lewis: "I remember the things I used to say: 'hip' and 'groovy' and 'neat.' I'm from a farm, and we said 'heck' and 'darn,' and I said 'garsh' a lot."

Westheimer: "The reason I say 'cool' is because that's the term my grandson used all the time when he was 5."

Folks: "I have a hard time picking between *b* and *c*. Those expressions are kind of silly, but then you think back and realize that they're kind of cute, too, a part of the life cycle."

QUESTION 7:

Arnot and Folks voted *c*.

Arnot: "I've contacted my investment banker, and I'm going to buy my own company. Here's something wild: I'm going to buy my old company and fire those guys."

Folks: "What's the reason for being forced to retire? If a person is doing his or her job well, that's just flat-out wrong. People are offered a package that may be very attractive, and they think, 'Well, if I turn this down, I may be kicking myself a year from now.' Then they take the package, and they're unhappy about it. They ought to get a good attorney to ensure that their rights are protected. And they ought to see what else is out there."

Westheimer cast her vote for *a*. "Why do you put the couch potato together with the golf? If it's somebody who has hobbies, then they should welcome not having to go to work anymore, assuming there's enough money. To sue could consume a couple of years in misery."

Lewis: "None of those. I wouldn't get a lawyer. If I wanted that job, I would act to find out who made the decision and see if there's a way I can turn this thing around—either by dealing with that person directly or with other people above him or her. I would probably have a couple of options and different income streams on the back burner."

QUESTION 8:

Arnot, Folks and Lewis voted *c*.

Arnot: "You call his agent, because you are younger and better-looking than he is."

Folks: "I couldn't care less—that's his problem. And *Legends of the Fall* wasn't all that great a movie."

Lewis: "Definitely *c*, but also too much information."

Westheimer picked *a*. "Is that guy, Pat—whatever his name is—going to be offended that I don't know who he is?"

QUESTION 9:.

Arnot voted *c*, Folks and Westheimer *b*, and Lewis had her own ideas.

Arnot [who's 47]: "What I'd really rather do is say, 'It's not your chronological age but your biological age that counts.' I've ripped up my driver's license."

Folks [41]: "It doesn't matter to me." [Asked whether it will matter when he's 61, he says no.]

Westheimer [67]: "I'm proud of my age."

Lewis [57]: "I think of age like hair color or height. It's a fact of life, and I'm no more pleased than the other person to get closer to the moment of mortality. I don't know what there is to be proud of, and it is devious not to be straightforward about it."

QUESTION 10:

This was a mixed bag.

Folks: voted *b*: "I'm fairly sensitive to what people say, and I'd want to see how they came up with that conclusion, whether there's any justification for it. I hope that I would conclude they were wrong."

Lewis: "I would do *d*—he must be off the wall and doesn't know me very well."

Arnot: chose *c*: "Assuming he's mispronouncing another word, I'd use kung fu on him."

Westheimer, after voting *c*, just giggled. ■

Lawrence Eisenberg is a novelist, magazine writer and a contributing editor to New Choices *magazine.*

DON'T GROW UP

Charles Schulz, the creator of "Peanuts," tells how he keeps his strip—and himself—from getting old.

By Andy Meisler

The Background

Good grief! It's been nearly 45 years since a "little round-headed boy" named Charlie Brown first bared his soul. It was on October 2, 1950, that he made his debut in a brand-new comic strip called *Peanuts.*

The strip's creator was Charles M. "Sparky" Schulz, a 28-year-old correspondence-school art instructor from Minneapolis. The slight, painfully shy former World War II infantryman—nicknamed by his uncle after Sparkplug, the horse in the old *Barney Google* comic strip—had already sold some drawings to the *Saturday Evening Post.* A subsequent proposal for a strip about children attracted interest from the United Feature Syndicate; a long but hope-filled train trip to the syndicate's offices in New York led to a deal.

From the start, *Peanuts* centered on a comedic repertory troupe of economically but elegantly drawn characters, including Charlie Brown, the eternal loser/good sport/survivor; Lucy, the no-nonsense pragmatist; Schroeder, the self-absorbed artist; Snoopy, the swashbuckling master of the imaginary adventure. All seemed to represent different parts of their creator's own complex personality.

Initially, a grand total of seven newspapers carried *Peanuts.* By the mid-1950s, however, the strip's gentle, uncannily perceptive humor had swept around the world like a wistful tidal wave. During the late 1960s, *Peanuts* and Snoopy-mania were at their height: There was a *Life* magazine cover, an Off-Broadway musical and regular television specials, plus books and greeting cards, dolls and clothes and other merchandise beyond reckoning. A truism from the strip—"Happiness is a warm puppy"—found its way into *Bartlett's Familiar Quotations.*

Although *Peanuts* may have lost some of its fad status in recent years, the strip still appears in more than 2,000 papers worldwide. Today, at age 72, Charles Schulz is a millionaire many times over. He is also the father of five children, ranging in age from 36 to 44, from a first marriage that ended in divorce in 1972. He has two stepchildren from his second marriage, to Jean Forsyth, in 1974.

Forty years of honors and riches have left Schulz surprisingly unfazed. Although many successful comic-strip creators employ gag writers and even ghost artists, Schulz still writes, draws, inks and colors all his strips himself. A recent visit to his Santa Rosa, California, studio found him two months' worth of strips ahead of schedule and surrounded by another week's worth in various stages of completion.

He has no plans for retirement. Although gracious and soft-spoken, he seems fiercely proud of his status as a productive popular artist—and still completely, almost compulsively, in touch with the insecurities, anxieties, joys and truths found within.

The Interview

An astounding thing has been happening to me the last couple of years. People come up to me and say, "Are you still drawing the strip?" I want to say to them, "Good grief—who else do you think is drawing it?" I would never let anybody take over. And I have it in my contract that if I die, then my strip dies. This is what my children want, too. They said, "We don't want anybody

else drawing Dad's strip."

People also ask me if there's any message or theme to *Peanuts*. I suppose it might be that Charlie Brown, in spite of always losing, never gives up. But really, I never think about that. I just think about how I'm going to get two or three more good ideas. I draw from day to day.

You see, I work just as hard now, if not harder than I ever have. I think I'm more particular about what I do. My drawing is so much better now—in spite of the fact that I keep reading in articles that I'm not as good as I used to be, and that some people even say I should quit now before the strip deteriorates. But that's nonsense. I think that if a person maintains decent health and can handle the grind, then this is one of those professions where you should get better all the time.

My biggest worry is that I could use up my life. I could use up everything that I have experienced, all the thoughts that I've had about playing baseball when I was a kid and playing hockey and falling in love and being rejected, and all of the other things that happen to us throughout our lives. As you get older, you draw upon these experiences and use them all up until, finally, you're just doing the same things over and over and over.

I also have a great fear of becoming boring. There are a lot of boring people around, and, unfortunately, I think older people can become boring very easily. The way to prevent all that, I suppose, is to maintain an interest in others and forget about yourself. It's a great crime to talk only about yourself and not to express curiosity about other people.

I have found that simply asking other people about themselves can be quite fascinating. My wife, Jeannie, is good that way. It's a little sad, but I find that when she and I are out to dinner with other people, we seem to be the ones asking all the questions. We'll say, "Oh, where were you raised?" Or, "What did your father do?" And oftentimes when we get home at night, I'll say, "You know, Jeannie, you and I were the only ones who asked any questions. Nobody ever asked me anything."

I gave a lecture once to a group of selected high-school students. I said, "Go home tonight and ask your parents where they met. Ask your dad what he did in World War II. Ask your mom if she went to the high-school prom. Talk to your grandmother, and don't just let the thing die; pursue the questioning. Do it now before it's too late." It's this kind of thinking that promotes cartoon ideas. Anybody can think of shallow cartoon situations, but I'm always trying to pursue something a little bit deeper. I suppose we're all at the mercy of the medium in which we work, and a comic strip doesn't give you that much room for a topic like death, but it can be there if you work at it.

I think you also have to make an effort to stay open to the world. I read a lot. I don't read simply for research or to get ideas; I read because I enjoy it. I took a college course in the novel a few years ago, and oddly enough I got an A in it. When I was a kid, I was a lousy student, the way Peppermint Patty is. I never knew what was going on, never did my homework, never did the reading assignments. This time I did all the reading and wrote a paper on Katherine Anne Porter's book *Pale Horse, Pale Rider*. As I wrote it, I pretended I was writing for *The New Yorker*. Afterward, the professor said to me, "I just want you to know that this is a perfect example of what a paper should be."

I also sit in front of the TV. I flip through all the channels. I'll start at 2 and go up to 60, and then when I hit *Northern Exposure*, I'll watch until Janine Turner is on. When she's not on anymore, I'll switch away again. (We almost met last year, but it didn't work out—and I was just crushed.) On the sitcoms, well, all everybody does is feed each other gag lines. They don't converse. Oh, and Jeannie and I always watch *Jeopardy* while we eat dinner. We try to get that last question. Once, I was a whole category!

More seriously, I think that there is a real danger of people thinking that what they see on TV is real life. From watching all the crime shows that are on these days, you get the impression that crime is all around us. Every time a woman pulls her car into a driveway, she's in grave danger. Crime just can't be *that* prevalent.

I think you have to make an effort to stay open to the world. I read a lot ...

I've always liked the funny papers. I'm a great admirer of certain strips, like *Mutts*, *Rose Is Rose*, *For Better or for Worse* and *Cathy*. I hold in complete disdain others that aren't any good or whose artists don't seem to be putting in the effort they should.

I think one of the other things that helps me keep in touch is the ice arena across the street, which I built 25 years ago. The place always has a wonderful mixture of people, from little tiny kids up to old people. I go there every day, and I do hear things now and then. In fact, that's where I first heard the expression "Joe Cool," which is how Snoopy happened to become Joe Cool from time to time.

I never envision my characters growing old, though a couple of them have changed over the years. Charlie Brown, especially, has grown less sarcastic, more gentle. Sally has become much more important. She's developed a personality all her own. She's either very bright or very stupid. It's hard to figure sometimes.

Maybe the real secret to not getting too old is not to grow up. I'm not a complete grown-up, really. I still feel out of place most of the time. At different times I've had trouble traveling and become almost agoraphobic. I'm always insecure and anxious. Somebody asked me in an interview recently, "What are you anxious about?" I said, "If I knew, I wouldn't be anxious."

I have some very good friends in different professions, and I was just with four or five of them a couple of weeks ago. One of them was having a birthday, and we all went out to lunch. And I suddenly realized that I felt a little bit out of place. See, I'm not a businessman, I don't know anything about financial affairs or banking or what attorneys do or things like that. All I know is cartooning, golf, hockey, books and reading and a few more things like that. It's a joy when I find somebody I can relate to.

I'm not Catholic, and I never will be, but right now one of my best friends is a Catholic priest. We play golf together every Thursday. And I have more fun with this guy because he is extremely broad-minded. He knows my fondness for theological thinking and spiritual searching and all of that. I can talk these things over with him.

Am I a religious man? I'll have to let someone else judge that. I'm a firm believer in the Kingdom of God, but I don't know about the afterlife—that baffles me. I think life is a mystery. I have no idea why we're here, where it all came from or where we're all going, and I don't think anybody knows.

But here's one of the things that helps me, personally, to survive. Years and years ago, when I was living in Minneapolis, I met a man who played first viola for the Minneapolis Symphony. And in one of our talks, he said to me, "You know, playing the viola to me is a lot like a religion." And I thought, That's nonsense. What does he mean by that?

But as the years went by, I could almost say that drawing a comic strip for me became a lot like a religion. Because it helps me survive from day to day. I always have this to fall back upon. When everything seems hopeless and all of that, I know I can come to the studio and think: Here's where I'm at home. This is where I belong — in this room, drawing pictures. ■

Andy Meisler is an editor at Los Angeles Magazine *and a frequent contributor to* The New York Times.

How We Deal with Growing Older

By Myrna Lewis

A recent study finds that people tend to have one of three basic attitudes about aging—and that a too-rigid adherence to any one can have negative consequences.

Researcher Anne-Linda Furstenberg, Ph.D., an associate professor at the University of North Carolina at Chapel Hill, based her observations on a series of interviews and focus groups conducted with 50-plus men and women. These are the three kinds of responses she recorded:

- **Type 1's** are those who advocate resistance to and denial of getting older. They believe that aging can be avoided and ignored, as in the response, "You're only as old as you feel."

- **Type 2's** accommodate and accept. They focus on dealing with and compensating for changes brought about by aging.

- **Type 3's** find the notion of aging filled with trouble and pain. They cope by finding solace in religion or other spiritual pursuits.

Problems arise when a person is unable to see life in any terms other than those of his or her basic type. "For example, denying age takes you only so far," notes Furstenberg. "While it can be useful to think of yourself as young at heart, it can be dangerous to think you can still drive a car with seriously impaired eyesight."

Furstenberg believes that people need to become conscious of which type they are and then find an appropriate balance of all three approaches. "Being able to shape a flexible response to age-related changes could be the key to managing growing older more successfully," she notes.

WHO AGE BETTER, MEN OR WOMEN?

Experts rate the sexes on their ability to hold off physical and mental changes—and report on the latest in anti-aging research.

By Andrea Atkins

You know the typical images from movies and TV: The older man is distinguished, wise and virile. The older woman is bent, cranky and usually a victim. Then again, on average, men die six and a half years sooner than women. So who age better, women or men?

British researcher and Oxford University professor Richard Doll, M.D., gives the prize to women. In fact, says Doll, women consistently have a better shot at living at least one year longer than men—until age 105. Only then, he says, is the mortality rate for men and women equal.

Since most of us won't get that old, here's a look at some things that happen as we age, how men and women fare and what, if anything, we can do about it.

Physical Changes

SKIN. Aging skin loses elasticity, collagen, fat and oil glands. The skin itself becomes thinner and often feels and appears drier. On top of that, according to Marianne Berwick, Ph.D., of Memorial Sloan-Kettering Cancer Center in New York City, skin cancer is a major concern for older people. In fact, more than half of all new cases of squamous cell and basal cell skin cancer are diagnosed in people over 65 each year.

Men versus women: According to some surveys, men spend more time in the sun than women and are less likely to use sunscreen. By age 80, men have twice as many melanomas, a potentially fatal form of skin cancer, as women. Women also tend to see a doctor when skin lesions are smaller, which may explain why women's survival rate for this form of skin cancer is better. Yet men have better-looking skin than women as they age—owing to one unlikely-to-change difference between the sexes: shaving. As men take whiskers from their face each day, they also slough away dead cells, which can make skin look old and dull.

What you can do: Most melanomas, experts agree, are caused by an intermittent pattern of exposure to the sun, but the way it works is baffling. At this point, the best advice remains to use caution. Whether or not sunscreens can prevent skin cancer in adults is a subject of hot debate among researchers, but it certainly won't hurt to use a sunscreen. Of course, stay out of the sun between 11 AM and 2 PM, and wear hats, long sleeves and long pants. In addition, on every birthday, have your birthday suit checked for moles and new growths.

As for day-to-day wear and tear on your skin, use gentle skin-care products and avoid overscrubbing. And, in lieu of shaving, women can use a skin-care product formulated with alpha hydroxy acids to freshen the look of their skin.

MUSCLES. After age 30, muscles begin to atrophy. The change, subtle at first, becomes noticeable over time in both men and women. "Even Arnold Schwarzenegger is not as strong today as he was a few years ago," says James Fozard, Ph.D., of the National Institute on Aging.

"Strength and endurance fall off after age 30," agrees John A. Faulkner, Ph.D., of the University of Michigan.

Muscle cells and tissue—unlike skin—says Fozard, do not reproduce. Once they're gone, others won't take their place. That's significant because, as muscle cells weaken and atrophy, you become less able to do everyday chores, such as walking up stairs or lifting and carrying heavy objects. Worse than that, says Faulkner, "weak muscles are much more likely to be injured."

Men versus women: Men develop bigger muscles, so the decline of strength takes longer, according to Faulkner. Hence, a woman in her 70s may find it difficult to walk to the grocery store, but her husband may be able to take over the shopping for an additional 10 years.

What you can do: "You can't do anything about the change in muscle," says Faulkner, "but you can ameliorate it with conditioning. And I would give the same advice to both men and women." Stressing the muscle is the only way to strengthen it, so if you're not involved in some form of strength training, either at home or at a gym or health club, you're not doing anything to stop muscle loss, notes Faulkner.

BONES. With age, bones become more brittle and lose their density. The result: increased chance of fracture. An estimated 250,000 Americans suffer hip fractures each year, most often due to falls.

Men versus women: As with muscle mass, men start out with greater bone density.

"Men start getting fractures about a decade later than women," says University of Chicago's Murray Favus, M.D. "Since men live shorter lives, they may not reach that stage."

"After menopause, women lose bone more quickly. Estrogen replacement therapy slows bone loss, which is why so many doctors recommend it," says Fozard.

What you can do: Exercise, exercise—and more exercise. "Studies have shown that a week of bed rest equals two years of aging on the skeleton," says William Evans, Ph.D., of Pennsylvania State University. The good news is that it doesn't take much exercise to have a positive effect. "Three to four days a week of walking for 40 to 45 minutes per day slows down the rate of bone loss—primarily from the spine," Evans says.

Do men or women exercise more consistently? No studies have answered that question, but Evans notes that when his center sets up exercise programs in the community, women enrollees far outnumber men.

HORMONES. Those chemical substances that travel around your body, causing all kinds of reactions in everything from sex organs to memory to physique, decrease as you age. Scientists are unsure whether the body suffers without them or simply has no use for them any longer. But hordes of researchers are trying to figure that out. A 1990 study by Daniel Rudman, M.D., found that men over the age of 60 given human growth hormone (hGH) for six months had improved energy, less body fat and more muscle mass. Unfortunately, a study released in 1996 stripped hGH of some of its Fountain of Youth pizzazz. Although most of the men in

The Latest Research

Meanwhile, Back in the Labs . . .

Can we learn to slow aging's inevitable advance? If we don't, it won't be for lack of trying. Researchers around the world are working in areas that range from diet to genes to hormones in an effort to slow the clock.

Cut the calories consumed by a laboratory rat, mouse or worm and it will live not only longer but better. In hundreds of experiments, animals whose daily calories were cut by 35 percent aged better than those that ate what they wanted.

Research of this kind led University of Southern California's Caleb Finch, Ph.D., to conclude recently that caloric restriction could extend the average human life expectancy to 120 years. So scientists at the National Institute on Aging (NIA) began restricting the diets of monkeys. They wanted to see if the effect holds for a species more closely related to humans.

"The kinds of biological changes we saw in rats and mice also occur with monkeys," says NIA's George Roth, Ph.D., head of the monkey study. Sure, the monkeys are aging more slowly, but they are hungry, Roth acknowledges. Are they happy? A behavioral study now under way will answer that question. But more important, that study seeks to identify the mechanism that slows down aging when food is withheld. If the researchers can find that, Roth notes, then perhaps they can develop a drug that would mimic the effect of caloric restriction without necessarily cutting calories.

Researchers have also identified several genes in worms and fruit flies that, when mutated, increase life span. But they caution that the relationship to genes that control aging in humans remains unclear. Scientists may be somewhat closer to an answer with the identification of a gene responsible for a disease with symptoms of premature aging. But they're still far from finding the genes that control aging.

And the use of hormones? Mitchell Harman, M.D., Ph.D., an endocrinologist with the NIA, says that work on human growth hormone is in its infancy. "We'll see the results of some large studies in the next few years, which will give us more information, but we'll need to experiment a lot more before we know what's going to work."

But, says Harman, the point of hormone research is not to help people live longer. "We're not trying to add years to life," he adds. "We're more interested in enabling people to feel better and not lose the capacity to work and play."—A.A.

this study who received the hormone showed the same physical gains, none gained strength, endurance or muscle ability, according to Dennis Black, Ph.D., of the University of California at San Francisco.

But the hormone hunt is far from over. "The potential is great," enthuses Owen Wolkowitz, M.D., also of the University of California at San Francisco. For example, Wolkowitz recently administered another hormone, DHEA, to a small group of depressed men and women between the ages of 50 and 75. The hormone not only lifted depression but improved memory as well, Wolkowitz says. Some researchers also believe that DHEA blocks the decline of the immune system. Melatonin, a hormone on the research hot list, has been shown in some studies to improve sleep and even sexual function. You can buy it in health food stores, but its real benefits—like those of most hormones—remain unknown.

Men versus women: In the 1940s, doctors discovered the dramatic loss of estrogen suffered by women at the time of menopause. Researchers are just beginning to understand the loss of hormones in men. Reduced levels of testosterone, for instance, have been associated with decreased libido and, possibly, stroke.

What you can do: If you're a woman, you've probably made your choice about estrogen replacement therapy. But beyond that, for the moment, you can do very little about hormone replacement on your own. If you're a man, keep posted for news about testosterone studies.

One benefit credited to melatonin, however, is that it acts as an antioxidant, and both men and women can up their intake of antioxidants. Antioxidants seek out the body's free radicals, the result of normal metabolic changes, believed to damage the body. You can eat your antioxidants in foods, such as whole-grain cereals and breads, green leafy vegetables and citrus fruits (which contain high concentrations of beta carotene and vitamins C and E), as well as take them in pill form. What's more, a study released in May 1996 showed that vitamin E supplements slowed age-related changes in the brain and the immune system in mice.

"Eventually, these age-related changes will occur, but vitamin E slowed them," says Marguerite M. Kay, M.D., who led the study at the University of Arizona.

Mental Ability

THE BRAIN. The older you get, the more slowly your brain works, says K. Warner Schaie, Ph.D., of Pennsylvania State University. With age, your ability to do more than one thing at a time also decreases. But, Schaie says, "it doesn't matter if you take a bit more time. The information, the vocabulary, the ability to use words, all continue pretty well into old age."

Men versus women: As they age, men lose brain tissue from the area that affects planning and inhibition at almost three times the rate of women, according to Ruben C. Gur, Ph.D., of the University of Pennsylvania Medical Center. Men's bodies compensate for the shrinkage, Gur notes, by running their metabolisms at a higher rate. When brain (or any) cells are pushed too hard by a racing metabolism, they can die. This may be one reason men die sooner than women. Women, on the other hand, start with smaller brains but lose brain tissue more slowly, Gur found. They also tend to maintain a lower metabolic rate.

What you can do: "Use it or lose it" applies to the brain as well as to muscles. Schaie and Gur agree that trying new activities, staying active and involved, and doing things you love are ways to stave off the slowing brain function that comes with age.

PERSONALITY. Were you a crotchety young man? Then you'll probably be a crotchety old man. Were you adventurous as a young woman? That sense of adventure will follow you to old age. "Personality doesn't change," says Barbara Waxman, a gerontologist in Kentfield, California.

Men versus women: Women tend to make more friends and remain more emotionally tied to them than men. That's significant because in a study of older people, "those with more social ties were less likely to be dead nine years later," finds Toni Antonucci, Ph.D., of the University of Michigan. "People who are productive and who receive and give social support live longer," says Yale University's Martha L. Bruce, Ph.D.

What you can do: Maintain social contacts—and make new ones. "Some people stop doing the things they enjoy when they retire—such as lunching with colleagues—and that's worrisome," Bruce says. Regardless of whether you're a man or woman, you'll age. Men may look better with the passing years, but they don't live as long. Although women live longer, their lives are not necessarily healthier; they suffer more from such chronic conditions as arthritis and osteoporosis. In either case, one day you'll look in the mirror and see an image staring back that you recognize only vaguely. "Our outer layer does change," says gerontologist Waxman, "but our spirits don't. In the end, it's a question of melding the two. You've got to manage the spirit to stay vital." ■

Andrea Atkins is a freelance writer who lives in Rye, New York, and writes frequently on health and related subjects.

Is there really a

MALE MENOPAUSE?

By Cyra McFadden

It sounds like a teaser for a TV talk show: "Male Menopause—Menace or Myth?" Although it's only recently become the focus of media attention, male menopause is a subject that has been debated for 20 years by doctors and researchers. Their goal: to determine whether it actually exists as a complex of clearly identifiable physical and psychological changes.

If it does, and if many men suffer negative effects from it, the condition may call for intervention in the form of psychological counseling, hormone-replacement therapy or both. If male menopause doesn't exist, we're inventing a problem and inviting men to grasp at solutions.

While scientists disagree about male menopause, the ultimate experts on the subject—middle-aged men themselves—express few doubts that it exists. I talked to a dozen men, ranging in age from 45 to 70, about their experience. Many shared 60-year-old songwriter and piano player Dave Frishberg's sentiment: "Gee, I hope there's such a thing as male menopause." Long pause. "Because if there isn't . . . what was that?"

Researchers who believe there is no such thing would answer that the physical and psychological changes men experience are just a natural process: getting older. They worry that men who buy the idea might start seeking unnecessary cures. And some regard

male menopause as nothing more than a handy excuse for the middle-aged man who ups and trades the family sedan for a Porsche and his wife for a 20-year-old aerobics instructor. Christopher Longcope, M.D., speaking at the North American Menopause Society's annual meeting in 1992, suggested that some people would rather blame their behavior on hormones than on psychological problems.

Longcope is a professor of obstetrics, gynecology and medicine at the University of Massachusetts Medical Center in Worcester. During the meeting he also made the point that although men do begin to produce less of the male hormone testosterone in their late 40s, its gradual decline "does not compare with the sudden plunge in estrogen levels and the cessation of ovulation that women experience during menopause." In other words, biology doesn't explain that familiar event, the male midlife crisis (the term is used interchangeably with *male menopause* in this country, along with *male climacteric*).

Other experts, kinder and gentler, don't write off male menopause as a myth. Unlike their female counterparts, obviously, most middle-aged men don't light up like Christmas trees with hot flashes (although rare cases, caused by a sudden drop in testosterone, have been documented). But, these experts say, men may still go through a version of the Change. An article that appeared in *The*

New York Times several years ago, written by science writer Natalie Angier, stated that, gradual though it is, "some researchers suggest that the drop in testosterone causes a broad range of symptoms, including a decline in muscle mass and strength, a build-up of body fat, a loss of bone density, flagging energy, lowered fertility and fading virility." At the very least, such changes call for an attitude adjustment by men, as well as understanding by the women in their lives. Who knows better, after all, that making the passage from youth to middle age isn't easy? Besides, misery loves company.

More dramatic than the physical changes, however, are the profound psychological changes that the men I spoke with described. Some of them were moving into Longcope's target period, the late 40s, when testosterone begins to decline. Others had already gone through the male menopause/midlife crisis and come out the other side.

Law professor Thomas M. Goetzl, 50, summed up a preoccupation they all shared: a heightened awareness that the clock is ticking. "You realize that life is finite and that most of it is behind you," he said. "You have the sense of diminished possibilities. If you want to be a cop, you have to be 18 to 35, so forget it—your choices are being precluded." Thus, if he's not happy, the middle-aged man may panic. "Not only may you be in a rut, but you don't have a lot of time to get out of it," Goetzl observed.

A writer in his early 50s described his textbook midlife crisis: In his late 40s, he realized that "I was living my father's life—job, paycheck, mortgage, obligations. I felt as if I were dying. And since we're not supposed to have these feelings, men feel desperate. We break out." Years after a painful divorce and extensive psychotherapy, he can't label the shakeup in his life as entirely positive or negative. "The thing I say to myself is that I'm not despairing anymore."

Only 52-year-old Fred Wickham, an artist and cartoonist, contended that male menopause was the product of societal brainwashing. "We're too susceptible to suggestion," he said. "Everybody goes through crises. If they happen between 35 and 69, they're *midlife* crises."

Maybe Wickham is onto something; maybe the widespread acceptance of midlife crisis does encourage men to get busy and have one, before the window of opportunity closes. Books and films on the subject abound. Barbara Ehrenreich writes in her 1983 study of male roles, *The Hearts of Men*, that as early as the 1950s "the literature of male protest" preached that "conformity destroys not only men's souls, but their very manhood." Avery Corman called his 1987 novel about a middle-aged man in a state of emotional upheaval simply *Fifty*. Even the 1948 movie *Mr. Peabody and the Mermaid* attributed William Powell's sightings of a fishy seductress to his passing over the 50-year mark.

Certainly male menopause can't be regarded as a private event; sociological and cultural factors enter in. But so do hard physiological facts. The middle years often involve the onset of such illnesses as diabetes, heart disease and colon and prostate cancer. Even the healthiest middle-aged man is physically compromised, and as if thinning hair and weakening eyesight weren't enough to contend with, these conditions may be accompanied by severe depression.

The physical problems middle-aged men experience can cause the depression, explains Chesley C. Herbert, a San Francisco psychiatrist. Or the depression can cause some of the physical symptoms, among them diminished sex drive. Stress can inhibit testosterone release. The interaction goes in both directions and may complicate diagnosis. "Over 20 years, I have seen a number of men in that general age range—from the mid-40s through the 50s—who complain of midlife crisis and sometimes decreased potency and libido," Herbert adds. "But in the absence of a clinical depression, with its marked changes in mood, thought and physiological functioning, it is often unclear which is the cause and which the effect."

While all the men I interviewed for this article played

down their physical problems (including, in one case, a life-threatening illness), all confessed to constant reminders of them. A 58-year-old executive still works out, but "at my age, men don't build muscle. You get stringy." Sculptor Richard Mayer, 59, sometimes wishes that he'd chosen another profession. "Working on a large piece, I think, 'My god, I'm going to have to lift this thing!' Also, the brass ring seems less distinct. It's even receding somewhat. I don't know if that's a function of my weakening eyesight or reality," he jokes.

Atlanta psychiatrist and author Frank Pittman reinforces Mayer's point. "Middle-aged men are seeing younger men who are more energetic. When they look in the mirror, they look more like their fathers every day. Their parents either die on them or are collapsing, and their kids are leaving home. Every day, they are going to become older, fatter, balder, weaker and less important to the world."

Women, too, get older and wider, I gently reminded him. The 58-year-old Pittman —author of *Man Enough* (Putnam), a 1993 book that examines stereotypes about masculinity—replied that, for men, there's an extra wrinkle: "Men believe their potency is necessary to get them loved." But at a certain age, "the genitals don't work the way they used to. . . . Not that men are impotent; but potency can't always be relied on. It depends more on circumstances and relationship; as a result, the man feels more dependent.

"When middle-aged men go messing around," Pittman added, "they're not really looking for new partners, they're looking for reassurance of their potency, for someone who will make them feel wonderful. They don't expect to get trapped and upend their lives. They expect it to be outpatient therapy."

A quicker fix might be medical treatment, similar to the estrogen therapy sometimes prescribed for menopausal women. Already, in Britain and in Europe, hormone-replacement therapy for men is readily available.

Although many American doctors believe that supplementing testosterone to increase virility also increases the risk of prostate cancer and heart disease, one consumer-health newsletter reported that prescriptions for injectable testosterone nearly doubled

Your Thoughts and Longevity

By Myrna Lewis

Thoughts and beliefs may be so powerful that they actually affect how long you live, according to research from the University of California at San Diego that was published in The Lancet. The study finds that Chinese Americans who adhere to a traditional Chinese belief system that links specific diseases with the year of birth, and who in fact develop those diseases, die one to five years earlier than normal. "We attribute these differences in survival time to fatalistic beliefs," says researcher David P. Phillips, Ph.D.

In Chinese medicine and astrology, people's fates are believed to be influenced by their year of birth. Birth years are associated with one of five phases—earth, fire, metal, water and wood—and each of these phases is, in turn, associated with a body organ or symptom (for example, earth with tumors, fire with the heart). A prophecy is seemingly fulfilled when, for example, people born in earth years get lung cancer. These people survive a significantly shorter time than cancer patients born in non-earth years, the study revealed. Why does this happen? "People with a strong belief-driven, fatalistic outlook about their health tend to feel more helpless and hopeless, and therefore more pessimistic about the future," explains Phillips, who analyzed the death records of more than 28,000 Chinese Americans and compared them with the death records of more than 412,000 Caucasian Americans. "On the other hand, some evidence from other studies suggests that optimism is associated with a longer life," he adds.

in the United States between 1987 and 1992. Look for the proliferation of European-style "rejuvenation" clinics with American-style marketing: "We'll put the tiger back in your tank!"

As the debate continues, we need to remember that for most men the map of middle life is not dotted with signs that read "Here Be Dragons." They don't suffer from sexual anxieties or debilitating depression. In fact, instead of perceiving male menopause as a menace, they may thrive as never before, enjoying their professional accomplishments and, if they have grown children, their relative freedom from parental responsibilities. Says Sandor Burstein, M.D., a longtime San Francisco internist: "There are a few people who get into crisis situations, but most don't. It's a matter of degree—just as some women don't really notice their menopause."

Some of the men in my informal study find midlife productive, marked by introspection and self-assessment. They see themselves moving toward acceptance and what sociologist and child-care teacher Jim Stockinger, 47, calls "a certain kind of equilibrium." He sees the process of transition as "a journey toward what the Greeks called wisdom. I really believe that there are stages in life that transform your being."

Even a diminishing sex drive has its good side. As a 70-year-old I talked to pointed out, "Nothing clicks off"—it's just that middle-aged men are not as enslaved by sexual appetite as when they were younger and constantly trying to cut to the chase. Dan Linn, 53, manager of a large paper-products firm, put it this way: "From the time we are kids, we're considered cool if we have a lot of girlfriends. I continually say that one good thing about getting into the 50s is that I'm not thinking endlessly about Sally Whozit a few desks away."

Frank Pittman believes that "if men feel that their productive life is over, that they are not going to be potent in a sexual, economic or creative sense, they go into a kind of emotional decline." He hastens to add that constructive solutions can take a number of forms and needn't involve fast cars and younger women.

Kevin Hughes, a 52-year-old attorney, is engaged in an exhilarating search for meaning. "In middle age, you can truly say to yourself, 'I am not my car.' I don't care how hip, slick and cool I am; I want to discard the impatient, intolerant, resentful parts of myself and cultivate those parts of me that are worth cultivating. I also want to latch onto things that are positive and distance myself from things that are negative." If this attitude is a by-product of male menopause, midlife crisis or whatever, someone should bottle it. ■

The author of the best-selling The Serial, *Cyra McFadden is currently finishing her second novel, a look at urban life, San Francisco-style.*

QUESTION & ANSWER

Sudden Personality Changes

Question

My husband and I have been married for 36 years. He had always been considerate and affectionate, but in the last few months he has changed. For example, at a party not long ago, when the host told him to sit next to me, he shouted, "Who wants to sit next to that old lady?" I was so hurt! We don't even touch each other anymore. He doesn't seem to realize or care how miserable I am. I'm still very much in love with him, but I don't know what to do.

Answer

Get your husband to a doctor immediately for a complete physical and mental examination. The clues that something is wrong are the sudden shifts in your long and happy marriage, the gross inappropriateness in a social situation and his insensitivity to your upset. Something may be happening to him that requres medical attention. — M.L.

WOMEN SURGE ON!

Why many women over 50 today feel more powerful than ever

By Celia Morris

"We shall not be in our prime before 50," Elizabeth Cady Stanton declared in that wonderfully certain way she had, "and after that we shall be good for 20 years at least." She was writing to Susan B. Anthony in 1857, when a woman in their part of the country could expect to live only about 40 years. Still, Stanton proved right: She died at 87 and Anthony at 86, and those great fighters for American women's equality were vital to the end.

Almost a century and a half later, when women's life expectancy had nearly doubled, I featured that quote in the invitation to my 50th birthday party, and in the eight years that have passed since I called on Stanton's powers of prophecy, she has been right for me and my closest women friends as well. Women of my generation who made it into their 50s with good health and enough money have found themselves at the most exhilarating time of their lives, and I am not playing Pollyanna!

For the happy truth of our era is that you don't have to be an exceptional woman, as Stanton and Anthony so clearly were, to find yourself, at 50, pleased with your life and work. We are likely to live much longer than our foremothers, and in relatively good health; we also have choices now that were unthinkable even in my mother's generation.

Women, of course, have always been the backbone of their communities as well as their families. But not only were they expected to let men take most of the public credit, they were supposed to be satisfied with the least prestigious, worst-paying jobs — if, indeed, they had the misfortune of having to work for pay — and their lives were thought to be on the downslide when their children left home.

Now, in the tiniest hamlets and the greatest cities, women are elders in their churches as well as ministers; they're proud of their work operating forklifts and flying jets; and they head the school boards in addition to teaching the children. When the system thwarts them, they

are far more likely than women of earlier generations to find ways around it. For instance, grocery-store clerks in northern California who were denied promotion sued Lucky Stores, Inc., and in late 1993 won a settlement of nearly $75 million that promised to change personnel practices throughout the industry.

"A revolution has occurred in the roles of women," concluded the 1992 Women's Voices Project, "and women's work outside the home has a major impact today on how they feel about their lives and the changes they look for in their own lives and their daughters'." This project sponsored the first national poll to survey women across class and race lines, and through it we discovered that an astonishing 84 percent of American women are satisfied with their family life and the same high percentage are basically satisfied with their jobs. A few organizations that have always depended on women volunteers now even have women presidents — Elizabeth Dole, for instance, at the American Red Cross, and Gwendolyn Calvert Baker at the United States Committee for UNICEF. (Both are over 50 and clearly in their prime.)

Women between 45 and 54 are almost twice as likely to work for pay as they were in 1950, along with 60 percent more of those between 55 and 64. And women in all parts of the economy are demonstrating an unprecedented resourcefulness. In 1991, under Labor Secretary Lynn Martin, a Commission on the Glass Ceiling was established. Its executive director, Joyce Miller, reported that 40 percent of the women who leave their jobs because they're stuck at work go out and start their own businesses.

Another example is the National Displaced Homemakers Network, which began in the mid-'70s as a support group for older women who had lost their husbands because of death or divorce and has now evolved into Women Work!, a national membership organization that directs women to more than 1,200 education, training and employment programs to help them achieve economic self-sufficiency.

As for women's traditional identification with their children, Maya Angelou (who at 64 would become President Clinton's inaugural poet) put it in a new perspective. After describing her son's departure for college, she closed her autobiographical book *The Heart of a Woman* by saying, "At last, I'll be able to eat the whole breast of a roast chicken by myself." Not only have women begun to insist that their husbands take on more responsibility at home and a larger role in family life, but they themselves are as likely to find fulfillment outside the home as within it.

This fall, when I went to my 40th high school reunion in Houston, it was thrilling to reconnect with the women I had known. All of us had grown up taking our American birthright of equality for granted, and many had been profoundly disappointed. Nonetheless, most were doing things our mothers would never have dreamed of. Some had gone back to college — whether for degrees that would lead to better jobs or for knowledge to enrich their lives. Several belonged to book groups that focused on women's writing, and many who'd never expected to work for pay had had a variety of challenging jobs.

Like most women of our generation, Ann Nicholl Chadwick, a talented pianist, hadn't taken her gift seriously when she was young. But in her late 40s she had become part of a chamber music group that made her work at her music as never before, gave her a profound insight into what life ought to be, and provided the most meaningful experience she'd ever had. Each musician was essentially a soloist, she said, but all had gradually learned to work together. "It was a metaphor for how I wanted to relate to others": The individual thrived as she merged into a group playing together.

None of us at that reunion exactly welcomed the bulges and sagging flesh, or the graying, thinning hair, but most seemed at peace with the possibilities inherent in the faces and bodies time had left us.

Then there are women I've met, like Terri Sanders, who had to use a ruse to get a job at an engineering firm in Indiana: She wrote her name with a *y* on the application form, knowing she was likely to be mistaken for a man, and at the interview she told the guys who said "We don't hire women" that she'd work for two weeks for free. She succeeded so well that she has moved gradually into a very responsible job at a large power plant, and the rap on her is "You can talk to Terri about anything, but you don't mess with her." Now on the verge of 50, Terri had a friend who went through a terrible experience of sexual harassment. When the leadership refused to take it seriously, Terri got herself elected a union representative and stood up for her friend's rights.

Crediting Oprah Winfrey with giving women the courage to take their feelings seriously, Terri was over 40 before she learned to express her own, and her newfound ability has been wonderfully liberating. Although our mothers would have blushed to mention a topic like menopause in polite company, for instance, Terri and her high school friends not only discussed it at a recent get-together, they passed around a delightful cartoon in which one woman says of another who seems not entirely with it: "She's waiting for post-menopausal zest to kick in."

And so I think of ours as an extraordinarily lucky generation—born as we were into traditional expectations for women, and living as we have into a wholly new time, when women can be astronauts, college presidents and governors, and people expect them to be. Those of us who have survived this momentous transition have lived far richer lives than 98 percent of the people in the history of the world.

While I think we value home life more than many younger women, we are far more aware of the breadth of human experience than our foremothers were. The barriers that isolated groups of people have fallen, and so we can enjoy a much wider range of friends. The schools I went to, for instance, were all-white and overwhelmingly Gentile. The late U.S. Congresswoman Barbara Jordan and I, in fact, were born within a year of each other on opposite sides of Houston, when it was unthinkable that we should know each other as equals, much less become colleagues and friends. But the civil-rights movement that captured the world's attention when we were in our early 20s has defused, though not destroyed, the attitudes that kept us apart. When Jordan wrote that my book *Storming the Statehouse: Running for Governor with Ann Richards and Dianne Feinstein* made her feel proud, I wept—and knew that nothing anyone else could say would have the power to move me so deeply.

I think of ours as an extraordinarily lucky generation . . . living as we have into a wholly new time.

But it is to the women's movement that women of our generation are the most profoundly indebted. In some cases, it encouraged personal friendships to evolve into political alliances, and in Texas, which may set the national standard for machismo, this eventually resulted in the unthinkable: the election in 1990 of a self-proclaimed feminist governor, Ann Richards, just two months after her 57th birthday.

While on the stump, Richards rallied her audiences by quoting ex–Houston Oilers coach Bum Phillips: "The first year we knocked on the door. The second year we banged on the door. And this year, we're gonna kick that sucker in!" On the day after her upset victory, the tart-tongued lady with the halo of white hair declared, "This is sociological change, not just governmental change. It means the doors are going to be open to everyone." Like Richards, most female political leaders with a national reputation, Republican and Democrat alike, are over 50—and all of them owe their victories to the women who constitute more than half of the registered voters.

Beginning in the 1960s, we've also been blessed by an outpouring of work from women writers, many of them now over 50, who have explored the female condition with breathtaking clarity and have broken silences that women had been enjoined to keep for millennia. They have taught us to see the put-down inherent in such phrases as "little old ladies in tennis shoes" and "You've come a long way, baby" and ultimately to realize that we hadn't really been living as equals with our male peers. (In 1993, when Toni Morrison, at 62, won the Nobel Prize in Literature, America for the first time had a Nobel laureate who focused on women.)

Prompted by the Anita Hill/Clarence Thomas hearings, all this collective truth-telling and political organizing coalesced, and in the fall of 1991, women all over the country told one another personal stories they had never told before. So many women gave so much money to female candidates that in November 1992 the number of women in the U.S. House of Representatives almost doubled to 48, while 4 more were elected to the Senate. Since one of the latter, Patty Murray of Washington, had run as "a mom in tennis shoes," no one is likely to belittle such women again.

For we are caught up in a thrilling process called synergy, which Governor Richards described as she saw it working in her own life: "The force of this campaign became greater than each of us could ever have been individually. There is an energy that is a fusion of people who are focused and working together." Women who hold conspicuous political positions or who rise to unprecedented heights in their professions give new self-respect and courage to essentially private people like us, who provide the votes and organizing skills that elect qualified women to office. And together we're succeeding in changing the laws. Our power resulted, in a single session of Congress in the mid-1990s, in the passage of 30 new pieces of legislation relating to women and children.

The emergence of so many women in their 40s and 50s into positions of real power ... makes me hopeful ...

My own work would be unthinkable without the support of many women. When I set off after the Hill/Thomas hearings to collect examples of sexual harassment and abuse for my book *Bearing Witness*, women from Tennessee to California, and from New York to Texas, volunteered to help me find the most compelling stories. Some worked in battered women's shelters and some in high-profile women's organizations; others were teachers, businesswomen, journalists, politicians or simply private people.

Over a period of 18 months, I listened to stories from 150 women—many of whom had never "gone public" before but who now understood that breaking silence was a necessary part of the process of empowerment. Lives changed in the course of an interview; a huge network emerged—one woman suggesting another, who suggested another, and so on; and the exhilaration we felt was breathtaking.

To be sure, as we approach the end of this century, our problems can seem overwhelming. But the emergence of so many women in their 40s and 50s into positions of real power, along with a binding commitment from women in every rank of society to work for justice, makes me hopeful enough to recall the words of the great Sojourner Truth, who was born a slave but who could say nonetheless: "If the first woman God ever made could turn the world upside down all alone, these women together ought to be able to get it right side up again."

Celia Morris's latest book is Bearing Witness: Sexual Harassment and Beyond — Everywoman's Story *(Little, Brown).*

As the years go by, do we grow...

CRANKIER OR MORE TOLERANT?

By Willie Morris

On the occasion of my 61st birthday, a comrade jocularly asked, "Do you see yourself growing more intolerant, or more tolerant?" It was a beguiling question and a very human one, touching on many aspects of aging; and because it titillated me, I have been thinking about it.

I truthfully believe I have grown more tolerant with time, and I will try to explain some of the reasons why. More than a year ago, almost coincidental with my turning 60, something exceedingly strange and unexpected began to happen in my life. I had always been an easy and heavy sleeper, but suddenly I began to awaken regularly at the first light of dawn, whereupon my precipitously troubled consciousness would enter into a hazy reverie of years long past, a drowsing yet sleepless musing often lasting as long as three hours or more. During these hours, I would dwell upon, in graphic and painful detail, one by one in aimless progression, specific past guilts of my lifetime: errors, transgressions, cruelties, fears —the back-stabbing of a long-ago professional colleague, or a deceitful act to a friend, or monstrous behavior to a person I cared for, or a dreadfully unthinking remark that hurt someone, and on and on in these old peremptory mists, almost as in a shadowy Fellini film. Not unlike Mr. Scrooge himself, I am visited daily now by these unrelenting spirits evoking my own accumulated neglects and flaws, not at night, as happened with-Scrooge, but in the morning.

One such morning, for instance, I was compelled to the recollection of my standing before the honor society of which I was a member at my university and successfully opposing the nomination of a young man who was about to be my opponent for the editorship of the student newspaper. On another, I was obsessed with the image of striking and knocking down a small African-American child when I was 12 years old. Or of telling my mother in a tantrum of bad temper that I did not love her. Or of mindlessly publishing off-the-record comments of a public official when I was 25 on a statewide paper and getting him into serious trouble. Or of angrily taking the wedding ring from my wife's finger when I was 32 and tossing it out the window of a New York apartment. Or of writing something at age 48 of an adversary that I knew bordered on libel. Or of making a buffoon of myself at age 50 at the wedding of friends by losing my composure and cursing the future father-in-law. Such venerable self-pities and selfish aggrandizements and awkward indispositions occurred in dozens of venues. The catalog is endless.

I do not know the sources of these horrific visitations and the dark, brooding nightmares that accompany them. I wish I did. But somehow they have begun to mellow me and make me a little more charitable—how could they not? They have helped me realize that I am far from perfect myself: that we are all flawed creatures springing from the ambivalence of our common inheritance and must pray for more indulgence of the fallibilities of our fellows. And with all this, some slight or injury or deception over which I have been aggrieved, from something that happened to me last week, or six months ago, or eight years ago, mysteriously begins to recede into the retrospective tally of my own complex and melancholy remembrances.

Not that I am lost in a delicate cloud of benevolence, but I feel I have become more forgiving of others' transgressions toward me. Here are some examples. Recently a man I thought a friend bitterly attacked me, grossly unfairly I thought, as a person and a writer in an interview with a newspaper. In earlier days, I would have responded with ire. Instead, after my initial anger, I tried to reflect on the reasons he had chosen to be so offensive, and let it go at that. Later, when a recent book of mine came out, a prominent magazine published what I considered the most abusively hostile review of any in my long lifetime as a writer, taking gratuitous liberties with something that took me three years to write. I have never once written to a book reviewer, but 20 years ago I would surely have answered this one in kind, or even gone so far as to confront the man personally. Now I let this drop also; this is part of the territory, I told myself.

Similarly, my recollections of past affronts—someone years ago who attempted to get my job, or a friend who tried to persuade my wife to leave me, or a stranger who wrote destructive letters about me to my professional colleagues—are no longer so enveloped in distant distrusts and paranoias but oddly begin to fit for me into some vast and profoundly unfathomable human puzzle.

Ironically, my spectral post-dawn visions come at the happiest time in my personal life: I have a loving and talented son, more money than I have ever made, a beautiful old house set in verdant Southern terrain, a new marriage more contented than I ever could have hoped for, two inspiriting stepsons and four exasperating yet affectionate cats who are now songs in the heart of this former feline misanthrope. From a long bachelorhood of divorce in the literary enclaves of New York and then in a sequestered college town to this tranquil landing near the place of my birth in Jackson, Mississippi, I am learning to see my existence as a whole, as a funny integrity, as part of the quintessence of life and death.

My recollections of past affronts . . . oddly begin to fit for me into some vast and profoundly unfathomable human puzzle.

Much of this is reflected in my own writer's calling. After a lifetime as a writer and editor of such magazines as *The Texas Observer* and *Harper's*, where my job involved tough criticism of those I considered adversaries, what I really wish to do now is write about people and places and things that intrigue me, that I admire.

Not too long ago, a widely read magazine offered me a very lucrative assignment for what would be its cover story on a prominent national figure. I pondered this offer, watched the man on television, listened to him on the radio, took notes, but finally told the editors I would not do the piece because I felt no human chemistry with him, indeed could not abide him or anything he stood for. At age 35, I would have taken the assignment with much enthusiasm.

There are other factors, too. I believe my returning home to the place of my birth has substantially mellowed me. I do not consider it odd that I often drive the 40 miles or so from the city where I live to the small town where I grew up and take long solitary walks, the streets and alleys so etched in my memory—the cemetery, the school, the house where my dog Skip lies buried in the backyard. I amble past the dwellings of the reprobates and charlatans we feared in that boyhood time, all long dead, everything evanescently touched by the patina of the vanished years.

In my first book, *North Toward Home*, I described moving to New York City and seeing everywhere people whom I thought I knew from my hometown. Now, on returning home after all the years, I see them in reality, running into them in restaurants or supermarkets, resuming conversations that might have been broken in midsentence decades ago. At the Jitney Jungle checkout last week, a vaguely familiar figure accosted me: "Do you know who I am?" In an instant I replied: "Billy Rhodes!" My warm-spirited boyhood pal and I discussed the ball games we played in and the girls we dated, and he brought out photos of his grandchildren.

As I age, and because I dwell in a relatively settled society, I perceive now more than I ever did the link between the generations—the continuity. It is not uncommon in my hometown for three generations of the same families I have known to still live there. I am constantly confusing the generations, talking with a son or daughter; but after a time I note an ancestral gesture, a customary expression, an incredible physical resemblance, a turn of phrase, and then I feel I am really talking with the father, or mother, who was my contemporary, or even the grandfather or grandmother. "It's been good seeing you, Thomas," I said at the end of one recent conversation. "I'm not Thomas," the man replied. "I'm Robert. Thomas is my grandfather."

I have grown more tolerant because I see that I do not have all the time in the world. My feelings of humility deepen the more frequently I look around a room, or a dinner table, and acknowledge that I am the oldest person present. Likewise, when my quirky subconscious sedulously whispers: "Is this at last the day you sit down at your worktable and nothing at all comes out? Ha, ha!" this diabolic interior traitor exclaims. "Nothing there at last!"

Time is a tricky fellow. Why is it that time passes so swiftly as we age? The moment has come for me to say that the one and only thing I am zealously intolerant of these days is the passing of time itself.

The moment has come for me to say that the one and only thing I am zealously intolerant of these days is the passing of time itself.

In childhood and youth, fool that I was, I wished time to pass quickly. I vividly remember sitting on a street curb at 15, holding my baseball bat and beseeching the years to go by so that I could play ball in Yankee Stadium or Wrigley Field. In my 20s, in Chartres Cathedral, the waning sunlight filtering through the magnificent stained glass, I felt almost mystically immersed in time as history, in the ineluctable unfolding of the ancient human drama. In my 30s, I was half oblivious to time, impatient as I was with matters of political and social reform. In my 40s, I took most to my heart William Faulkner's dictum, "The past is never dead, it's not even past," past and present deeply linked for me in continuum. In my 50s, as I revisited New York City, I felt I had hardly made a ripple on that mutable place and that time in my youth had somehow deceived me. Now, as I enter my 60s, I am beginning to view time as a difficult and most honored adversary.

As I write these words on this page, I am pausing to gaze out the windows of my workroom. It is an unseasonably warm winter's forenoon in the deepest South. Down below me on the broad sloping lawn, I see the first robin bathing herself in a little puddle. In the distance, my beautiful wife is strolling languidly toward Purple Crane Creek, followed by my irascible cats Spit McGee, Mamie Harper, George W. Harper and Bessie Graham. The five of them are silently examining something in the grass. Could it be the first crocus? They seem so *together* there, caught for me in bittersweet frieze, in the belonging of the Lord's earth. They touch me deeply, and I implore: Stop, Time, you tricky fellow! Stop right now! ■

Willie Morris was editor in chief of Harper's *magazine from 1967 to 1971. His latest book, recently issued in paperback, is* My Dog Skip *(Vintage), a remembrance of his childhood in the South.*

How To Deal With Midlife Regrets

By Myrna Lewis

1. I wish I'd taken more risks in life .... ☐
2. I feel I've wasted too much time .... ☐
3. If I knew then what I know now, I'd have made some important choices differently .... ☐
4. I fantasize about what my life might have been........ ☐
5. I wish I had the courage to be more spontaneous ...... ☐
6. I'm critical of myself for things I do .... ☐
7. I wish I'd spent more time with good friends.......... ☐
8. I feel I've made too many sacrifices for other people ... ☐
9. I feel cheated about not doing enough for myself...... ☐
10. I've made too many self-centered choices............ ☐
11. I wish I were less impulsive in my decisions and actions . ☐
12. I worry about decisions after making them .... ☐
13. I think about the career I didn't pursue.............. ☐
14. I wish I'd balanced work and personal life better....... ☐
15. I wish I'd taken more risks in career moves .... ☐
16. I wish I'd tried harder in school .... ☐
17. I wish I'd pursued my education during a different period in my life .... ☐
18. I should have gone for a higher level of education .... ☐
19. I wish I'd married earlier or later than I did .... ☐
20. I wish I'd chosen my partner more wisely .... ☐
21. I wish I had (or hadn't) ended my marriage .... ☐
22. I wish I'd made different decisions about having children .... ☐
23. I worry about the mistakes I made as a parent .... ☐
24. I wish my relationship with my parents was better ..... ☐
25. I wish I'd worked harder at expanding my circle of relationships .... ☐

Most people are unhappy about some of the choices they've made over the years. Unfortunately, some of us can become so consumed by second-guessing that we are unable to move on with our lives. Richard Gotti, Ph.D., a psychotherapist and professor of human behavior at SUNY Empire State College in Albany, New York, helped devise the following quiz for people to better grasp what areas of life they feel regretful about.

For each of the statements above, choose the number that best represents your response and enter it in the box at right. Enter 1 if the statement is not at all how you feel; 2 if you feel somewhat that way; 3 if you feel moderately that way; and 4 if it very much reflects how you feel.

SCORING. Add up your total score. For every question unanswered because it doesn't apply to your life, add 1 to your total score. Find your regret level below:

TOTAL SCORE

81–100: A high level of regret. Requires working at some coping skills.

51–80: An overall moderate level of regret. May require some work on specific troublesome issues.

31–50: A low level of regret. Either you are coping effectively or tending toward some denial.

30 and below: Either you are lucky in not feeling regret or you aren't allowing regret to surface.

If you find you have serious regrets, Gotti recommends the following steps:

1. Give up the idea of being perfect. Develop compassion for your personal limitations and consider why mistakes may have been made.

2. Begin to make amends with people with whom you have problematic relationships.

3. Try to find positive lessons in choices that you now regret wholly or partially.

4. Finally, Gotti advises, "Seize the moment! Without denying our regrets, we can remind ourselves that they are part of the past and that we are free to make wiser use of the present."

Adapted from Overcoming Regret: Lessons from the Roads Not Taken, *by Carole Klein and Richard Gotti, Ph.D. (Bantam Books).*

AGEISM

The disease America won't cure, and should

By Aljean Harmetz

The chronic illness faced by a majority of older Americans is not arthritis or high blood pressure but the much more insidious disease known as ageism. It is implicit in newspaper articles that ask whether 73-year-old Bob Dole wasn't really too old to run for president. It is explicit when a young doctor says that aches and pains are to be expected "at your age." It is devastating when an employer badgers you into accepting early retirement and hires a younger person to take your place. And it is life-threatening when politicians suggest rationing health care for the elderly.

The word *ageism* made one of its earliest appearances in the dictionary in 1976, but George Manitzas doesn't need a dictionary definition. A fifth-grade teacher in the Los Angeles city schools until he retired in 1992 at age 65, Manitzas later dyed his white hair and gray beard red for his role as Henry VIII in a play reading. "I don't care how kind and wonderful we want to be toward senior citizens, the younger ones get first place in line," says Manitzas of his three-month experiment. "The public reacts to looks. I got more attention more quickly from everybody I dealt with. It's an internal feeling of acceptance versus arm's length."

Almost everyone over 60 has been bruised by ageism—whether in the workplace, in health care, in the careless words of the media, in the entertainment provided by movies and television, or in the day-to-day mindset of our culture. Over-60s are routinely maligned, frequently discrim-

inated against and too often ignored. They are fighting back by forming pressure groups and by asserting themselves in their choice of doctors, stores, products, political leaders and social activities.

In some occupations, ageism starts much earlier than 60. Dena Dietrich, who at age 67 chairs the Seniors' Committee of the Screen Actors Guild, says, "For a long time, actors have been knocked out of work almost completely after they turn 40 or, at the latest, 50. And there's an extra problem facing us vital older actresses. When I go on interviews for commercials, if there is a grandmother character, she's a stooped, gray-haired little old lady who can just barely walk up the steps. These days, that's ridiculous. It's unrealistic. But nine times out of ten, the advertising executive will pick one of these sweet little old ladies."

Such decisions don't hurt just the actors involved. By presenting these false images of older people in movies and commercials, advertising executives and casting directors are helping to perpetuate negative stereotypes that influence the way younger people treat their elders.

Robert N. Butler, M.D., who claims credit for coining the word *ageism* in 1968 when he was chairman of the District of Columbia Advisory Committee on Aging, has defined it as a "disease" of "negative attitudes and practices that lead to discrimination against the aged." Butler, a professor of geriatrics at Mount Sinai School of Medicine in New York, has also warned that the growing number of older people in Europe (by the year 2030, for example, more than a third of all Germans will be over 60), as well as in the United States, may lead to a fiercer ageism.

"A threshold that might be regarded as an achievement has, instead, come to be regarded as a burden," Butler wrote in *Generations* magazine in 1993. "What should have been a celebration has become a sense of threat."

Whatever they may lead to, the demographics of the future are inexorable. In 1800, half of all Americans were under the age of 16, and few Americans lived past the age of 60. But a raw pioneer country needed only strong men and fertile women to build and populate all those empty states west of the Mississippi. Today, the average American's life span is 75. In 2030, according to the Census Bureau, one in five Americans will be over 65; and by the middle of the next century, 18 million Americans will be over the age of 85.

So a young country that has always made a joke of old age must now come to terms with it. And part of coming to terms means changing the terms with which the American language characterizes the old: *frail, feeble, wrinkled, gaga, doddering, over the hill, senile, cronelike, out of date, withered, fuddy-duddy, old biddy, old lecher, old fool.*

The problem with getting rid of stereotypes, however, is that there is always some truth in them, and people will grab at it. Indeed, many elderly people —particularly those over 85 whom doctors define as the "old old"—are frail. Statistics vary, but, at a minimum, Alzheimer's disease affects over 13 percent of the old old. However, according to a study released by the Census Bureau in May, 1996, Americans between the ages of 65 and 85 are healthier and better off financially than ever before. Yet their chance of staying healthy is undermined by many of the men and women who provide their health care.

Mack Lipkin, M.D., a 53-year-old internist in New York, tells of a woman in her late 70s who fell and broke her arm. Her 40-year-old doctor recommended that she get her glasses checked and told her not to take any tranquilizers or other drugs that would make her sleepy. He implied that her age had made her clumsy and unable to see well. As it happened, the woman had a brain tumor, and although she survived, her life was threatened by the delayed diagnosis.

Lipkin, who is the director of primary care at New York University and a specialist in doctor-patient relationships, says that a number of physicians grumble about older patients because they require more time. Citing a 1986 patient-care study, Lipkin notes that "people between 65 and 85 take an average of two minutes more per visit. They may have more problems and may talk and undress more slowly. That's not a big deal."

One of the most common complaints of older people is that doctors and nurses refuse to listen to them. If a son or daughter takes a parent to the doctor, the doctor routinely ignores the patient and talks to the younger person instead. "My mother broke her hip and had to go into a nursing home for six days," says Beth Mann, who is employment coordinator for the California Department of Aging. "My mother was in the room with me, but the nurse asked me, 'Can she stand and pivot?' I said, 'I don't know. Mother, can you stand and pivot?' Then the nurse asked me, 'What does she like to eat?' I said, 'I don't know. Mother, what do you like to eat?' Finally, I said, 'Mother broke her hip. She didn't land on her head.'"

Butler thinks that medical ageism starts in medical school, where the first older person the students encounter is usually the cadaver they dissect. Says Robin Frasier, M.D., a Los Angeles psychoanalyst, "I have always felt ageism had to do with the fear of being old and being disabled and not being strong and vigorous. The young—to prove how young and vigorous and how far from death they are—frequently don't notice older people, or, if it's impossible to ignore older people, they mock them."

People who are too polite to mock the elderly often patronize them instead. The late Maggie Kuhn, a Presbyterian Church executive who founded the Gray Panthers after church rules forced her to retire at 65, had a chance to give a lesson in ageism to President Gerald Ford two decades ago. When Kuhn and a number of other activists were invited to the White House for the signing of a bill that regulated pension plans, Ford asked her, "And what have you to say, young lady?" Kuhn answered, "Mr. President, I'm not a young lady. I'm an old woman." As she wrote in her autobiography, "I just couldn't help reminding him that his words weren't a compliment."

One of the most common complaints of older people is that doctors and nurses refuse to listen to them.

Although my hair is not gray and I spend my weekends running an English cocker spaniel through agility courses, I had a taste of the same experience when my doctor at a Kaiser-Permanente medical facility in California retired last January. My new doctor greeted me with, "How many years young are you?" Although I explained that I found his question unappealing, he repeated it twice on my second visit. I chose another doctor.

Older people are also subtly infantilized by being referred to as "sweet," "little," "cute" and "dear." Similarly, "old age" has been turned into "the golden years." (That other euphemism, "the sunset years," never caught on, perhaps because it was too unsubtle a reminder that life inevitably ends in death.) Older people have also been ghettoized as "senior citizens."

The media have a spotty but improving record in combating ageism in print. In the recently revised stylebook at the *Los Angeles Times*, reporters are encouraged to use the term *senior citizens* with caution and to avoid using the word *oldster* at all since it "is often regarded as patronizing." In almost every case, the stylebook suggests, it is best simply to use a person's specific age.

Paul Kleyman, who edits *Aging Today* magazine for the American Society on Aging, says that by the autumn of 1996, approximately 18 major daily newspapers—including the *Richmond Times-Dispatch*, *Milwaukee Journal Sentinel* and *Philadelphia Inquirer*—had assigned a reporter full-time to senior issues, while another 25 or 30 papers had a reporter on the beat half-time.

"But the media have a split personality in the coverage of aging," says Kleyman. "One day you pick up your paper, and there is a terrific series about caregiving for your older parents and all the difficulties it entails, and the gaps in the long-term-care system that leave people in the lurch. The following week, you pick up the same newspaper and read an article from the Washington bureau about how entitlements for seniors are costing too much. There is no coordination between the local reporter who tries to understand the complicated issues involved in an aging America and the political or economic writer in Washington."

One of the worst recent examples of ageism in the media was economist Lester Thurow's *New York Times Magazine* article on May 19, 1996, which accused the elderly of "bringing down the social welfare state" and "threatening America's economic future" by getting too much income and health care from the government. *The New York Times* chose to illustrate Thurow's article with a drawing of a lethargic-looking elderly man and a lumpish elderly woman sitting comfortably atop bags of money.

"If you begin to do what ageism does—to focus all of society's problems in terms of one demographic group—what's to prevent any of us from being the subject of blame for who we are?" asks Kleyman.

Because state and federal laws protect older people from being fired because of their age, ageism in the workplace is usually less blatant. But it is powerful nonetheless. "It's just a feeling you get," says a 60-year-old New Jersey bank manager who has asked not to be identified by name. "You just

know that if there's an opportunity for further education paid for by the bank and you're over 50, don't bother applying. And you're pretty sure that when a job promotion opens up, it would be silly to apply. But you can never pin anything down. I'm sure the corporation could come up with five other reasons why I—or someone else my age—wasn't promoted."

Ironically, the industry that provides America with its dreams is one of the worst workplace offenders. "Don't send me gray hair," show-business agents are told by network and studio executives, and they aren't speaking only of actors. Beverly Hills plastic surgeons perform face-lifts on directors as well as actors, and in order to get in the studio door, writers have been known to pretend that their 28-year-old sons and daughters are their writing partners. Indeed, for movie and television writers, "it's generally understood that if you're 35 or 40 years old, you have to start forgetting your career," says Mort Thaw, who founded the age-discrimination committee of the Writers Guild of America West in 1981 and chaired the committee until 1993.

Star writers—Academy Award–winners or others with well-known names—are an exception. "Otherwise," says Thaw, "the perception has always been that older writers are dated. We were told that as the executives, particularly in television, got younger and younger, they did not want to see their mothers or fathers or grandfathers coming into their offices to pitch story ideas. A top woman writer who was about 70 had written a treatment for a romantic movie of the week, and the treatment had met with great favor. So she came in to be interviewed by a 28-year-old woman executive, who made it clear that the writer would not be hired to turn her treatment into a script. The executive asked her, 'Do you think you can write a script about two young people?' After the interview, the writer told me, 'This is my story, and these are my characters. Does she think I have forgotten love?'"

Says Thaw, "You do not lose the ability to write because you're 70. Your talent does not wither away. Your talent is enriched."

His lament for writers could be echoed by bakers, bricklayers, salesclerks and secretaries who want to continue working but find themselves fired or forced to retire too soon—and not only in America. In 1970, according to *The Economist* magazine, 70 to 80 percent of men aged 60 to 64 were still at work in European Union countries. By 1990, only 35 to 40 percent of that age group were still working.

Up to now, ageism has not been a hot topic, except to people affected by it, and the very fact of society's indifference diminishes the older citizen. The psychological mindset that infantilizes, patronizes or ignores everyone who has lost the first flush of youth leaves millions of older Americans feeling denigrated and useless. When only the young are valued, older people can fail to get the health care that would save their lives or make their lives less painful. When young workers are promoted and older workers are discarded, the impact on a generation that wants to contribute to society is immeasurable; and, significantly, the stereotypes of slow-thinking older adults upon which these hiring decisions are based have often been proved wrong. For example, although reflexes get slower as people age, a 1984 study of typists between the ages of 19 and 72 showed that while the older women had slower reaction times, they worked as quickly as the younger women by processing the material in a different way.

"You do not lose the ability to write because you are 70. Your talent does not wither away. Your talent is enriched."

There is, however, some hope that ageism may be at least lessened, if not stamped out, and it lies in the sheer numbers of the huge baby boom generation whose advance guard has just turned 50 and whose members will represent more than 25 percent of the U.S. population within a decade. "The baby boomers are transforming every age they pass through," says the Screen Actors Guild's Dena Dietrich. "At a recent U.C.L.A. conference for advertising people on ageism, it became clear that the advertising industry will have to think in terms of more mature consumers, since the population of 18- to 34-year-olds is declining every year."

So alert, active, vigorous maturity may yet be given its due... by necessity. ■

Aljean Harmetz is the author of Round Up the Usual Suspects: The Making of Casablanca *(Hyperion) and* On the Road to Tara: The Making of Gone With the Wind *(Abrams).*

Age and Boredom: An Issue of Well-being

By Myrna Lewis

Boredom can be a real problem during retirement, according to Norman D. Sundberg, Ph.D., professor emeritus in the Department of Psychology at the University of Oregon in Eugene. "A newly retired person can feel disengaged from mainstream roles, and finding interesting ways to spend time can prove difficult. Most important, boredom is a major risk factor for depression."

Of course, many retirees adjust quite nicely to their new lives. To help you prepare for important life changes, it may prove helpful to know just how easily you get bored. Take the following personality test, adapted from the Boredom Proneness Scale developed by Sundberg and Richard Farmer, Ph.D.

Circle your answers and then read the scoring information at the end.

1. It is easy for me to focus on the activity I'm doing at any given moment. **TRUE FALSE**
2. I frequently feel at a loss about what to do next. **TRUE FALSE**
3. Visiting friends who show home movies and go on and on about their vacation is my definition of boring. **TRUE FALSE**
4. It's easy for me to find something interesting to do or see in any situation I find myself in. **TRUE FALSE**
5. Waiting in line at the supermarket or bank makes me really restless. **TRUE FALSE**
6. New ideas pop into my mind frequently. **TRUE FALSE**
7. I wish I could find something more interesting to do in my life. **TRUE FALSE**
8. My friends would describe me as a creative and imaginative person. **TRUE FALSE**
9. I'm so busy with my various activities that I couldn't possibly take on anything new. **TRUE FALSE**
10. I need a lot of change and excitement to feel happy. **TRUE FALSE**
11. Most of the time, I feel that I'm working below my capacity and abilities. **TRUE FALSE**
12. It's quite easy for me to entertain myself. **TRUE FALSE**
13. I frequently feel that time passes too slowly. **TRUE FALSE**

Scoring

For questions 1, 4, 6, 8, 9 and 12, give yourself 1 point for each FALSE answer and 0 points for each TRUE.
For questions 2, 3, 5, 7, 10, 11 and 13, give yourself 1 point for each TRUE and 0 for each FALSE.

When you add up your points, a score of 0 means you are at the lowest point on the boredom scale, and a score of 13 means you are at the highest point.

"A score of 5 and above indicates that boredom may become a problem for you," says Sundberg. "It's important to remember that increased boredom is not inevitable with aging. A high score on this quiz should be interpreted as a warning sign to begin taking action now by consciously cultivating a variety of interests that are useful and rewarding."

LEARNING THE NEW INTIMACY

A best-selling author's tips for improving communication between the sexes and heating up longtime marriages

By John Gray, Ph.D.

Imagine that men are from Mars and women are from Venus. Eventually you connect emotionally and romantically with someone from the other "planet"; you fall in love and get married. For a while, you and your spouse instinctively focus on each other, enjoying good conversation and great sex. Whether or not you acknowledge that your needs, preferences and behaviors are significantly different, you're in tune with each other. But over the years, you unconsciously settle into certain rhythms that come to define your marriage. Meanwhile, passion slowly fades. By the time you're in your 50s, you are oblivious to the inherent distinctions between you and your spouse.

To break free of damaging patterns and restore the romance in your relationship, you need to incorporate communication—both words and gestures—based on the recognition that men and women are different. You expect your partner to think, behave and react as you would, but words don't always mean the same thing to men and women. For instance, a man says to a woman, "What's the matter?" and she says, "Nothing." He automatically interprets that response in his Mars language: "Nothing is the matter that I can't deal with by myself. If I want to talk about it, I will, later." However, in the language of Venus, "nothing" means something is the matter. A woman thinks, "If you love me, you'll take some time to ask me more questions." It's important to remember that men and women are from separate "worlds"; you shouldn't take everything your partner says literally. As you learn to interpret each other's language, your conversations and discussions—even your arguments—will become more open, satisfying and honest.

Communicating with your spouse requires more than just "talking it out." In even the most mundane situations, how you express yourself is as important as what you say. For example, Barbara wants her husband Lee's help with a small chore. She might say, "I have four big bags of groceries in the car, and I need that food to make our dinner. Could you bring them in?" Instead of this lengthy, indirect request, she should say, "Would you bring the groceries in from the car?" Here, Barbara isn't nagging or making Lee feel guilty; she is merely asking for help.

Learning to Support Your Spouse

Understanding your differences can free you of the struggle of repeatedly doing things for your partner that don't work. For example, a man tends to provide solutions to his wife's problems, but she wants empathy; a woman commonly tries to change her husband's habits, but he craves acceptance. Instead of automatically giving what you'd want to receive, you can learn to provide what your partner needs—so he or she, in turn, can satisfy your needs.

When a man is stressed or upset, he typically withdraws into himself—into his "cave." The greatest gift his wife can give him is not trying to get him to open up. For example, when Henry feels depressed about work, his wife, Madeline, initially asks, "What's the matter? Let's talk about it." But Henry doesn't want to talk. The more Madeline pushes him to talk, the more he pulls away from her. Eventually it becomes impossible for them to come

together. When Henry finally says he's ready to talk about it, Madeline is likely to resent him. This is understandable, for when a woman feels down, she wants her partner to say, "What's the matter? Is it something I did? Let's talk about it."

Henry's response is especially familiar to the 50-plus women who hear it. They immediately say, "That's my husband! I thought I was being helpful, but encouraging him to talk has been counterproductive." The solution? A woman should take some time for herself — for friends, support groups and activities. The best thing for her is a life so complete that she's not totally dependent on her husband for emotional fulfillment.

Left alone with his problems — and freed of the pressure of pleasing his wife — a man will eventually work his way out of his foul mood, gradually becoming warm and responsive. For example, I was in my cave the other day, which meant my wife was getting zip of warmth and caring attention from me. I wasn't doing it purposefully; I just wasn't able to give at that time. Bonnie very wisely chose to go on a shopping spree, which is something she enjoys. She came home very happy, thanking me for what she bought. I had been sitting there in my cave the whole time, but essentially I got credit for her happiness. And this started to draw me out of my cave.

Women have their own method of dealing with emotional swings. When a woman feels hopeless or empty inside, she enters her "well." She needs to be filled up with love from her husband. A man gets frustrated when his wife goes down into her well because he doesn't know how to make things better. Rather than try to "fix it," he should support his wife with attention and unconditional love. When a woman feels that she can be heard and understood, she automatically begins to rise back up from the well. And only then is she capable of expressing love and affection.

Changes After 50

At midlife, 50-plus couples face a major communication obstacle: role reversal. Men naturally become more in touch with their feminine qualities; women, with their masculine qualities. Ideally, we'd finally meet in the middle. Instead, many 50-plus men actually become more outgoing and talkative. Whereas a big chunk of a man's need for acknowledgment was once met through his career, he now looks instinctively to his wife to fill him up. But she can't possibly give her husband all the love and attention he craves, and suddenly she thinks, "He talks too much.

I don't even want to talk to him anymore." She should practice saying, "Honey, I need you to listen to me first." A woman must feel that she can still count on her husband for support, even as he becomes more emotionally dependent on her. If a woman sees that her husband is too needy, she may become so independent that she no longer turns to him. Women in this stage of life are likely to pull away and have less to say to their spouses.

Just as women seek fulfillment outside the marriage, older men especially should partake in other activities, such as volunteer work or a hobby-career. A man should have contact with others who value his service or benefit from his expertise and kindness. When both partners have temporary "escape routes," they are less likely to smother each other, and they become more open to supporting each other in a loving, beneficial way. Once you and your spouse strike a balance—an agreed-upon system of give-and-take—you will have laid the groundwork for reworking the romance into your relationship.

Romance: Back to the Basics

What makes men feel romantic toward women is not so much what women do for them but how women respond to what their partners do for them. That's the big secret both men and women must grasp. Over the years, however, you and your spouse may start to take each other for granted. When a woman no longer expresses appreciation for her husband's romantic gestures, he loses the motivation for romance. Understandably, resentment builds on both sides. Here's my favorite example of this:

One night, about 10 years into our marriage, as my wife, Bonnie, and I were leaving a restaurant, I opened the door for her—a small but important romantic gesture. At the same time, another man walked up and opened the other side of

When both partners have temporary "escape routes," they are less likely to smother each other.

the double door for my wife. She walked through the door, looked at the stranger, gave him a smile and said, "Oh, thank you so much." What the tone of her voice said to me—and to any man—was, "You didn't have to do that, and you did it anyway. What a wonderful gentleman you are. Now, my husband—he has to open the door because I do his laundry." If I weren't aware that such oversights commonly occur in relationships over time, my feelings would have been hurt. In this case, I might figure, "Why bother opening the door if she's not going to appreciate me for it." This may seem like a minor quibble, but even an unintentional slight can be hurtful.

A man needs his wife's positive reinforcement, but it doesn't always have to be verbal. By the time a couple hits 50, they should devise other means of expressing appreciation for each other in order to rekindle the flame. I suggest that couples start by looking back to the first years of marriage. What were some of the things the husband did? How did the wife respond? Remember those times and retrieve those habits (even if you don't feel like it), because they've been lost but not forgotten. It's kind of like priming the pump; you just have to get that old-fashioned connection going.

One evening, Arthur surprises Julia by bringing home a bouquet of flowers. Even if Julia is suspicious and doesn't genuinely feel a lot of warmth for this gesture, she should try to express some sense of gratitude. Slowly but surely, Arthur does more and Julia responds. He does a little more, she responds a little more. And they start reviving the emotional energy in their marriage. However, if Arthur doesn't take the initiative, Julia needs to get him to do things so she can show her appreciation. She should ask directly, but gently, for small things: "Honey, would you hold the ladder while I change the lightbulb?" Then, as Julia thanks him, Arthur senses her gratitude.

When a man doesn't feel appreciated, he loses his attraction for his wife. And if a woman doesn't sense that her feelings are heard and respected and that her needs are being tended to, she loses her attraction for her husband. When the attraction fizzles, a couple usually stops having sex—which can break the emotional connection. Ultimately, the relationship between a man and a woman is inextricably linked to their relationship in the bedroom.

Improving Communication in the Bedroom

Sex is a touchy topic for many couples, even those who've spent years together. Rather than remain silently unhappy in a marriage devoid of sex—or good sex—a couple can seek an outside source for help. My advice is to find a book about sex and read it, either out loud to each other or separately, and discuss it later. Once the issue is out in the open, it becomes easier to understand the problem and solve it.

After years of marriage, an interesting shift in the sexual dynamics between a man and a woman occurs. It's extremely common for 50-plus women to be more in touch with their desire for sex and their male peers to be less in touch with it. I have counseled plenty of couples who struggle with this delicate situation. Consider Brad and Sarah, who have been married for 25 years. While Sarah now feels like a teenager, suddenly wanting more sex, Brad feels that his sexual needs have long been rejected. For years, Sarah focused on raising the kids and tending to domestic activities; yet, come 50, she has more time for sex. But since Brad resents that Sarah was disinterested for so many years, he's unable to retain his desire for sex—or romance.

Many men over 50 are no longer instinctively aroused; they need stimulation—just as women need foreplay. Biologically, it's perfectly normal for older men to not be as quickly and automatically aroused as they once were. After 50, a man may be capable of enjoying wonderful sex and not even know it. He merely needs help getting in touch with his erogenous desires. But here's the catch-22: A man becomes reluctant to initiate romantic activities because he's unsure whether his wife will respond. Meanwhile, she's waiting to be romanced by him. When a woman feels romantic, she'll want to have sex—and that desire arouses him. But before a man can be turned on by his wife, he needs to feel that he can please her. To avoid confusion, a husband and wife must establish a means of communicating their sexual desires to each other.

When You're in the Mood

Couples who have been married for many, many years and have a great sex life generally share a very clear set of rituals that lead to sex. Designating signals can eliminate the misunderstanding that may otherwise interfere with sex. For a woman over 50, a signal may be the way she dresses for bed. Instead of her basic flannel nightgown, she may wear some silkier, more elegant bedroom attire. This sends her husband a subtle, but obvious, message: "I'm in the mood. If you initiate, I'll respond." Even if a man initially feels tired and unmotivated, he'll notice that his wife looks especially pretty, that she's in the mood for sex. Soon, he finds himself wanting to make love to her.

A more confident woman could say to her husband, "Honey, I just want you to know that when I take a long, hot bath and the candle is burning, if you are in the mood for sex, I certainly am." Or, she might write him a little note expressing a similar sentiment. One couple I counseled had an unusuaL—yet effective—method. The husband had once mentioned to his wife that eating pistachio nuts made him more virile. Whenever she wanted to have sex, she put out a dish of pistachio nuts. Each couple can create their own rituals through trial and error. Maybe the husband brings home a particular bottle of wine; the wife might cook a certain meal. The possibilities are endless. With a romantic ritual, the message is clear: She's not pushing sex on him; she's not demanding. And that opens the door for change.

The Key to a Happier Mars-Venus Alliance

Remember that you're never too old to change, as long as you're being nurtured correctly.

If a man senses that his wife is trying to change him, he cannot change. He gives up because her actions and reactions imply that he can't succeed. Instead of criticizing, she must say to him, "All these years I've been trying to change you, but I realize that it's I who need to change." She focuses the change on her own attitude about the way he is—the way she approaches him with requests and the way she responds to his moods. When a woman says, "I need to stop what I've been doing and start doing other things," her husband sees that she has the potential to be happy. He can succeed, so he becomes motivated to change.

Men sometimes ignore the need for improvement and give up entirely. Before a man can get his wife to open up, he needs to recognize all the situations in which he has stopped trying. He could say to his wife, "I realize I've been doing all these things that have been insensitive and unsupportive. I've been neglecting you. And this is not what anyone needs." A man should be specific when mentioning the things he regrets doing, as well as the things he didn't do. Rather than attempting to change his wife's feelings—to talk her out of moods or solve her problems—a man can demonstrate through his actions that he's able to satisfy her needs.

The reality for couples over 50 is this: Men need to validate and embrace women's feelings; women must validate and embrace men's behavior. Only by understanding what motivates each other to change—and by sharing the responsibility for improvement—can a man from Mars and a woman from Venus work toward better communication, more romance and an all-around happier relationship after 50. ■

John Gray, Ph.D., is author of the best-selling Men Are from Mars, Women Are from Venus *and four more Mars/Venus titles (all from HarperCollins).*

Making Your Intimate Conversations Better

By Myrna Lewis

It's no surprise that a major way people achieve intimacy with their spouse is by talking. But what many couples don't realize is that the wrong kind of talk can stifle further communication and threaten the foundation of a relationship.

"Intimate talk becomes particularly important for couples when other distractions, such as children or work, are no longer there to fill the void," says Suzette Haden Elgin, Ph.D., author of *Genderspeak: Men, Women, and the Gentle Art of Verbal Self-Defense* (John Wiley). "One way to stay close is to converse without using what I call linguistic booby traps, which leave no room for your partner to respond."

Elgin says that common booby traps include using names and epithets ("You sexist pig!"), diagnoses ("You're only saying that because you're so tired"), direct commands ("Take off that awful tie"), prophecies ("You're going to hate yourself in the morning"), sermons ("Decent people stick to a budget and don't spend the way you do"), unsolicited advice ("Here's what I'd do if I were you") and what she calls hijackings ("You think you had a bad day? Listen to what happened to me today").

"You may not be able to eliminate these structures from your speech entirely," says Elgin, "but you can become aware of them and realize that they can block your efforts to foster intimacy. Above all, what you must do before speaking is to ask yourself, 'What can my partner possibly respond to what I'm about to say?' If you can't think of an answer, then say something else for which you yourself can think of a range of responses."

How to rethink your relationships and ...

BE A BETTER SPOUSE OR COMPANION

By Gene Cohen, M.D., PH.D.

Finally, you're middle-aged. Mortgage payments no longer faze you—who knows, maybe you'll sell and move to a cozy college town. Your kids have graduated from knapsacks to briefcases, from senior proms to honeymoons. There's not a midlife crisis looming anywhere. In fact, life has never looked so ripe with opportunity. So, how's your marriage going?

Until midlife, our emotional and daily lives fall into place around common transition points—childhood to adolescence, college to work, marriage to parenting. But once children are raised and professions established, life progresses without clear markers. Life past 50 used to be a short stage, but its boundaries have expanded significantly, allowing many of us who outlive spouses or broken marriages plenty of time to forge a close tie to someone else. Today the fastest-growing segment of the population consists of people 100 and over—an encouraging sign to those of us who hope to remain thriving individuals for many years.

But hand in hand with the increased potential for longer and healthier middle years comes an enhanced possibility of venturing into new, separate directions, a prospect borne out by the growing number of older adults getting divorced. Given how much of life stretches before us, now is the time to figure out whether the most important relationship in our lives still rates an A—and if it doesn't, be ready to improve it.

How Midlife Relationships Are Thrown Off Balance

Sometime during your 50s, life may become, for the first time, uncluttered. Instead of dodging distractions, you plot ways to spend your free time. Like a quiz-show contestant selecting prizes hidden behind numbered doors, you're delighted by the possibilities. Opening any of those doors, though, can have consequences for your relationship that you never anticipated.

I've often observed how the simple pursuit of a new interest can jar a marriage. Let me explain with an example: A fellow named Craig, who is semi-retired and whose kids are all working, decides to take a sculpture class. Craig is intrigued by sculpting, of course,

but he's not expecting much more than a fun learning experience. After a few sessions, though, he feels reinvigorated. He can't quite put his finger on it, but he senses that this engaging hobby that's brightening his perspective is a wake-up call.

By contrast, home suddenly seems static. Nothing there inspires the same fresh outlook he gets from his sculpting classes, and he sees no channels for his newfound energy. He's begun to suspect that his wife, Pamela, resents his new avocation. Unfortunately, Craig's hunch is right: Pamela feels completely eclipsed.

In another scenario, it is a sudden loss of time together that delivers a hard jolt to a relationship. Consider this example: During the years since their youngest child left home for college, Grace and Paul have contentedly followed a daily pace set by his consulting job, her part-time volunteering and their shared devotion to gardening.

When Grace accepts the demanding position of volunteer coordinator at the local museum, she and Paul have to reinvent the rhythm of their married life. Though genuinely pleased for his wife, Paul is unhappy that her new schedule will cost them the domestic routines they now relish. Who can blame him?

It is hard work resurrecting a relationship when the stresses of parenting and professional life have lifted; once we've adjusted to this calmer midlife landscape, few of us would choose to be jostled again.

We're bound to notice when a mate's attention is drawn away. But just as important to the well-being of a marriage is a less perceptible influence: outside relationships. A wife's enduring friendship with a golfing buddy, for instance, may bolster her marriage in myriad ways — until her pal develops a serious illness and withdraws. Without the steady support of his strong friendship, she is forced to face the weaknesses of her marriage.

None of us can afford to have our social network shrink — though inevitably it will.

Restoring Equilibrium

Luckily, it doesn't require major engineering to right the balance of a relationship. And the person who feels left out by a mate's new kick doesn't have to respond by kicking back. Pamela needn't sign up for piano lessons to fill the void created by Craig's enthusiasm for sculpting (though that's a perfectly good idea), and Paul doesn't have to return to full-time work so that the demands of Grace's new job are less painful. Both Pamela and Paul must act — but, surprisingly, just a small reciprocal action can counterbalance an unanticipated stir in a relationship's dynamics. If it's the right move, the dislocated partner regains his or her footing.

How do you know what the right move is? As a start, assess where your relationship is off-kilter. Make four lists: activities involving you and your spouse; activities involving you, your spouse and others; your solo involvement with others; your spouse's solo involvement with others. To each list add several new possibilities — relationships and activities — you could be pursuing. This isn't intended to pinpoint trouble spots or to prescribe new directions — those must come from you. But it can have the same clarifying effect as a first pair of bifocals.

Pamela's answer to Craig's sudden passion could be to do something new on her own, but there are countless other ways she can recharge her life. Maybe she schedules a weekly lunch with her best friend, something she has intended to do for years. Or maybe she and Craig decide to play tennis together every Saturday morning. Both of these possibilities fall within the framework of your lists; in the end, the choice of action is highly individual.

Thinking about what is most missing from his life since Grace started "camping out" at the museum, Paul knows it is the quiet evenings they habitually shared. Although he wants to make Grace aware of that loss, he doesn't want her to think he's a bad sport who can't cope with her success. When his son casually suggests that Paul and Grace should reserve Friday night for themselves each week, he welcomes the idea. But because it implies displeasure with things as they are, he can't bring himself to propose it to Grace. Finally, he enlists his son as messenger—a role the son, who has noticed his father's distress, willingly accepts and effectively performs.

In life, of course, one-step solutions are as hard to come by as winning lottery tickets. Conversely, it usually takes more than one bump to derail a marriage. I remember a 50-something married woman who came to me for help. She had been depressed much of her life, though she had never received steady treatment. She had started having affairs, one of which her husband knew about. And she had grown increasingly weary of her work as a teacher. Her husband, an engineer, was just as dissatisfied with his profession. These two people were almost a caricature of midlife crisis: Their former anchors no longer held fast, and they were adrift.

The wife responded well to psychotherapy and a brief round of antidepressant drugs. Once she had improved, they focused on reconstructing their relationship. After casting about for ways to come together, the couple settled on a first step: throwing dinner parties. Frivolous as that idea may seem, it worked well for them. They both were good cooks who enjoyed perfecting their skill and who collaborated comfortably in the kitchen. Saving their marriage, though, took much more—a shared commitment to altering their relationship and one partner's determination to conquer her depression.

When Your Closest Relationship Is Not with a Spouse

Through divorce, illness, death or just natural affinity, a person's closest midlife relationship may be with a friend, sibling or child. Whether your closest tie is to a spouse or someone else, it's easy, given the narrower focus of middle age, to fall into the trap of overinvesting in one relationship. Let's say it is a widow who discovers over time that her daughter is her most trustworthy confidante. Imagine her reaction when her daughter announces that her husband's new job means a move to a different state. The widow's imminent loss feels irreplaceable, which, in truth, it may be. But it doesn't have to devastate her life.

The widow who is about to lose her closest connection would quickly see from the four lists that she must diversify her interests. She might begin a class at a local college, for example. Besides having a diversion, she would be among people of different ages. Most likely, she would find the exposure to younger people not only stimulating but comforting. To ensure that her relationship with her daughter survives unharmed, she'd be wise to stock up on stationery or become conversant in E-mail and plan a visit—even before the moving van leaves town.

None of us can afford to have our social network shrink—though inevitably it will. Finding the right activities and companions throughout your life is as tricky as finding the right job—and just as crucial. Stimulation and challenge keep the mind sharp and morale up. And gentle nudges from caring peers ("You should keep that doctor's appointment," say) help to keep life on course.

The Greatest Risk Is Denial

To return to the opening question, "So, how's your marriage going?": If you can answer it with a heartfelt "Great," there's no need to worry. But if you have to pause and consider, or if a good friend recently asked, "How *are* you two doing?" don't hesitate—act.

At one time, I studied why some older people were markedly fulfilled and content. An explanation all these satisfied souls offered was that they now had the time to tackle any misunderstanding as it arose. The upshot was that a slight rift in a critical relationship never turned into a breach. For them, that was one of the great gifts of growing older. ■

Gene Cohen, M.D., Ph.D., is director of the Center on Aging, Health and Humanities at George Washington University.

TRAPPED IN MARRIAGE?

When to leave — why to stay

By Claire Safran

Last month, Marge and Joe Hamilton* gave a party to mark 25 years of marriage. Marge bought a new dress, but the occasion did not go well. "That dress makes you look fat," Joe told her as the guests were arriving. "You did it again!" he whispered an hour later. "The ham is too salty." At the end of the evening, he summed it up for his wife this way. "After all these years," he said, "you still don't know how to give a decent party."

*Names have been changed to protect the privacy of the individuals described.

All in all, it was a very tarnished silver anniversary. Marge is a long-suffering victim, bound in marriage to *el exigente*, as she calls him behind his back. She tries not to respond to his criticisms, partly because her answers only encourage him, partly because she half believes him.

Battered by words, she used to tell herself that she put up with it for the sake of the children. Now that they're grown, she has other reasons for staying. "Where would I go?" she wonders. She knows that the odds of a woman over 50 starting a new relationship are slim. As Joe has often taunted, "What other man would have you?" A full-time homemaker, she doubts she could find a job — "beyond Burger King, that is." If it came to a divorce, her share of their assets would not stretch very far. "On my own," she asks, "how would I survive?"

There's no official head count of people caught in unhappy, unrewarding or stale midlife marriages. According to Anna Beth Benningfield, Ph.D., past president of the American Association for Marriage and Family Therapy, they are a significant minority, about 15 percent of the post-50 wives and husbands she sees.

Some partners linger out of inertia. Some, like Marge, are stuck out of fear of poverty or the unknown. Others, especially women, are pinned in place by a sense of duty, convinced that it's up to them to "fix" the man and the marriage. Studies of alcoholic marriages, notes Louise Morgan, Ed.M., a Fairfield, Connecticut, counselor, show that men tend to leave their addicted wives but that women tend to stay with their alcoholic husbands. For their pains, they often get called names like "enabler" and "co-dependent."

Should wives or husbands who are unhappy day in and day out just sigh and stay put? Can they — or should they — head for the door? "Marriage becomes a trap when you think you have no choices and no control over what happens to you," explains Betty Carter, M.S.W., director of the Family Institute of Westchester (New York). "But most people have more choices than they realize."

Her friends feel sorry for Marge Hamilton, but marriage counselors can be stern with such a person. As they see it, she's made her choice — to be a victim. "Some nights, I dream that I've fallen down a dark hole," she says. "I try to scream for help, but no one hears. Even in my dream, I know that I'm not making a sound."

In fact, it's not too late for Marge to find her voice. Instead of wishing that Joe would change, she could save herself by changing herself. It may be scary, but she could make a new choice — to take charge of her life. She could go back to school, do some volunteering or find a part-time job; in other words, she could do whatever would build her skills and sense of competence.

Such a move could make it easier for her to leave the marriage, with less chance of turning into a bag lady. It also could make it easier for her to stay, with a newfound self-esteem and the courage to negotiate better terms with her husband. "Marriage is a system," explains Lonnie Barbach, Ph.D., a psychologist and co-author of *Going the Distance* (Doubleday). "If one person makes a change, the other person can't keep responding in the same old way."

Mostly, it's wives who feel trapped in marriage. Yet husbands, too, can feel cornered, says Carol M. Anderson, Ph.D., professor of psychiatry at the University of Pittsburgh Medical School. Anderson explains that men often feel "trapped not just in a relationship but in a role, shackled to the obligations of being the provider."

For many men, however, work is a sanctuary, the source of most of their satisfaction and sense of identity. Although more and more women are applying that male secret to themselves, many experts agree that women continue to define themselves by their connections to other people. When that part of life isn't working, it's like "a hole in the heart," as one woman I interviewed said.

"This generation of wives counted on marriage to make them happy," explains Anderson, author of *Flying Solo* (Norton), a wise new book on women living alone. "These women bought the Cinderella story," says Anderson. "It promised that they'd live 'happily ever after,' but it stopped short of telling them how. It didn't tell them very much about Prince Charming, either."

For Liz Jameson*, the prince turned out to be a workaholic, good at making money but scared of spending it. For 32 years, Liz and Walter* have been at war, shouting at each other about money, fighting over how to raise their two children. They seem to connect only through high decibels. Friends wonder why Liz stays in "the marriage from hell," as they call it.

On her own, Liz could live in modest comfort on her federal pension and with some financial support from Walter. "But I stayed this long," she says. "I earned some luxuries." She's afraid of being lonely and having to scrimp like some of her divorced or widowed friends. "Better the devil I know . . . ," she says. She thinks divorce means that you have "failed as a woman." She hangs in there, but she's angry about it.

"Walter never wants to go anywhere," she complains. Two years ago, he finally agreed to go on a group tour of Alaska, but once again he let her down. The day before take-off, he announced that he couldn't leave his business. Liz screamed, wept and then went by herself. "And guess what?" she says, smiling. "I had a good time." Since then, they've been leading parallel lives. If Walter wants to stay home, Liz still goes out, sometimes alone, sometimes with a friend. "It's not what I want," she says, "but it's what I can have." Because Liz sees their bargain as a choice, says Anderson, she doesn't have to feel trapped and out of control. Mind games, it seems, do count.

Liz's worst fear used to be that Walter would get sick and she would have to spend her days nursing him. Last year, he was diagnosed as having severe hypertension. Walter still works long hours, but now he comes home and cooks dinner for both of them, "because he doesn't trust me not to put salt in his food," Liz explains, only half joking. She has found her silver lining: a role reversal. "For the first time, he is taking care of me," she says. The bitter fights are less frequent now. Walter's new health-consciousness has also given them something they can do together—work out at the gym. "With all his faults," Liz admits, "I realize I'd miss him if he were gone. And I think he'd miss me."

Few marriages are perfect, but few are nonstop misery. "He doesn't drink, beat me or run around. What more can I ask for?" says one of my friends, Lilly Morgan*, an excruciatingly humble wife. Other women have made the same comment to Dr. Benningfield. "It comes as a surprise to some women that they have a right to demand lots more," she notes. "The married couples who have the best chance of being healed are those who, at some point, were happy together."

Once upon a time, Mary and Tom Billings*, for example, were passionately in love. Along the way, in the hurly-burly of child rearing and dual career building, they lost each other. Now they have turned into that familiar couple often seen in restaurants, the man and woman who must be married because they have nothing to say to each other. Turning 50, Mary feels trapped by boredom. She has begun to weigh her choices. "On the one hand, I like being part of a couple," she admits. "We're 'the Billings.' Our social life is built around that." She cherishes the history and the children they share. On the other hand, she yearns for more companionship and intimacy. So, sitting across the table from him, she thinks, "Thirty more years of this? Uh-uh!"

"Marriage is a trap when you think you have no control. Most people have more choices than they realize."

"She doesn't have to just sit there," says Benningfield. "A wife can take the initiative for breaking the routine." She could introduce something as simple as a walk before dinner, as challenging as a sport neither of them has ever tried, or as unexpected as an erotic video.

As psychologist Barbach sees it, a wife can jump-start her marriage by trusting her husband enough to tell him what she feels and needs. Expressing your needs directly can make a difference. For example, Mary and Tom Billings are redoing their home, and, like many couples, they're arguing about it. He's in charge, she heckles from the sidelines. The disorder is driving her crazy, but she hasn't told him that. If she had said, "I can't stand so much disorder," he might have considered her view. He might have said, "Okay, let's do it one room at a time."

In marriage, there are no guarantees. Some can't be saved; some are worth the try. But if there's still a flicker of love and loyalty, wives and husbands have a chance to change the patterns that have trapped them both. ■

Claire Safran writes about social issues for various national magazines.

Top 5 Topics to Discuss Before Remarrying

By Myrna Lewis

This year, an estimated 250,000 people over age 50 will remarry in the United States—a statistic that guarantees a fair amount of discussion about retirement plans, property, adult children and other issues unique to later-life marriages. "Many of these problem areas should be dealt with before the ceremony," says Jane Hughes Barton (herself a widow who remarried), educator and author of Remarriage after 50 (Roger Thomas Press).

Based on Barton's interviews with dozens of "second-timers," here is her list of the top five subjects to explore with your future spouse:

- **Whether or not to have a prenuptial agreement.**
If you choose, you can work with a lawyer to spell out arrangements for shared and separate finances, inheritance provisions for surviving spouses as well as adult children and anything else you want to acknowledge formally.

- **Where to live.**
Besides geography, consider whether one or both of you want to take advantage of the one-time $125,000 exclusion from capital-gains tax on the sale of a house when you're 55 or older. (Each of you can take it if you sell before you marry.)

- **Sharing household tasks.**
How will you divide the chores of daily living? This could become a major issue.

- **Intimacy and sex.**
"There are many ways to express affection and closeness besides sex," notes Barton. "The key is whether your partner is able to respect and respond to your needs in a loving way."

- **Compatible values.**
How does each of you feel about honesty, family, faith? If two people share similar core beliefs, their marriage has a better chance of lasting.

A Husband May Not Be Good for Your Health

By Nissa Simon

Rather than serving as a calm haven from the emotional stresses of daily life, marriage itself may actually raise a woman's blood pressure. Researchers at Duke University evaluated the effects of type of occupation, amount of job strain, and marital status on the blood pressure of 99 men and women with mild hypertension. They found that occupation and marital status—but not necessarily job stress—increase blood pressure. As reported in the *Journal of Psychosomatic Research,* the men and women with high-status occupations, such as executives or professors, have significantly higher blood pressure both during their workday and in laboratory testing of mental stress. But marital status affects only women—with married women having higher blood pressure than their single sisters.

WHY WOMEN OVER 50 HAVE AFFAIRS

. . . and what we can learn from their bitter-sweet experiences

By Deborah Mason

The women would talk only on the condition of anonymity. And it had to be on the mornings their husbands were at work or the weekly golf game, on the afternoons when grown children would not drop by. Two of the women shooed grandchildren out of the room before we began. In their 50s and 60s, the women then poured out to me the biggest secret of their lives: their love affairs.

Joan, a 58-year-old secretary from Kansas, has come to the point of second-guessing her choice. In an interview, she told me: "If I'd ever known it would go this far, I never would've gotten into the relationship."

Some affairs have gone on for years; most are with men who are married—old friends of the family, co-workers and, in two cases, former high school sweethearts. Like Joan, every woman says that the passionate charge of the connection has stunned her, unsettling her ideas of how a middle-aged woman, mother or grandmother "should" act. As part of a generation unswayed by the sexual revolution and groomed to be eternal "good girls" who hold life together for everyone else, they say an affair often makes them feel torn in half.

To admit the affair in the first place was not easy. In a national *New Choices* survey by EDK Associates of 500 women ranging in age from 50 to 70, both married and single, only 4 percent actually owned up to an affair. But, significantly, 24 percent more said they knew of at least one 50-plus woman who is having or has had an affair. So did therapists from across the country, five of whom in one week told me they had two or three such women as clients. The therapists were also bound to secrecy.

The Secret No One Wants to Know

Indeed, this is a secret so carefully guarded—and so rarely suspected—that almost half the husbands of the women whose affairs the survey uncovered have never found out about them. Do the husbands just assume an affair is the last thing on a 50-plus wife's mind? After all, most people still have a hard time using the words *sex* and *older woman* in the same sentence.

"This is a secret we don't want to know. It's too threatening," says Sonya Friedman, Ph.D., clinical psychologist and author of *Secret Loves: Women with Two Lives* (Crown). "We can't accept the idea of women having affairs yet—so certainly not your grandmother."

In my follow-up interviews with people in the *New Choices* survey and with another small group, the women themselves said that one of the biggest surprises was finding themselves in affairs in the first place. Betsy, 53, a Vermont chemist in a near-sexless marriage, describes how she and a younger, married colleague started having long telephone conversations. When she went out with him for what she thought was a casual drink, he stunned her by grabbing her hand and telling her he had a crush on her.

"I was really not looking," she says. "I hadn't even been aware that we were 'flirting' up to that point, if we were. I was in perimenopause; I could no longer imagine walking into a room and turning someone on—I thought that part of my life was over. Not to mention the fact that I was married. But I also started feeling excited; I literally lost the power of speech." Soon afterward, they started an affair.

Like many of the women we talked to, Betsy had routinely bought into the idea that she was out of the running—not only for an affair but even to register on the attractiveness scale, given our culture's preference for young bodies and its habit of measuring women by their looks. Mention "affair" to a 50-plus woman and chances are, her first reaction will be like that of one of my friends: "For me, it would be a matter of thighs. Mine. Plus, I'd be worried he'd see my cellulite." Given what the women having affairs told me, cellulite was the last thing on their lovers' minds.

"If I'd known it would go this far, I would not have gotten into the relationship."

— Joan, 58, a Kansas secretary

As with Joan and Betsy, names and some identifying characteristics of the women in this article have been changed to protect anonymity. But they are from all parts of the country, showing the national sweep of our findings. What emerged from the interviews was that precisely because a woman is over 50, her affair takes a dramatically different shape from that of a younger woman's. Many of its reasons are more surprising, its dangers greater, its pleasures sweeter and its rules more pragmatic, more "mature," if you will.

My Husband Won't Talk to Me

There is one familiar reason, though amplified by age: Those who are married say their husbands simply don't pay enough attention to them, let alone tell them they are beautiful or make them feel desirable. Indeed, almost one in three women surveyed cite a lack of closeness in a marriage as a reason a woman would have an affair.

"I have a hard time getting him to talk to me," says Marjorie, 57, a Tennessee housewife who has a near platonic relationship with her husband of 35 years. "It's sad. I feel I've grown and have a broader outlook on most everything. To this day, I could go out somewhere and dance until the place closes. My husband doesn't even like to dance."

Middle age and late middle age can bring on marital discontent—children gone, suddenly alone together in the house, maybe confronting health problems or the emotional dislocation of retirement. Almost 4 out of 10 women surveyed, 68 percent of whom were married, see it as a time of particular marital stress. Even so, women entering affairs don't describe their marriages as terrible. "Distant" and "routine" are more the rule.

"To me, affairs are symptomatic of intense marital conflict. But it doesn't have to be people ripping each other's faces off; it can be quiet, underground conflict," says Judith Gilbert Kautto, C.S.W., a Chappaqua, New York, therapist who specializes in putting marriages back together after an affair. "In a way, affairs can, initially, stabilize a situation: They either deal with an issue in a marriage —or help people avoid it."

A Chance to Unwrap the Sexual Self

With 50-plus women's affairs, sex seems to be the issue more often than anyone would imagine. Raised to keep their sexual selves under wraps, they are more comfortable talking about their need for "emotional closeness," as they did in the survey. But tellingly, 73 percent went on to insist that women over 50 are much sexier than people think they are. In a follow-up interview, Marjorie told how, on a visit to her sister in Arkansas, she met a married man seven years younger—who not coincidentally loved to dance. They started an affair that lasted almost four years, the first two of delirious intensity.

"The whole thing was such a high—oh gosh, it was such a high! I can't even remember feeling that way when I was 20," she says. "We both enjoyed sex. We really got into it. And we talked about it—it was all so open. What I found out was that I was not as inhibited as I thought; a lot of it was the man I was living with."

Sally, 51, a Seattle teacher, divorced with grown children, expresses even stronger satisfaction. In her recent affair with a married former high school sweetheart, she says she had the first real orgasm of her life.

It's Not About Revenge, or Missing Out, or Even Age

Hearing the women talk and reading the *New Choices* survey dispel a number of myths.

One, that a primary reason for a midlife affair is to retaliate against a husband for having one: Only 6 percent of the women surveyed who had an affair, or who knew of someone who did, say it was because of a husband who had strayed. (A revenge affair in a marriage, say therapists, often serves to finally do it in.)

Two, that women have affairs in midlife because they feel they "missed out" earlier: 54 percent of the surveyed women were married between ages 18 and 21, and the husband was the first sexual partner of 76 percent of all the women, but neither fact had much impact on their feelings about marriage or affairs. Indeed, a mere 11 percent have fantasized about one since turning 50. Clearly, these women don't feel especially "deprived."

And finally, only 1 in 10 of the women surveyed even mentioned age as a reason for an affair, neatly dismantling the cliché of a "woman of a certain age" wistfully grasping at one last chance for love.

"Age? I never gave it a thought," said Joyce, 59, a Pennsylvania real estate agent with two grown children, who divorced her husband of 24 years, then entered into an 11-year affair with a married man. "We used to laugh about the fact that he was five years younger. And I'm completely gray—the 'Centrum Lady!' I'd say, 'Hey, you're over the hill, and I'm just coming into my own, sexually and everything else.' "

Another reason for an affair, as articulated by Ruth, 61, a Texas social worker, is as a bandage for a wounded ego. After her husband of 21 years, father of her four children, left her to marry his young secretary, she started an affair with a former high school boyfriend who was married. "I felt so used up. Suddenly, there he was, blindly adoring. And for the first time in a long time, I thought, 'I am attractive; I am interesting.' He gave me a vision of myself as a single woman who could make it on her own. I was playing a new role: utterly desirable. That's the way it is in an affair—you're playing a part. And man, is it fun."

But it isn't easy.

A Difficult Decision

Raised at a time when, for the most part, only "bad girls" had sex before marriage and only "tramps" outside of it, these women rarely took lightly the decision to have an affair. Whatever her religious upbringing or marital status, almost everyone described an agonizing struggle with her conscience.

"I spent almost a year telling him, 'No way. Stop calling me,' " says Sally, the divorced Seattle teacher who took up with her high school sweetheart. "Even now, to hear the words that I had an affair with a married man—I just can't fathom that that's what I did. It has always been a taboo for me. Plus, I'm staunchly pro-women, and I didn't want to hurt his wife." Said another, "I figured that I was going to die and go directly to hell. That's the kind of upbringing I had."

Once the affair starts, the good-girl training often resurfaces in another way: The 50-plus woman needs to view the relationship as somehow "monogamous"—even if she is married. Indeed, almost every one talks about her lover as if he were another husband. "I haven't gone out with anyone since we started seeing one another seven years ago," says one single woman, 55, having an affair with a married co-worker. "When it ends, it's going to be like another divorce."

Many of the women take pains to emphasize the longevity of the affair, as if to make it more respectable. Says a 60-year-old widow who has had two affairs: "They haven't been one-night stands, you understand. The last one was for four years."

For both married and single women, the solid friendship and equality in their affairs seems to be crucial—maybe because they have never had either in their marriages; maybe because, unlike the compliant creatures they were at 20, they have come into their own and need to feel free to speak their minds.

"I could talk to my lover about anything, say exactly how I felt about things, and he could accept it," says Joan, the Kansas secretary who started her 10-year affair with a married co-worker near the end of her own marriage. "He probably knows me better than anybody. We could be in the kitchen drinking coffee or out in the country mushroom hunting and be totally happy."

A 50-plus woman's seasoned savvy also helps to preserve the affair's secrecy. Says therapist Gilbert Kautto, "In most cases, older women are more mature than younger women about the way they handle an affair, and much more discreet. They don't leave motel receipts lying around."

The Risks: "If people knew we were having an affair, they'd probably think we'd lost our minds."

They have good reason to be careful: At this age, the risks of an affair are enormous. Even if her husband has been quietly complicit—secretly relieved that she is no longer pressuring him for sex or attention, or having an affair of his own—it is the woman who pays the biggest price when her affair surfaces. Six out of 10 women in the poll agreed that wives 50 and older risk more disapproval from society than husbands that age do.

"What happens is that a man becomes a 'stud' and a woman becomes a 'whore.' This is still not considered 'what women do,' " says sexologist Carol Botwin, author of *Tempted Women: The Passions, Perils, and Agonies of Female Infidelity* (Morrow). "And husbands are much less likely to forgive than wives are in the opposite case, so she stands a much greater chance of risking her marriage." The survey agrees: Almost one out of five married women who had an affair ended up divorced.

Most of the women interviewed shudder at being held responsible for upsetting the stability of family life, even a cozy nest of grandchildren.

"If people knew we were having an affair," says Joan, the Kansas secretary, "they'd probably think we'd lost our minds." In the end, these women know that holding the family together is still seen as their job.

Many say grown children are potent lightning rods for guilt. "An affair reveals your sexual self to them—and your disloyalty," says therapist Gilbert Kautto. "As we get older, most of us try to tighten bonds, make amends: We don't want to leave this earth with our children seeing us as bad people."

The married women I interviewed were also bluntly

pragmatic about the other major danger of an affair—financial risk. "Security. That's what's keeping me where I am right now," says Marjorie, who fell in love with a younger man. "It would be tough for me to build another life at this point. And I sure don't want to go back to work."

Most were also clear-eyed about the realities of single life for an older woman: the bleak dating market with AIDS and the many men their age who, one woman growled, prefer "a 30-year-old arm charm."

What seems to be most at risk for older single women seeing married men is their self-respect. Says Joyce, the Pennsylvania real estate agent in the 11-year affair, "Occasionally, in the beginning, I'd get taken out to dinner. Somewhere very remote. Then that became a hassle. I used to bug him, 'Let's do something. I feel like a prisoner here in the house.' "

When It's Over: No Regrets?

In real life, 50-plus affairs are not the sunlit idylls described in *The Bridges of Madison County*—nor are they as tidy in their resolution. Joan, the Kansas secretary, ended her affair with her co-worker when his wife became seriously ill. "I told him, 'I wouldn't want you to leave her. She needs you more than I do.' And you know what? I wouldn't have respected him if he had left." Joyce is still reeling in bitterness after finally ending her long affair. "Now I see that he was never going to leave his wife. I wasted 11 years. I'm 59 years old: I'm not young anymore."

Betsy, the chemist, is still devastated by the nasty end of her affair with a younger colleague: He accused her of undercutting a project of his wife's (she is also in their field). "He and I are very angry at one another. And we're still in the same workplace. It's turned into a nightmare." But

"Once I saw that my lover wasn't as sensitive as he seemed, I began to think I'd better make a go of what I have."

Betsy has a new insight: One reason he was attracted to her was that she was accomplished and wellknown in their profession. "And that affected how he saw me physically," she says. "We are so used to the idea that a man is considered attractive because of who he is, the power he has. We just haven't lived in a time when a woman is seen to be attractive because of who she is and her stature in her field—not because of her physical shell."

For married women, the survey finds, resolving their affairs usually means staying in their marriage. At the same time, 60 percent whose affair has ended say they have no regrets; few feel guilt. Those women who admitted to affairs said their confidence increased and they felt encouraged to think about their own needs for the first time in their lives. In addition, says Sonya Friedman of those she studied, "They are grateful for this experience of being loved."

Why They Stay Married

The women also tell why, in the end, they stayed. "I've put in so many years," said Marjorie, the Tennessee housewife who ended a four-year affair. "And I mean, I've got a 'nice' husband—he's a good man. If he beat up on me or didn't support me, it would have been easier to leave."

According to the *New Choices* poll, 46 percent of the women emerged with their marriages pretty much the same as before. "The only thing the affair changed," says Marjorie, "was that it helped me deal with the absence of sex easier. But it also let me know that it's out there; it can be had."

Betsy says her affair was a factor in recommitting herself to working out her marriage. "Once I saw that my lover wasn't as nice and sensitive as he seemed, I began to think, 'Well, I'll never really get what I want. And I don't feel like starting over by myself at this point. I'd better make a go of what I have.' " She and her husband went to a therapist together. "Now we are really on the mend. We're trying to figure out how to be together and not to be at war. What I'm looking for now is a comrade, a partner."

"An affair can give a glorious feeling of being chosen that can provide a woman with tremendous confidence," says Gilbert Kautto. "But if you're in one, you can't possibly have an intimate relationship with your husband — not really. And if intimacy is what you're after, an affair is not going to do it for you."

Her words underline the ambivalence that all the women expressed. According to psychologist Friedman, most married women in ongoing affairs hammer out a pact with themselves: "They say, 'Look, I made a decision a long time ago, and I'm holding to that. And I have to pay my own conscience price.' Their needs overrode their guilt."

Long after an affair ends, the ambivalence can persist. Says Betsy, "Now that I'm in a much better phase of my marriage, I would feel that it would be wrong. And yes, I think an affair is a very dangerous thing. But irresistible, irresistible." ■

Deborah Mason is a contributing editor to New Choices *magazine. She also contributes regularly as a writer for* The New York Times.

Sex, Marriage, Self-Image: What We Believe

How do women 50 and over feel about themselves, their sexuality and their impact on others? *New Choices* commissioned a national survey by EDK Associates, a New York–based public-opinion research company, to help answer these and other questions. And the results were reassuring. Contrary to popular belief, most women at midlife are positive about themselves, their marriages and their roles in society. Rather than taking a seat on the sidelines, they are often actively changing the rules they live by. And, for a small but statistically significant number, that includes rules about fidelity.

The report is based on a scientifically valid sample of 500 women aged 50 to 70 across the country, selected randomly and interviewed by telephone during April and May of 1994. Among its findings:

- Almost 1 in 2 women agree that "now it's my turn to come first, instead of other people."
- 65% disagree that "the older a woman gets, the less attention people pay to her."
- Almost 3 in 4 believe that "women over 50 are much sexier than people think we are."
- 52% are still married to their first husbands.
- Almost 4 in 10 find middle and late middle age to be a particularly stressful time for marriage, with health problems topping the list of reasons.
- 81% would marry the same man, if they had it to do all over again.
- 1 in 3 agree that not enough emotional closeness in her marriage is the main reason a woman might want to have an affair.
- 6 out of 10 agree that wives 50 and older who have affairs risk more disapproval from society than husbands of that age do.
- 28% have had an affair or know someone who did.

Women who had affairs had only a 60% chance of hearing a woman friend's true opinion about the affair — positive or negative. Women who have had affairs or know of a woman who did reported that:

- 34% met their lovers at work.
- 51% had lovers of the same age.
- For 57% the affair lasted at least one year.
- 60% don't regret the affair.
- Almost half of the husbands never found out about the affair.

—D.M.

TO FEEL CONNECTED

How to get the most out of your changing relationships

By Gloria Hochman

Less than a decade ago, Cynthia and Harry Mercer* were struggling to adjust to the emptiness in their lives. For the first time in 20 years, their house had no children in it. Their son, Donald, had taken a job in England and might stay permanently. Their daughter, Leslie, a college student, had determined that she wouldn't call home more than once a month. And Cynthia had become estranged from her closest cousin, Elinor, after an argument about the man Elinor planned to marry. Cynthia says that period was the most difficult of her life.

Cynthia never guessed then that 10 years later, at age 57, she would feel content about her children, be closer to her cousin and enjoy a new, exciting intimacy with her husband.

The pivotal event for her, she remembers, was the death of her mother in the winter of 1986. In the hospital for several months, her mother had fought her way back from near death six times. Although the doctors insisted that she was terminally ill, Cynthia believed that her mother's will to live would pull her through, that she was invincible.

Her mother's death jolted Cynthia into the realization that life is fragile. She emerged from a year of intense grieving with a simple goal. She must live the rest of her life as a challenge, an adventure. She must love her husband, free her children, nurture relationships with friends and family. This vision, she says—this capacity to develop a new kind

Names have been changed to protect the privacy of the individuals described.

of intimacy with the most significant people in her life—was her mother's final gift to her.

Cynthia's situation is not unique. Somewhere after midlife, something happens that makes most of us recognize that there are more years behind us than ahead. It may be, as in Cynthia's case, the death of a parent that nudges us to confront our own mortality. We become, after all, the next in line. It may be the intrusion of a health problem — our own or that of someone close to us. Sometimes it is a final coming to terms with unrealized dreams, ours or those we had for our children.

Or it may be just the mellowing that comes with time—less need to win, less patience with pettiness, more willingness to let go of past injuries. Often we rearrange our priorities dramatically. "As people mature, they become resigned to the exhaustion of living—getting through each day and dealing with strains that require enormous energy," says David Leof, M.D., a San Francisco psychoanalyst. "As we get older, we don't want to use that energy to fight old battles. We need to use it in rich and productive ways."

Many people in their 50s and 60s focus that energy on a new and surprising kind of intimacy, one that allows them to view the final third of their lives as an intriguing opportunity—an intimacy with themselves.

This is a time of life when many men and women, perhaps for the first time, get to know who they really are," says Nancy K. Schlossberg, Ed.D., professor of counseling psychology at the University of Maryland in College Park. "Once you pass 50, you often feel freer to take risks. You can figure out what you want to do with the rest of your life, what your needs and limitations are. If you don't know yourself, how can you become intimate with someone else?"

Cynthia, who spent most of her married life as a homemaker, says that's what happened to her. Instead of living through her children and her husband, she learned in therapy to articulate what was important to her. "I realized that I hadn't figured out what I wanted to be when I grew up," she says. "Time was running out. I could sit and moan about my losses—my children living far away, my mother's death, my cousin's absence. Or I could take care of myself, learn more about me and then use that information creatively so I could live to the fullest."

Cynthia's life now includes a degree in nursing that she earned after her mother's death, a satisfying job in a small residence for emotionally disabled adolescents and a fresh viewpoint. "When I changed, the people around me changed, too," she says. "Had I gone to school earlier in my marriage, I would have tried to clean the house, cook the dinners, do all the shopping. Now I tell my husband that he is responsible for dinner on Tuesdays, Wednesdays and Thursdays. He protested at first, but he also gained new respect for me in response to the new respect I have for myself. There is more romance and fun in my marriage now than ever before."

"When someone shifts to explore aspects of himself that had been dormant or undeveloped, every relationship he has will be affected," says Dr. Leof. "Everyone will get to know a slightly different person. In some cases, relationships may not survive. In others, they will deepen." In Cynthia's case, they deepened. As she felt better about herself, her children sensed that she had less need to live through them. And they drew closer. Cynthia's cousin responded to her overtures; they talked about their relationship and how to renew and enrich it.

But a personal reassessment does not work that way all the time. Sometimes it convinces a person to search for real intimacy outside marriage.

"Ten years ago, when I was 45, I wasn't capable of putting my needs into words," Jeffrey Wilkins says. "I think I was unaware I had any needs. My wife, Helen, was in graduate school and had a briefcase full of her own emotional baggage, my children were still young, and I felt a serious responsibility for everyone's well-being. Everyone's but mine.

"When my father died three years ago, my own mortality hit me hard. I became conscious that we have only one life to live. It became unacceptable to me to waste it. I asked myself what I wanted for my life, and several words came to me — words like joy, romance, love, travel. For the first time, I knew that I had to make some choices."

Jeffrey's first choice was to try to push his marriage into a new dimension that would be more satisfying to both him and his wife. It didn't work. He felt that Helen couldn't shake loose from what he describes as "enmeshment with our children," nor could she respond to his need for emotional intimacy. After 27 years of marriage, Jeffrey moved out.

Since then, he has developed a relationship with Susan. "We both want the same things out of life — always to make time for each other, never to take each other for granted, never to be so tied up in our work that we can't be spontaneous, go out for a bike ride or a picnic. I want Susan to love the real me, and I want to love the real her. I would have preferred this kind of intimacy with my wife, but that just wasn't possible."

Most mental-health experts agree that after children have left the house, good marriages get better; poor ones can become unbearable or not fulfilling. "If two people build their life around the children and create nothing for themselves, they will feel tremendous loss," says Caryn Stark, M.S., a psychologist in Philadelphia. "But if they had a healthy relationship to begin with, these can be the best years. The stresses of child rearing are over, and women especially often feel liberated. They can go back to school, embark on a new career, have the time to cultivate relationships with friends and family. There may be opportunities to travel, to be creative, to meet new people, find new hobbies. Life is learning how to adjust to losses and finding ways to cope. Instead of grieving while your child is on his journey through life, it makes sense to figure out how to be on your own journey."

Jenny, just turned 60, discovered an intimacy with herself that enables her to embrace life.

Jerry Davis, a Chicago lawyer who just celebrated his 63rd birthday, says that he wouldn't trade this stage of life for any other. He has cut down on his hours at work so that he can pursue an old interest in writing, and he is now halfway through his first novel. He also thinks he has become less stubborn, more flexible and more accepting of other people's flaws. "I don't always have to be right," he says, "and I've stopped needing to prove a point. Life's a great teacher."

Jerry feels a renewed intimacy with his wife, Nancy, who has been a legal secretary for eight years, because she, too, is following new paths and presents him with provocative challenges. In the past year, they have enjoyed several firsts — white-water rafting, ballroom-dance lessons, a costume party on New Year's Eve. "We are curious, adventurous and just have a good time together," he says. "Our sex life isn't bad, either."

But even when children don't live out their parents' dreams, parents can live out their own. Jennie, just turned 60, discovered an intimacy with herself that enables her to embrace life with zest although her 31-year-old daughter, Merilee, is an alcoholic and frequently threatens suicide.

"At first, my husband and I argued all the time about what went wrong and who was to blame. We tried to get Merilee connected with good professional help, but often she resisted, insisting she could manage herself. I was so depressed, there were days I couldn't get out of bed. But somewhere a little piece of me struggled to be free."

Jennie's freedom came the day she closed the bathroom door when she was taking a shower. "I used to keep the door open in case Merilee called, in case she was threatening suicide again," Jennie says. "When I stopped doing that, I knew I had turned the corner."

What Jennie calls her "reawakening" came after she went to Al-Anon, a self-help group for relatives and friends of alcoholics. There she learned that she could not control anyone but herself. She was not responsible for her daughter, and if Merilee rejected her help, she could not save her.

"That was so liberating," she says. "It allowed me to refocus on myself. I began to see that my role in life had been to get everyone's approval, to make sure everyone liked me, so I was afraid to be vulnerable with anyone. And when you can't be vulnerable, you can't be intimate. Once I realized that intimacy is not about sex but about talking and sharing feelings, my husband and I were on our way to a new closeness that enables us to survive our daughter's tragedy."

"Intimate relationships are critical, especially at this time of life," says Carolyn Subin, M.S.W., a psychiatric social worker at the New York Hospital–Cornell Medical Center, Westchester Division. "Figuring out how to feel connected is the key to fulfillment."

Too often it remains an elusive key for single men and women in their 50s and 60s. As Jill, a twice-divorced woman who recently turned 62, says, "You need someone who is there for you, to whom you are the most important person. I haven't given up on finding that, but it is getting harder."

Jill has turned to her female friends for intimacy, each for different reasons — Monica because she lives in the same building; Laura because they both love the theater; Gail because they enjoy talking about books and movies; Sarah because they share 25 years of memories. "We're all in the same lifeboat," Jill says, "and we look to each other for comfort and support. You must keep those connections going."

"Each of us looks for intimacy in different ways, in different places," says Dr. Leof. "No one says on his deathbed, 'I didn't make enough money.' What they say is 'I haven't loved well enough. I haven't given enough. I haven't listened enough.' These later years offer a luxurious opportunity to embrace intimacy in a more fulfilling way. It can be a wonderful season of harvest." ■

Gloria Hochman, an award-winning jounalist, is co-author with Patty Duke of A Brilliant Madness: Living with Manic-Depressive Illness *(Bantam). She lives near Philadelphia.*

Pet Names Can Enhance Your Marriage

By Myrna Lewis

Couples who use pet names and other private expressions with each other have better marriages, according to a new study. Researchers Carol Bruess, Ph.D., and Judy Pearson, Ph.D., of Ohio University studied 154 couples (ranging from newly married to married more than 50 years) to assess their use of pet names, rituals and other private communications.

The report concluded that "couples who use such expressions have created a 'culture of two' that both reflects and reinforces their intimacy and can lead to even greater closeness."

The researchers examined partner nicknames (such as Puddin', Buttercup, Sweat Pea), nonverbal expressions of affection (winks, squeezes) and codes for sexual invitations, such as saying, "It's time for ice cream." Also studied was the use of teasing insults, such as calling a partner "Marge"—private language for "You're acting like Marge from the TV cartoon show *The Simpsons*."

"Such language and gestures introduce playfulness into a relationship, which contributes to marital intimacy," says Bruess. "This has special importance after age 50, when many couples have raised their children and have time to make their marriage a priority again." She adds that couples who want to introduce new bonds into their marriage should try using new pet words and phrases. "Even if it feels silly, your partner will understand, and that's the whole point."

WHAT KEEPS US FROM CHAOS

Arthur Miller on the meaning of family

By Susan Cheever

The Background

Arthur Miller has seen a lot, but he says that very little has changed. The world is different; the family endures. "I think the tie between parents and children is the basis of social existence, quite frankly," he says. "Where it doesn't exist, you have chaos."

Miller, born on October 17, 1915, is the playwright who has defined the modern American family—the difficulties between parents and children, parents and the community, parents and their dreams. His life—his painful divorce from his first wife, his marriage to Marilyn Monroe, his refusal to bow to the inquisition of the House Un-American Activities Committee about his political alliances, his happy marriage to photographer Inge Morath, his championing of the rights of writers—is also a compelling drama of struggle, success, temptation and redemption.

Miller grew up in a prosperous Jewish neighborhood in New York's Harlem. In 1929, when he was 14, his father's coat-manufacturing business failed, and the family moved to a small house in Brooklyn.

Jolted by this collision with the dark side of the American dream, Miller saved his earnings from a job at an auto-parts warehouse until he could afford to go to the University of Michigan. His first play, *Honors at Dawn*, was written in 1936 during his sophomore year, and won the university's Hopwood Award. By 1944, *The Man Who Had All the Luck* had been produced on Broadway, followed by *All My Sons*, which won a Tony Award and the Drama Critics Circle Award. In 1949, he was awarded the Pulitzer Prize for his haunting, perfectly American failure story, *Death of a Salesman*, about the tragic Willy Loman.

Since then, Miller has become one of the world's most eminent playwrights; his latest play, *Broken Glass*, opened in New York (1994) and London (1995). Much of his work describes the modern family in general and the modern father in particular, a father nearly crushed by the moral and emotional difficulties that come with authority in a world ruled by circumstance. Both precious and fragile, Miller's families are people under siege from the pressures of the community and from their inner longings. His own family, including four children from his first and third marriages, has survived the odds he knows so well. "I have heard the word 'Grandpa!' from a girl of 2, a boy of 6 and a girl of 14, Bob's kids," he wrote in *Timebends*, his wonderful 1987 autobiography. "There was no denying the resistance to that word — my God, I had hardly begun! What are these small persons doing in my lap repeating that terrible accusation with all its finality? How confidently they imagine that I am Grandpa. And this makes me wonder who I imagine I am."

Miller lives in the Connecticut farmhouse he bought more than 40 years ago. As we talk on the afternoon of the Fourth of July, he swings in a rope hammock strung across the porch, which is furnished with a table he made in his woodworking shop. His German shepherd, Lola, lies in the shade, occasionally glancing over to see if there's any chance of a ride in the car or an imminent meal. Speaking in his low, gravelly voice, Miller answers questions with wit and a reluctance to take himself too seriously, both of which make it easy to forget his accomplishments. During our conversation, Inge brings him the first raspberry of the summer from their garden.

The Interview

My own family was of the greatest importance to me. I had a mother who was culturally hip — she managed to see all the latest musicals, she could play the piano and sing all the songs, and she read popular novels. She thought that being an artist was wonderful. My father loved actors, but he was a businessman.

When I went off to college to be a writer, I had to pretend I was going to be a newspaperman because my father couldn't imagine being anything without being on a payroll. So the two sides of my family were very useful to me, and from that mixture I gained a perception of what this country is like.

I have been different as a parent from my own parents. They made it very overt that I should succeed. They took successful people far more seriously than failed people. In my generation, on the other hand, we were all involved with social issues, and the whole idea of individual success and failure was mitigated by that awareness. I never pressed my children one way or another. I assumed that the best way to teach them was to be an example rather than make a speech — I made a few speeches, too, I suppose — but my hope was that they would be successful on their own terms, whatever those were.

I have the feeling that, when it comes to the family, very little has changed. There was a time in the '60s when the idea of the nuclear family was supposed to have gone over the bridge, or under the bridge and out to sea . . . it wasn't supposed to exist anymore. I knew then that it was nonsense. Children require a family, even though more and more people are divorcing. Growing up without a stable family background wounds them in a way and leaves them directionless. I think the need for family is a biological need.

In places like Israel and Russia and socialist countries,

they had the idea that all you needed to raise children was enough milk or porridge and somebody to wipe up. They even thought that it was deleterious for children to be with their biological parents. That idea failed. When it comes to the family, I'm afraid we're back to square one.

The young human has to feel some security, and that security depends on his identification with the parents. Something that's simply an objectification of care, an emotional Horn & Hardart where you push a button and you get fed, doesn't work. We know all that from the animals. If you watch monkeys or higher-level simians, it's quite obvious that they require a relationship with an adult that's a safe one.

Years ago, in 1957—this now seems a hundred years ago—I was going to write a film about what was then called juvenile delinquency. It was before kids got guns. I spent about six months in Bay Ridge, Brooklyn. I could pick out the boys who had fathers who were operating as fathers, and those who didn't. The ones who had fathers would be as aggressive as the other boys, but when it came to going out and robbing, or going where they knew there was going to be terrible violence, these guys didn't go. They weren't regarded as cowards because everyone understood they had fathers who would beat them if they put their lives in danger.

On the other hand, the family is at odds with the community. When it's working well, the family is working to protect its members against the claims of social responsibility. In fact, the early socialists always regarded the family as the prime enemy because it interfered with the rule of the state over the individual. If you look at countries like Italy—where, in effect, there has not been a government since the fall of the Roman Empire—the family is intact. The ultimate social expression of the family, which is the Mafia, even calls itself "the family." That's what they live by, and a more anarchic society is hard to find.

The young human has to feel some security, and that security depends on his identification with the parents.

When the community goes bad, the family becomes symptomatic. For example, if you have unemployment over a certain level, it will begin to destroy family life: As the father becomes unable to provide, he will lose his authority, and the mother will go crazy. That economic base has got to be there. You can't expect people to subsist on a creative and peaceful level if they are really up a tree as to how they're going to eat next week.

What about my own family? My first divorce was painful and probably traumatic, but the two children I had in that marriage (they're 50 and 47 now) are terrific. I met Inge when I was in my 40s; we've been married 32 years. The secret of a great marriage is to have a wife who listens to you. It's a magical confluence of events, and it's amazing it occurs at all. We've solved some of our problems by ignoring them. This is probably the most long-term, safest solution ever devised by man: ignoring things. In our case, it helps that we're both artists, so that one knows that the other is an idiot of one kind or another and not supposed to be a regular fellow. I go into my studio, and nothing is important except that machine with the paper—and Inge knows what that's like because she's a fanatic with the camera. She's got her darkroom, and she goes in there and that's it. Other wives would feel that the artist has turned his back on them, that they are competing with something, and therefore their value is less.

Sometimes you look at life and figure it's all for nothing—that you didn't do what you wanted to do or you should have done, or that you did what you shouldn't have done. Then life seems a waste, and you're simply old. Other times, you feel as if you've made an impression in the cake of ice that we live on. That's an important thing for a lot of people, including me. I don't think you can write as long as I have without it crossing your mind that you're outliving yourself, that the work will remain. I'm writing a piece now about people my age whose paths cross again—so I'm looking at the enormous span of time that I've occupied, and I'm really shocked at how long it is. It always seemed to me to be quite short, but lately I'm impressed with still being able to get up out of a chair.

America is an amazing country—it's never the same from one period to another. It's always looking ahead. Other societies are mostly looking for the past. They're nervous because they can't reproduce the mythology of history; we're searching for a track into the future. I was raised by a generation of immigrants, and that had a big effect. My father was one of those men who always thought of America as the place of miracle and wonder. They never got over it. A place of miracle and wonder: In some part of my head, I still feel the same way. ■

Susan Cheever's most recent book is A Woman's Life: The Story of an Ordinary American and Her Extraordinary Generation *(William Morrow). She is also the author of five novels and two memoirs, including* Home Before Dark *(Bantam), about her father, John Cheever.*

Building a Stronger Mother-Daughter Bond

By Myrna Lewis

"My mother doesn't understand me!" is a complaint you would expect to hear from a teenage girl, but according to new research, it may be a common perception among midlife daughters as well. The good news is that there are a number of ways that mothers and daughters can improve their communication and achieve greater mutual understanding.

The findings come from a study conducted by Karen Fingerman, Ph.D., an assistant professor of human development at Pennsylvania State University in University Park. She asked 48 pairs of mothers (average age 76) and daughters (average age 44) to describe past conflicts between them and how they perceived each other's behavior during such times. The mothers consistently saw their relationships with progeny in a more positive light than their daughters did. "Even when daughters say they are upset with their mothers or report that they engage in negative behaviors, such as yelling at or ignoring their mothers, the mothers report the conflict with a positive glow," notes Fingerman. "This can leave the daughters feeling let down by their mothers' failure to pick up on their true feelings."

Why do mothers misinterpret such messages from their daughters? One possibility, says Fingerman, is that "the older women have a vested interest in seeing themselves as good mothers, and so they cast their daughters in the best possible light. They also believe that, as parents, they are more aware of their daughters' feelings than is actually the case."

So what's an adult daughter to do? If the relationship is a relatively good one, says Fingerman, it may be more important for you to try to accept your differences than to attempt to change your mother's outlook. But if you really want your mother to see your point of view, you need to get your grievances out in the open, according to Roberta Galler, C.S.W., a psychoanalyst and therapist in private practice in New York City.

"Making peace doesn't have to mean silencing your voice," notes Galler. "Entering into conflict often enables real intimacy and connection. If you bury serious conflicts, you may achieve a safe but false harmony. It takes courage to speak one's mind and heart, but it's worth the effort—especially if you approach your mother with love, respect and empathy."

INEVITABLE FAMILY RIFTS

. . . and how to handle them

By Susan Littwin

When my Aunt Edith died, she wasn't on speaking terms with her two brothers and three sisters because she had taken a ring from my grandmother's finger after her death. "Mama wanted me to have it," was the explanation she gave her furious family.

I was in college at the time and had long since lost interest in the quarrels of my mother's contentious yet—until then—inseparable family. But even I knew that no one really cared about the ring. I overheard the analysis by my mother and aunts and uncles over their endless cups of Sunday tea: Edith had never helped care for Mama. Her childlessness had made her fussy and self-centered. And did it matter that she was the eldest when she had done so little for the family?

I never heard Aunt Edith's side of the story because we never saw her again.

Estrangement is the knock-on-any-door family secret, the dark corner we prefer not to talk about. Photos of smiling relatives at weddings and other gatherings can reveal much if we consider the people who aren't there—the parents, stepparents, adult children, sisters, brothers and in-laws who live on the other side of the rifts that split so many families.

Some rifts have serious causes, such as abuse or alcoholism; others have seemingly minor, even puzzling, beginnings.

"There are no new rifts, just a widening of imperceptible cracks begun in youth," says Roger Moss, Ph.D., a professor of psychology at California State University, Northridge. Family therapist Monica McGoldrick, M.S.W., author of *You Can Go Home Again: Reconnecting with Your Family* (Norton), agrees and says such divisions "track way back to childhood issues—for instance, to children who feel they didn't get as much as another sibling but perhaps put out more than their fair share."

Rifts often occur at times of intensity—births, deaths, marriages, divorces. "Distancing and cutting off are ways that family members navigate stress," says Harriet Goldhor Lerner, Ph.D., a clinical psychologist at the Menninger Clinic in Topeka, Kansas, and the author of *The Dance of Intimacy* (HarperCollins).

For a decade or more, such popular therapists as John Bradshaw and Susan Forward urged us to dump our toxic families, put an end to codependency and learn to nurture our inner child. Today experts are drifting back to the view that family members are connected by a powerful force of nature.

Some psychotherapists warn that when you forsake your family, you forsake a part of yourself and bury emotions that may resurface like torpedoes later on. "If you stay cut off from your own first family," Lerner adds, "you will find it difficult to be on solid ground in other relationships or in a family of your own."

But mending rifts is a complex and unpredictable process. Lyndia Wurthman and Doug Gregory are both in their early 50s. She is a university administrator; he is a supermarket meat manager. Doug has been married for 32 years and is devoted to his two daughters and two grandchildren. Lyndia is single again after three divorces and goes in and out of relationships. They are odd-couple best friends who meet for long lunches and talk on the phone for hours at a time.

**Names have been changed to protect the privacy of the individual described.*

They are also brother and sister who reunited four years ago after an 18-year rift.

Their long estrangement began abruptly. Doug had stopped speaking to their mother after a quarrel with her newly acquired fifth husband, whom Doug considered a self-aggrandizing liar. "It's him or me," Doug told her.

Not long after, Lyndia called to give him a sisterly lecture. "You should be talking to your own mother," she said, in tones that, she admits, may have been holier-than-thou.

"I don't need any of you," Doug said as he hung up.

By then, Doug had a wife and two daughters, and he lived in the bosom of his in-laws. He saw his own first family as dysfunctional. His oft-married mother drank too much and had moved them constantly from one home to another. Even their grandmother had a bizarre aversion to family ties. "She wouldn't be called 'Grandmother.' We had to call her Elizabeth," he recalls.

But Doug had lost sight of what he had shared with his sister while growing up. "We were all we had," he says. "We were each other's family."

After the phone call, Lyndia remembers, "the days became weeks and the weeks became months and the months became years. We both put it in the back of our minds. Oh, that. I won't deal with that now." But the loss hurt more deeply than either admitted.

When Doug's wife asked him what he wanted for his birthday four years ago, he immediately answered, "My sister." His wife understood, and the couple began doing detective work to locate Lyndia. Doug's wife hit on the idea of calling the alumnae society of the Catholic high school Lyndia had attended. The nun in charge refused to give out Lyndia's number, but she did call her. "Do you want to speak to your brother?" she asked.

"Yes!" Lyndia cried. She called him that night, and they spoke for two hours and then agreed to meet for dinner. "It was like falling in love," she says now. "You don't know what you've missed till you get it back."

They have both gained more than a confidant and best friend. Reconnecting turned out to be a kind of therapy. They see in each other how their early life affected them, and they have discovered odd likenesses that survived separation and differing paths.

Their reconciliation has, not so incidentally, provided an aunt for Doug's children and an uncle for Lyndia's, and removed what might have been a troublesome veil of mystery.

"Sibling rifts are often a displacement of anger felt toward the parents," notes Mark Goulston, M.D., a Los Angeles psychiatrist and author of *Get Out of Your Own Way: Overcoming Self-Defeating Behavior* (Perigee/Berkley). "Even adults are afraid to get angry at their parents. The unspoken fear is, 'What if they abandon me?' "

That fear of abandonment can affect siblings in different ways. "If parental love is limited, each child develops a way of dealing with it," says Roger Moss. "One may spin into the family while the other spins out. And often the one who spins out is mad at the other for currying favor." Once reconciled, however, they can accept their past and be less rigid.

Kinship matters, it seems, even in dysfunctional families.

Doug and Lyndia's story had a fairy-tale ending. The rift between Marcus*, 54, and his 26-year-old daughter, Lisa*, was probably more typical. They had not been close since his divorce, when his three children were toddlers. His former wife, he believes, constantly told the children that their father was not doing enough for the family financially. When Marcus's second wife made her feel unwelcome, Lisa cut off relations with her father.

The estrangement lasted through Lisa's teen years. They attempted a reconciliation five years ago, beginning, symbolically, with money. Marcus co-signed a car loan for her. When she defaulted and the car was repossessed, he found himself with a court order to pay the remainder of the loan. Lisa agreed to pay him back in small amounts every month, but she never made a payment or explained.

They did not speak again until four years later, when Lisa learned that her father was to have cancer surgery. She went to see him at the hospital, but even then a bitter exchange about the car loan renewed their mutual silence.

"Do you want to wait . . . to tell them you love them? Does it matter so much who makes the first move?"

It was during Marcus's recuperation that he had an insight: Life was fragile and time short. He sent Lisa a birthday card and included a note saying that he had forgiven the loan because he didn't want anything coming between them. Lisa called a few weeks later and then visited him on Father's Day.

They are not close now. They speak on the phone once or twice a month and see each other less often. "But it's something," Marcus says. "Maybe it's the best it can be."

Was such limited success worth the trouble? Staying in touch, says Stephanie Goldstein, Ph.D., a clinical psychologist in Long Island, New York, "will allow them to gradually explore their history and learn from what happened, instead of being cut off from feelings connected with the family."

Even efforts that end in rejection can yield powerful benefits, McGoldrick says. Gilbert*, 50, a big, lumbering, kindly man, is the mayor of a small Midwestern city. He has kept his political enemies in the fold but cannot repair a mysterious breach with his father. They have had no contact for more than three years, since his father and stepmother, newly married, spent a week with him and his wife and their four children.

"The visit went well," Gilbert says, then his face clouds over. There was a small altercation when he asked his stepmother not to put sugar substitute in a dessert she was preparing because the chemicals disagreed with him. She seemed annoyed, but the moment passed. At the end of their stay, the older couple said warm good-byes. Gilbert never heard from them again.

Gilbert has written and sent greeting cards but has gotten no response. When he tried calling, he found that their phone had been disconnected. A relative later told him that they had moved—without telling him. Was it the sugar-substitute incident? Something else? Unable to solve the mystery, Gilbert thought he had an olive branch to offer. When he was about to be inaugurated as mayor, he got their new address from the relative and invited them to the ceremony. They never responded.

Too hurt to pursue them any further, Gilbert has given up. For now, at least.

"If I were working with Gilbert, I would challenge him," says McGoldrick. "He's giving up out of fear. I would have him keep pursuing the father through the relative. I would suggest he write a 'heavier letter,' telling him how much the relationship means to both of them."

Even if another attempt ends in rejection, McGoldrick says that Gilbert will benefit: "He'll know that he's left the door open, and one day his father might walk through it. The hurt won't go away, but if he didn't open up and try, it would hurt even worse every time he thought of his father."

Other therapists agree with McGoldrick but are perhaps more cautionary. "It's important to try to work out estrangement within a family, but you also have to keep your personal integrity. There are circumstances when a person has to say, 'No more,' even if it means disconnecting," says Goldstein. She tells of a woman patient in her mid-50s whose authoritarian parents required childlike compliance. When she appropriately stood up to them, she and her husband were ordered out of their house. She has since written letters and tried to meet with them, but her parents will accept nothing less than total and abject apology. "If she has to act like a child to have her parents love her, the relationship won't work," says Goldstein.

Those who want to end a long chill might take a lesson from Marcus—and not wait for a crisis like his cancer surgery to act. After the Oklahoma City bombing, Goldstein persuaded a woman to reach out again to her estranged son and daughter-in-law. "Terrible things happen, and you have no control over how or when. Do you want to wait till someone is sick or dies to tell them you love them? Does it matter so much who makes the first move?"

In *You Can Go Home Again*, McGoldrick suggests a practical exercise to overcome anger. Consider the family history from the estranged relative's point of view: "If you think of your father as an arch villain because of the awful way he treated you, explore his early life and think about how his family viewed him as a little boy."

Goldstein often suggests letter writing as a way to break the ice: "It allows the other person to read what's been said without having to react right away." McGoldrick asks clients to write letters, even if they don't send them. "It lets them get the anger out."

"It's safer," says Marcia*, who wrote to her daughter, Pam*, after a three-year rift broken only by angry phone calls and aborted visits. "I knew that Pam had withdrawn to figure out where she was in life, but I wanted some communication."

When nothing else worked, Marcia sat down and spent a long time composing a letter. "I bared my soul," she remembers. "I laid out all of my feelings, but I made it clear that I cared about the way she felt."

Pam spent a few weeks digesting the letter and then called and suggested that her mother visit her at her home in another part of the state.

"It was an emotional meeting. We both cried," Marcia recalls. "Pam was afraid and not quite ready, but she wanted her family back."

Greeting cards are another way to make a good start at rapprochement; you might even send them to the children of the estranged relative as a toe in the water.

To McGoldrick, what's in the heart is more important than the method of repairing a rift. "Come from a place of generosity, not fairness," she says. "Get out of the notion of tit for tat. It's not giving in or diminishing yourself but sensing that you're part of something larger, that you don't stand alone in the world."

I hope my Aunt Edith knew that. ■

Susan Littwin is the author most recently of The Fertility God *(Turner).*

THE POWER OF MEMORIES

The private codes that link us to parents, children, friends and sexual partners

By Penelope Lively

Memory gloriously defies chronology. I carry in my head a shuffled pack of cards — an assortment of brilliant frozen moments quite without sequence. Some are more than 50 years old, others date from last week or two months ago — there is this great submerged raft of experience from which a handful of shining fragments floats to the surface.

Why do we remember one event so vividly and another not at all? Why are trivial incidents scored deep into the mind while seminal moments have apparently been extinguished? This is the territory of the analyst and not my immediate concern. What I am interested in is the power and sustenance of memory, the ways in which it props us up and supplies a lifeline to other people.

Memories are often fused with a physical background. My grandmother's big garden in Somerset, England, is a focal point for me. My own children came to be as fixated on the place as I was, and now my granddaughter is exploring its secret places. I have photographs of three generations of toddlers staring down into the same ornamental pool. I don't remember my photograph being taken, of course, nor do my daughter and her child, but the three of us are linked by this place and our separate memories of it.

Each of us remembers in privacy, and each set of memories is unique. Memory is an isolating factor — but it is also our most abiding link with others. It is that skewed vision of the same experiences that binds us to parents, to children, to sexual partners and to friends. Marriages are fueled by memory — and sometimes destroyed by it. It cannot be shed, and in the last resort, it is the crucial substance that may restore calm and sanity at the worst moments: The awareness that this particular person is inextricably entwined with what lies within your head—even if at that moment you feel more like throwing a saucepan than proffering a cherished recollection—makes a difference.

Relationships are precarious in the initial stages precisely because they lack this ballast. The second meeting in a burgeoning love affair is enriched by the memory of the first; the process of establishing a relationship is the construction of this desirable platform of shared experience. "You" and "I" become "we"—there is not just the convergence of two lives but the emergence of an indestructible joint existence. A private code is being created, a system of personal references to which no one else has access, to be summoned up simply by a word or a glance. "They exchanged looks" runs the fictional cliché. No, they called up a complex set of memories.

The memories we share with friends are vital in another way. They tether us to our own previous selves. "Gracious!" I think, noting the gray thatch and the softened face of an old friend. "So that's what I look like now." But I see her also as the 20-something she was when we first met, and that memory is as much a reality as our thickened waistlines and unsprightly steps are today.

We're the same people, essentially—it's just that a chunk of time has somehow gotten in the way. And once again a private code springs into existence—the knowledge we both have of certain times and certain places and, indeed, of each other. We don't remember the same things in the same way, but we share a well into which we dip our buckets. No wonder people value familiar faces and surroundings; they are necessary if we are to retain a sense of identity. It is a brave soul who strikes out alone into an alien world.

Our childhood memories "are all that we can retrieve of the pristine way in which children perceive the world," says Lively.

Plenty do. Many have the experience thrust upon them: the refugee, the immigrant. I was born English in Egypt, spent my childhood there and came to England to live when I was 12, never having known the place. I felt uprooted and desperately homesick for the country in which I had grown up. This experience was a pale reflection of those grimmer examples of upheaval, but it gave me an insight into the vivid nature of childhood recollection when it is sharpened by abrupt departure. My earliest memories are of another world; they seem to lie behind glass, clear but entirely inaccessible.

I have tried to write of this odd childhood in a memoir, *Oleander, Jacaranda*, and to examine in the process the nature of childhood memory, which seems to me distinct from subsequent memory. That handful of early images that each of us carries in the head is, I believe, all that we can retrieve of the way in which children perceive the world—a vision that is without preconceptions because it is freed from the confines of adult experiences and assumptions. It is a pristine vision—the Wordsworthian vision of "the splendor in the grass"—and an anarchic vision as well, the perplexity and amazement of Lewis Carroll's Alice confronted with the contradictions and confusions of Wonderland.

I remember gazing, transfixed, at a praying mantis, experiencing with such intensity the translucent structure of that strange insect that the sight is with me still. I remember the mechanical repetition of the Lord's Prayer when I went to bed—words that meant nothing to me but that, for some inscrutable reason, had to be intoned each night.

Children are themselves learning about the operation of memory along with their miraculous acquisition of language. My daughter, when aged about four, used to try to communicate her idea of when something had occurred with the phrase "a long time ago not as long as all that," by which she meant a couple of weeks or so ago; it was her first attempt to capture in words the passage of time. Recently, I watched her own daughter, nine months old, crawl determinedly toward the shopping bag from which I had brought forth a toy for her on a previous visit. An object had sparked a memory.

This discovery of the memory process is a crucial part of growing up. It establishes identity and also helps us to achieve maturity. We need to place ourselves within the context of time, to recognize the fluidity of life, that we are never static but always a part of the inexorable onward rush of things. This is all too apparent when you are 50-plus, but it is not when you are 5 or even 15, and it is a necessary perception if a person is to escape the egocentric vision of youth. I endured a miserable adolescent period at a boarding school only by means of the gradual recognition that time would pass, that this calvary would eventually end, that it was not a life sentence.

Memory, in one of its most powerful and pungent forms, can erase time. My grandmother has been dead these 20 years, but in my mind's eye she is still going strong, bent double in her garden, dealing with a recalcitrant weed or teasing me for striking adolescent attitudes. I see her face and hear her voice. Nobody is extinguished so long as they survive in the memory of another.

It never fails to astonish me that presence and personality transcend death in this way—that we are so welcomely haunted by these tenacious ghosts. Maybe it is this phenomenon that prompted the concept of souls in limbo in classical mythology—the gray hordes waiting to cross the river Styx into the underworld. But the dear departed in my head are not gray at all. They are the Technicolor people that they were in real life, and I see their preservation not as souls in purgatory but as spirits redeemed for a little longer—just so long as I am still around myself.

"Watching my granddaughter now, I sometimes wonder what she is stashing away of me in her memories."

There is this marvelous sense in which personal memory defies the law of flying time—my grandmother is weeding in her rose garden forever, not just for an afternoon in 1950 or 1960 or whenever it may have been; friends and acquaintances are in fine fettle, hitched forever to some moment of my observation. And the converse of this is, of course, the unnerving thought that each of us is thus nailed down in the recollection of others. Watching my six-year-old granddaughter, I sometimes wonder what she is stashing away of me and of her immediate world as she goes about this involuntary process of laying down memories.

We cannot choose what to remember or how to remember. Scientific discussion of the strange process of memory operation is unable to explain these choices. The analysts have their say, of course, but the accumulation of the apparently random set of baggage that each of us carries with us and by which we set so much store remains a mysterious and provocative business.

As a novelist, I have been interested in trying to create fictional discussions of the nature of memory—what it does to people, whether it is a crutch or a millstone, how it functions at different points in life. I can't come up with definitive answers; all I can do is what any serious writer of fiction tries to do: explore and reflect the human condition. And if there is anything that is profoundly human, it is the capacity for memory, both the majestic and conflicting matter of collective remembering—of history—and the intimate and equally shifty process of private memory. The disputes of lovers and spouses, of parents and children, are about differing perceptions of what has happened just as much as are the arguments of historians.

Today, my daughter and I can laugh about our significantly different interpretations of the occasion on which she, aged six, persuaded her younger brother to eat potentially poisonous berries. I remember parental panic and a rush for medical advice. She recalls bewilderment at the unnecessary fuss when all she'd intended was to exercise some older-sister clout and see if he'd do it. Not quite on the same scale as opposing interpretations of the French Revolution, but memory up to its games again all the same, distorting and manipulating the past—as it transforms and enriches the present.

Penelope Lively was awarded England's prestigious Booker Prize for her 1987 novel Moon Tiger *(Grove Press). Her latest book is* Heatwave *(HarperCollins).*

How to Communicate Better with Your Adult Children

By Myrna Lewis

It's never too late to improve your skills as a mother or father, says Philadelphia author and parent Sylvia Auerbach, "especially when you consider that in this era of increasing longevity, many of us will spend 30 or more years in relationships with our children after they've become adults." Auerbach explores this concept in her new book, *How to Be Smart Parents Now That Your Kids Are Adults* (Silvercat), the writing of which, she says, helped her to clarify the following Five Rules of Parenting:

1. Learn to listen.
"That also means paying attention to what's not being said," notes Auerbach. "If your child always says a quick 'fine' when you ask how he or she is doing, and you don't follow up with further questions, then you're really not communicating."

2. Don't be judgmental.
"Recognize that times change and that new viewpoints might be called for."

3. Respect yourself and your rights.
"Don't be a patsy for your kids. You can say no."

4. Don't be afraid to let your kids know if you and your spouse differ on how to treat them.
"Children of all ages need to learn over and over again that there can be two completely different and equally valid approaches to the same situation."

5. Be sure to pay attention to your sons as well as your daughters.
"These are tough times for American males," says Auerbach. "There is a huge focus on women and how well they help each other on a personal basis and in a variety of support groups. Meanwhile, men are grappling with a mix of old expectations and changing roles, and they don't have nearly the same emotional-support system to rely on."

Ideally, families should be

VOLUNTARY ASSOCIATIONS

By Richard Rhodes

Whom would you die for? I used to ask myself that question when I was still trying to figure out who I am and what I value. The one certain answer I found, somewhere along in parenthood, was: my children. I have a son and a daughter, Tim and Kate. They're grown now, in their late 20s, and I still feel that way. When family succeeds, it's the most valuable gift anyone can receive.

Family values has become a workhorse phrase, two words harnessed to haul every sort of load. But the two words are unevenly yoked and don't pull equal shares. The parents of a murderer still love their wretched child, or try to. Family hitches somewhere behind values, on a trace extending all the way back to caves and Serengeti campfires. It's linked to biology, however much we clever primates have elaborated on and sanctified it.

Values, in the sense we mean the word today, came later, occupying the space where biology amplifies through altruism to become social, the space Hannah Arendt called "the human world." Family doesn't automatically confer value on its members. Some family values you don't want to meet in an alley late at night.

Repeated scientific observation confirms the subtle genetic partisanship of families. ("I would lay down my life for my two brothers — or my eight cousins," the British biologist J.B.S. Haldane is said to have quipped once, dramatizing the

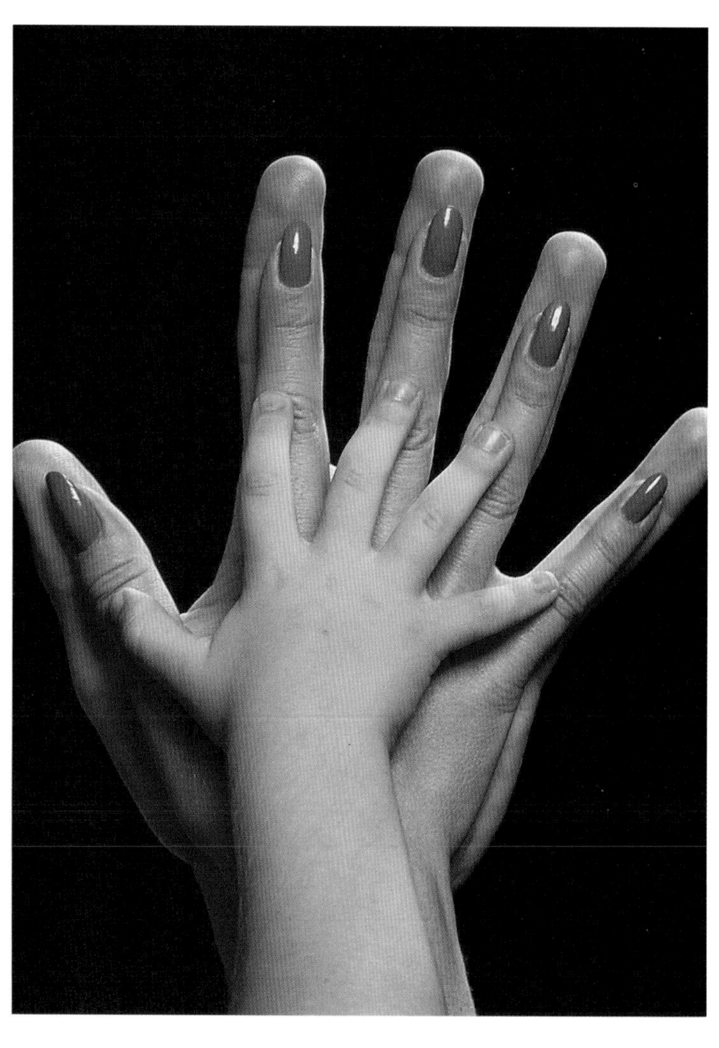

relevance of affinity.) The cruelty of stepmothers, women unrelated to the children they're supposed to nurture, is legendary. I knew such cruelty at first hand. Ignorant as yet of genetics, I used to wonder that my stepmother's own children survived to adulthood and actually loved her. (I know there are wonderful stepmothers. Their stepchildren shall rise up and call them blessed.)

I'm not sure, but I think the 1992 Republican platform's invocation of "family values" was supposed to be a pitch for the old patriarchal family: Dad and Mom and the kids, Dad in charge, speak when spoken to, yes sir, no sir, no cuss words, virtue intact until marriage, Mom czarina of the traditional virtues of children, cooking and church. Which is a fantasy on the order of a Grimm's fairy tale at the end of the 20th century, when Dad's worried about losing his job, Mom has to work to make ends meet, "cooking" means microwaving, everyone in the family has an opinion (not to mention an attitude) they'd be happy to defend on Oprah, the old Anglo-Saxon four-letter words have cycled back into vogue (as they do every other half century), and teenagers are such lucrative consumers that marketers have divided them into a population subgroup of their own. (I still don't understand where they get the money to buy all those CDs and sneakers—guilt-ridden parents?)

Family and values can even be—and often are—in terrible conflict. I read recently of an upright citizen who found his father 30 years after the man had abandoned him, discovered he was a swindler of elderly widows, and turned him in. The dissonance in that story makes the hair stand up on the back of my neck.

I ought to stop and present some credentials.

When I was a child, after Mother died, my family consisted of my father, my older brother, Stanley, and me. The three of us lived for my first 10 years in boarding houses, occupying one common room. Dad and I shared a double bed. Stanley slept on a cot.

I remember Dad as quiet and loving. A man who worked with him on the railroad says he was a nice guy, but loquacious and deeply cynical. I remember Dad as nurturing. Stanley says he spanked us often and hard. When I was raising my own children, the idealized version I remembered of my father—revealed later to be contrary to fact—served as a model for me of parenthood. That which was bitter gave forth sweetness; whence, then, do family values come?

Dad remarried when I was 10, and Stanley and I acquired a stepmother. I wrote about the traumatic two years that followed in my memoir *A Hole in the World*, and I won't repeat the whole story here. It's enough for you to know that on July 29, 1949, a compassionate judge removed Stanley and me from the beatings, torture and starvation we had suffered for two years at my stepmother's hands. I still have the commitment paper the court issued that day. It says that we were "neglected children," but we had been more than neglected; we had been actively and viciously abused. The abuse of children within their families had barely come to public attention in 1949.

My stepmother lived by cowbird values. Like that small parasitic bird, which lays its eggs in the nests of other birds, she commandeered the family's resources and forced Stanley and me out. Dad acquiesced and we lost him. Although I think he was an abused husband, at some level of his soul he chose to value being married more than he valued the health and safety of his sons. He wouldn't even protect us from a beating, much less die for us. My brother and I were lucky we got out alive.

The court sent us to a secure, benevolent, rural boys' home in Independence, Missouri, the Andrew Drumm Institute. My traditional family shrank down to two, but for six years an institutional family bolstered it. If I learned family values anywhere, I learned them at Drumm. Vigorous, altruistic teachers apprenticed Stanley and me and 30 or 40 other boys to the Protestant work ethic; we acquired such an extensive kit of skills that we would never again feel helpless. I made a list once of only a few of the skills I learned at Drumm. Ranging from chairing a meeting to butchering a steer, from blacksmithing to building a shortwave radio, it went on for half a page of fine print.

Elaine Scarry, who teaches literature at Harvard, wrote several years ago in her remarkable book *The Body in Pain* that material objects (like the hoes and stoves and tractors I learned to operate at Drumm) incarnate human creativity, and their purpose is the alleviation of pain: Chairs give us rest from gravity; cream, separated from milk, makes butter to flavor our food; lamps push back the darkness. All these small inventions wish us well. Drumm taught me that human work is dignified not because sentimentalists praise it but because its products are inherently compassionate.

One epidemic family value that Americans might reconsider is the conviction—dogma these days at state social-service agencies—that any ersatz family setting, even an abusive foster home, is better than the best institution. Institutions such as Drumm aren't merely communal; they're familial, like a good prep school. Drumm felt especially intimate to me because farming reconnected me emotionally with the mother I'd never consciously known (a suicide, she died when I was one). Before Dad remarried, he'd taken us to the cemetery once a year and pointed to the ground, the bluegrass sod, and said, "Your mother's buried there." At Drumm, the maternal earth gave up its bounty into my hands: tomatoes, beans, peaches, apples, corn. I'm on the board of trustees now, keeping the place alive.

Stanley graduated and went off to California to seek his fortune. A year later, I went far away to college on a scholarship, feeling like an alien recently arrived from the far side of the moon. I had no family within 1,500 miles. My freshman year was the loneliest of my life. But I met someone and fell in love, and when that didn't last forever, I met someone else and fell in love, and in time, after college, we married and started a family.

We can't choose the family we're born into, but we choose whether to stay affiliated or disconnect.

Child abusers were usually abused as children; why don't all abused children abuse their children in turn? The truth is, there are two possible outcomes to abuse: acknowledgment and denial. Those who acknowledge their abuse and especially those who work it through in therapy, as I did, aren't condemned to repeat it. Which brings up a subtler point about family values: They're practiced, not preached. I scolded a group of Southern Baptists recently. I told them that spanking children was child abuse and that they should take another look at the expedient evangelical conviction that sparing the rod spoils the child. There's even a scurrilous book, popular in certain Fundamentalist circles, that purports to teach parents what size dowel the Bible instructs them to buy. Why should children who are beaten with a pious rod before they're old enough to speak believe in a universe of love?

As a matter of principle, I never hit or spanked either of my children. Their mother did, one of the disagreements between us that eventually led to our divorce. I don't mean to sound self-righteous, only to report an understanding I came to that was one positive outcome of my own experience of abuse. I didn't punish my children physically because I believe absolutely that to do so, even with good intentions, is destructive. It's illegal in our society to lay a hand on another adult; the name for such an act of violence is assault and battery. We get away with physically punishing our children only because children aren't considered fully human under the law and therefore have little recourse except in the most egregious cases of abuse—and because they are smaller than we, and vulnerable.

There are any number of ways to protect and guide children besides punishing them physically, the same ways we use to relate to fellow adults: negotiation, distraction, discussion, appeals to conscience — if all else fails, a stern invocation of authority. With Tim and Kate, I tried them all. Under such democratic limitations, children may not always do what we want them to do. My children didn't, which was certainly frustrating sometimes. But other adults don't always comply with our requests and demands, and we accept their right to choose; why should we demand dictatorial authority over our children, and what do we teach them thereby?

Once Tim and Kate became teenagers, I tried to influence them primarily by serving as their most reliable source of information. I emphasized that they were responsible for themselves, for their choices, for their lives. Along with many of their peers, they both went through a period of experimenting — and they both came out the other side as responsible, productive adults. (Family values can work in reverse. How many of us have sworn we would not be like our parents? My children grew up sharing the high-wire financial life of a self-employed writer, balanced one month and wobbling dangerously the next. I'm sure that's one reason they chose to become professionals; Tim is an architect, Kate a molecular biologist.)

I don't think I was the world's best parent during my children's youth. I was struggling with serious emotional problems, part of the post-traumatic stress disorder that haunts victims of abuse.But Tim and Kate rank high among the world's best kids. That's not just their dad talking; they are natural leaders, and many of their peers agree.

Because of my childhood, I've always been conscious of how fragile family is. I've come to believe that that's a strength, not a weakness. We can't choose the family we're born into, but we certainly eventually choose whether to stay affiliated or to disconnect. Some children disconnect not bodily but by challenging traditional family values. Family is a democratic entitlement that I hope no rock-ribbed diktat will ever enforce. I learned enough about coercion by the time I was 12 to last me a lifetime. One truth I soaked up in my stepmother's cauldron was that voluntary associations are the only associations people can trust.

Although family isn't exactly voluntary, I think it is every parent's responsibility — the cardinal family value — to work to make it more so. My ideal family is one in which every family member would rush down to the recruiting center to volunteer, if he or she hadn't already been dragooned. ■

Richard Rhodes won the Pulitzer Prize for his 1986 book The Making of the Atomic Bomb. *His latest book is* Deadly Feasts: Tracking the Secrets of a Terrifying New Plague *(Simon & Schuster).*

Family-Reunion Jitters

By Myrna Lewis

Question

I'm in charge of planning a family reunion for my mom's relatives, some of whom are problem cases. Two of my aunts have been feuding since childhood, and one black-sheep cousin is likely to show up in some outrageous motorcycle outfit along with his electric guitar and latest girlfriend (the last one had a ring in her nose). Should I simply not invite these troublemakers?

Answer

I say invite everybody— and join the human race! We all have feuders and oddballs in our families; some of us may fall into those categories ourselves. According to *Reunions*, a magazine designed to help plan reunions of all sorts, eccentrics are a great part of a family's entertainment, providing everyone with something to talk about.

To make things even more interesting, organize some family games and put your aunts on the same team. That way they will have to cooperate if either of them is to win. As for your cousin, gather the littlest family members and beg him to play some children's songs on his guitar so they can sing along. The idea is to keep a sense of humor and a generosity of spirit— and you just might inspire some new ways of viewing old family issues.

"MOM AND DAD, I'M GAY"

What it was like for one family—the emotional fallout and adjustments—when they heard those words from their adult son

By Joanmarie Kalter

They say that every parent of an adult gay child remembers precisely the moment they first learned; they remember the time, the room, the weather.

In Vivian and Maurice Cooperman's case, their then-26-year-old son Abe asked Vivian to go for a walk. She was puzzled because it was Passover, and she was busy preparing a big seder dinner. Yet there was something in Abe's voice that said this was important. She remembers that they walked for 20 minutes on that spring day and had circled back home, almost to the doorstep of their rowhouse in Philadelphia, when Abe stopped, turned to her and said, "There's something I have to tell you."

Vivian had had no idea that her son was gay, and yet in that instant she knew exactly what he was about to say. "I said, 'I don't want to hear it.' And he said again, 'I have to tell you.' And we stood in the middle of the sidewalk, and I began crying because I knew what was coming."

Her husband Mac—as Maurice is known—took it more calmly. As mother and son walked in the door, Vivian recalls, "I said, 'I can't live with this secret. It's too big.' " Mac saw her tears, and the tale came tumbling out.

"All I said to him then is I love him," says Mac, "and he's the same kid that walked out the door a few minutes ago. I told him I don't really understand what it is to be gay, but I guess with some time I might."

Inside, however, Mac churned with a wave of protectiveness. His first thought was that Abe might get beaten up for being gay. And he worried immediately about the threat of AIDS.

Since that day six years ago, the Coopermans have learned that their sorrow and fears were typical. No one knows for sure what proportion of the population is gay (studies show a range from 1 to 10 percent), or how many choose to tell their families. What is clear is that those who tell tend to wait until their 20s or 30s, when they're financially independent and no longer risk having their parents cut off funds for college. The parents then are well into late middle age, feeling settled in their way of life, finally secure in their ability to handle a complex world. Suddenly they're allied with a despised minority, subject not only to the prejudice of society but to their own. The knowledge launches them on an unexpected journey, and for many it begins with a powerful grief.

"I did a lot of crying," says Vivian. "In the beginning it was the only thing I could think of. It's like 'gay' was written all over the sky, in red lights. My world fell apart."

She and Mac sit in the family room of their suburban home in Bensalem, Pennsylvania, two miles from the city where they raised their three children—son Zev, now 35; Abe, 32; and daughter Camie, 25. As they share their story with a visitor, their home speaks, too. Large portraits of each of their children decorate the living room walls. Two dogs, one cat and a bird share the premises. This family's values are traditional. Mac, 56, a dispatcher for a forklift-truck company, began dating Viv when she was in high school. Viv, 54, raised the children and worked at odd jobs to earn some extras for the family.

She compares her process of adjustment to the way one recovers from the death of a

loved one. There was shock, denial, depression. When she cried, she says, it was for the death of all the dreams she'd ever had for her son. That he would marry, have children, be respected by others. She cried for the fact that he must have feared to tell them, afraid he'd lose their love. Most of all, she says, she cried for the struggle she suddenly realized he had lived with for most of his life. "I can't imagine!" she says. "Knowing this thought has been going through your head for years, and it's completely the opposite of what society tells you is normal. It must have been like hitting a wall and there's no opening."

Indeed, Abe says he was afraid to disappoint his parents. He describes his father and brother as "Archie Bunker types," casually and habitually telling gay jokes. He knew they all believed that straight is right and gay is wrong.

So he learned, from as far back as grade school, to dissemble, to feign interest in girls and later to date—even, with one girlfriend, to contemplate marriage. For a period in his teens and early 20s, unknown to his parents, he numbed the pain of all this through alcohol and drugs. "They just didn't realize what I was going through," he says now. "How could they, when I wasn't letting them in?"

"There were clues," says Vivian. "A restlessness that I attributed to adolescence. And I still feel remiss in not having pushed him harder to talk."

Their daughter, Camie, whose interest in the arts had brought her many gay friends, took the news best. Mac and Vivian expected their boisterous son Zev, with whom Abe had shared a bedroom, to react explosively. He didn't, but his subdued manner covered a turmoil that lasted years.

Although Mac was outwardly more composed, he suffered, too. "He suffered in silence," says Vivian, and in different, fatherly ways. The whole family was relieved when Abe told them he was HIV-negative, and careful. But Mac still worried that being gay made Abe's life harder. There'd be discrimination, condemnation, maybe even violence. "He didn't want me to have to bear the brunt of someone else's ignorance," Abe says.

And so, as often happens, as a gay son came out of the closet, his parents went in. Suddenly, Mac and Vivian had a secret they were loath to share. Whom could they tell? And how? They feared that friends would drop them, that relatives might reject them, that co-workers would think less of them.

For Vivian's part, "I needed to wait until I wasn't so hysterical. I didn't want people to pity me. I didn't want to have to defend my emotions. I wanted to be able to understand what my emotions were before I said anything."

Yet as the months went by, Vivian felt her relationships blocked; she avoided friends and family; she withdrew. "You talk about your kids, about their lives," she says. Even a simple question like "How's Abe?" she now dodged.

Finally, about six months later, she resolved to tell her aunt. This was an aunt whom she cherished, with whom she'd spoken every day for 40 years, and yet who, as an Orthodox Jew, was unlikely to ever understand or accept Abe as gay. Vivian went three times to her house, intending to tell her, but it was only on the third visit that she was able to say, "I have something to tell you." The aunt cried and, as expected, has never fully accepted it. But Vivian had "come out" that day, at least a little bit.

Mac's forays happened at work. "At first I felt, 'Don't even mention it!' " he says. But after a while, he found himself responding defensively to the same jokes he himself used to tell. "So I'd say, 'Someone near and dear to me is gay, and I would rather not hear anything like that.' " With a few people, in time, he came out directly—sometimes to comic effect.

A co-worker, noting his protestations, said, "Oh, you're gay?" "And I said, 'No, I'm not, but somebody near and dear . . .' " "Well, who?" "I said, 'Well, my son is.' " "You're kidding!" "No, why should I kid?" Mac picked up the phone and called Vivian to back him up. (She wasn't home.)

At first they hesitated to attend the self-help group Parents and Friends of Lesbians and Gays (PFLAG), to which Abe had steered them. Mac thought no one would be there "because no one else in the world had a gay child or would talk about it. Obviously." And Vivian imagined that "we'd walk into a room with people so distraught you couldn't talk to them sensibly."

. . . they found themselves and Abe reversing roles: He became their guide and teacher.

Instead, the room was crowded with some 50 friendly and loving people, all dedicated to supporting their gay family members. Vivian recalls, "No one said, 'Why are you crying?' They knew damn well why I was crying! To have someone else understand how I really felt, even without my saying anything, was very comforting."

Vivian read incessantly and was helped—as many members of PFLAG seem to be—by learning that nothing she and Mac did had caused their son to be gay. She had not been a smothering mother, nor Mac an absent father. "Of course, you look for things," says Mac. "We asked ourselves, 'What did we do wrong?' Well, we didn't do anything wrong. It's not a choice—it's something he was born with, and it's very natural for him."

Curiously, they found themselves and Abe reversing roles: He became their guide and teacher. "Oh, God, yes. He mothered us," says Vivian. "He said, 'Ask me anything you want and I'll answer you.' And there was nothing he wouldn't willingly answer."

Vivian postponed telling her 85-year-old mother. "I gave myself the excuse that she wouldn't handle this problem well. And I didn't want to handle her." So Vivian hinted, but that was all. Then one Sunday she and Mac hurriedly stopped in to drop something off; they were on their way to their monthly support-group meeting. Vivian's mother said, "I think I know where you're going, and I think I know why. Is Abie . . . that way?" Not only had she guessed, but she took it completely in stride.

Perhaps what most heartened them was Abe's new partner. Five years ago, and a year after breaking the news,

Abe settled down in a serious relationship that has lasted to this day. "That helped them a lot," says Abe, "because they could see that he cared about me and I cared about him."

Vivian describes the relationship as "absolutely wonderful. I would not trade having [Abe's partner] in our family now for anything under the sun, and I never would have expected to say that." As Mac, in his more basic way, puts it, "They're like married people, not any different. They have jobs"—Abe is an administrative assistant at a corporation—"and a house and a dog, and life goes on."

The Coopermans' adjustment was a gradual process. "I don't think I realized how far I'd moved until it was finished," says Vivian. Ultimately, they had come to a decision. Their goal was to keep the family together, and to do that they would have to change, to embrace and honor the fact that Abe was gay.

What they had not realized, though, was how that process would transform them. Vivian, for one, had grown up in a restrictive home, afraid to speak her mind with her mother and excruciatingly shy in public. In high school, she says, "I would take a zero rather than say something." As her own children grew, she expected them to follow a path she approved.

Then along came Abe's news—and the incontrovertible fact that her child would lead his own life. Vivian began to feel so strongly about the need to champion him — and to help other families accept their own gay children — that something within her shifted. She began to speak out, even taking on the presidency of Philadelphia's PFLAG and became a home-care specialist for AIDS patients, caring less what other people thought and more what she believed.

"Somewhere inside me was a person who'd been scared to death but got unscared," she says. Mac nods: "There was somebody in there hiding."

"It's not to say I don't still get nervous," she goes on, "but it doesn't paralyze me like it did. I never would have expected that to be a by-product of having a gay kid, but it's okay!"

As for Mac, he's certainly less the Archie Bunker than he once was. Steering the family Oldsmobile into the city for the monthly PFLAG meeting, with Vivian in back and a visitor next to him, he pokes fun at himself: "I'm more open to gays, but I still have fixed ideas about a lot of things."

The skies above are changeable; with the outline of the City of Brotherly Love ahead of us, we drive from a rainstorm into sunshine and back into rain. Perhaps he is speaking about himself when he muses that "heterosexual men always have to prove how macho they are." The windshield wipers slap against the window. "I guess I do let more emotion come through," he allows. "We're two late bloomers."

He stops briefly at the rowhouse that Abe and his partner share to drop off some videotapes. Out comes Abe, a handsome young man in blue jeans with a warm smile. "So," says Mac as we pull away, "does he look gay?"

As the PFLAG meeting nears its start, some 80 people gather in a large room of a church. They are mostly gray-haired, rounded, in late middle age. Some stand in groups, chatting and laughing. Others take a seat alone. Mac stands smiling in the back, greeting newcomers near a table laden with books and pamphlets. Finally, Vivian gets up and calls them all to order. She jokes about the weather, makes announcements and assures everyone that their confidentiality will be respected. Her voice is loud, forthright and confident.

On the drive home, the skies have cleared and Mac seems energized, talking about a shaken father he greeted who only two weeks ago learned his son was gay. For the first time, Vivian is quiet. She seems tired, swallowed up in the large backseat. She inquires about her visitor's two-year-old son and suddenly brightens.

"Enjoy him!" she says, leaning forward. "They're delightful when they get older, too, but things come along that you just never expected . . ."

Joanmarie Kalter has written for The New York Times, Columbia Journalism Review *and* TV Guide *and is a contributing editor for* New Choices *magazine.*

GRANDPARENTING IN THE '90s

New rules for a new era

By Sey Chassler

Welcome to the ups and downs of modern grandparenting. Many of us experiencing the role for the first time feel younger, more energetic and less formal than our own grandparents and parents did when they were our age. At the same time, our children's ideas of child rearing may be very different from the views of Dr. Spock, to which we once pledged allegiance. And such factors as living in far-flung communities and coping with our children's increased divorce rates make it more of a challenge for us to play a meaningful part in our grandchildren's lives.

But if the road to successful grandparenthood is a bumpy one, we're fortunate to have a guide in T. Berry Brazelton, M.D., an internationally renowned scientist, practicing pediatrician and best-selling author whose books include *Toddlers and Parents* (Delta) and the new *Touchpoints: Your Child's Emotional and Behavioral Development* (Addison-Wesley). He is also the founder of the Child Development Unit of Children's Hospital in Boston and co-founder of Parent Action, a national advocacy group based in Baltimore. Indeed, it was no surprise to find this ardent advocate for children and parents at the White House standing alongside Hillary Rodham Clinton and former surgeon general C. Everett Koop when President Clinton presented his administration's plan for national health care on September 20, 1993.

As an ardent advocate for children, T. Berry Brazelton has his hands full.

T. Berry Brazelton and I have been friends and colleagues for more than 20 years. (He wrote a monthly column for *Redbook* magazine when I was its editor in chief.) Not long ago, we met in his office in Cambridge, Massachusetts, to identify the ways in which grandparents of the '90s can best do their jobs.

1. Don't Try to Compete with Your Children or the "Other Grandparents"

When your first grandchild is born, all the excitement is reminiscent of what it was like when you first became a parent. Once the joyous fact of a new life sinks in, however, many of us start to worry about how our child is going to perform in a parental role. Brazelton says that when we see our children begin to act as parents, "we get a little jealous — and competitive — and wish that they would do things our way. But you can't tell your child, 'Do things my way.' That's very destructive to anybody's self-image. And competition like that undermines the grandchildren."

His advice in this common situation is to "remember that your best job as a grandparent is to be supportive. If you really think that things need to be changed, sit down with your children and try to understand the reasons for the way they deal with their children."

Your children are not the only ones who can spark conflict. "A grandfather and grandmother came to my office with their daughter to talk about some problems they were having with intergenerational parenting," Brazelton recalls. "But suddenly the grandfather blurted out that he had strong feelings of competition with the grandchild's other grandparents. He said, 'You know, we are not poor, but we aren't wealthy, either. These other folks have a big place on the ocean with a boat, and when Kevin comes back from visits with them, all he can talk about is how great they are—and about that boat. I resent these people even though I hardly ever see them. How can I keep from letting Kevin know how I feel?' "

Brazelton reassured the grandfather that such feelings were common and that "the best things you can give to your grandchildren are love and time. The danger is in trying to seduce your grandchildren by giving them bigger or more expensive gifts, hoping they'll remember you better. They aren't going to remember you for things like that anyway. The great reward of being a grandparent is that your grandchild, like your mother and father, loves you for yourself—and for no other reason."

2. Don't Be Too Quick to Claim Disrespect

Most of us are under the impression that our grandparents were treated with great respect by the rest of the family, including the youngest ones. In a more formal age, that was probably true. But in today's more relaxed climate, we often run into what we perceive as disrespect on the part of our grandchildren: We are disobeyed, we sometimes get called nasty names and we can even become the target of a thrown toy.

But all might not be what it seems. "If you are going to take 'disrespect' personally, you'd better understand the reasons for it," says Brazelton. "Grandparents need first to know something about child development and the various stages of childhood. A five- or six-year-old doesn't act out of disrespect. What she is trying to do is balance the passion in her that occurs while she is deciding which relatives she wants to be like and which she doesn't. I call it the sorting-out phase. A passionate response like throwing a toy at you is usually a child's way of showing how much he cares for you. For him it may be a kind of intimacy. He is looking for a response from you. If you think about disrespect this way, it will be a great help to you and your grandchild."

3. Discipline: Use with Caution

One of the stormiest topics for grandparents and parents revolves around discipline—especially when the elders think their children are being too lax. "Exercise some restraint," Brazelton urges.

"You don't want to endanger what your own children are doing with their children. Don't get into it, but if you must, you'd better have thought out how you want to handle discipline. If you're impulsive and overreact, you'll lose respect and might do something you don't believe in.

"Children want and need limits, and when they get out of hand, it's a way for them to find out what their limits are. Keep in mind that discipline is not punishment—it's teaching."

I had a chance to put Brazelton's advice to work one recent weekend. I was playing by our pond in upstate New York with our 6- and 10-year-old grandsons and our 3-year-old granddaughter. Suddenly, I found myself in the midst of a revolution. The 6-year-old decided to dump pailfuls of sand from our tiny strip of beach into the pond. I asked him not to because he was rapidly depleting the amount of dry sand the little girl was playing in. He ignored my requests several times, and soon the older boy joined in the fun and the sand was flying everywhere. I was about to blow up when I remembered Brazelton's words.

So I switched from anger to explaining how difficult it is to lug 700 pounds of sand

More Advice from Dr. Brazelton

- You can make every grandchild a favorite by spending some special time alone with her or him once in a while.
- Avoid spanking. It sends a message that violence is okay.
- If playing ball or jumping rope takes your breath away, don't do it. Tell the little ones that you wish you were their age. They'll love you for letting them know they can beat you at something.
- If your daughter or son says, "You were never that nice to me," don't resent it. They are recognizing that you have learned something since they were kids. Graciously acknowledge that you have learned a thing or two.
- If you are stuck in a discipline gridlock, ignoring the child is sometimes the easiest way out. Or just say: "You can't do that when your mom or dad is around, and I'm here to help them. Don't do it when I'm here, either."
- If a child flares up, let the feelings burn themselves out —and then say, "Wow, you stopped yourself! That was wonderful!" Next time, the child will try harder to be wonderful.

to replenish the beach. I told them that I was glad they were having fun but that I surely didn't want to do that job again. They not only stopped, they were impressed by my strength.

4. Clear the Air about Stepgrandchildren

Families aren't the same as when we were younger. How does one deal with the stepchildren who came with your divorced child's second marriage? Are you supposed to love them? Is it proper to call them your grandchildren? Should you feel free to talk about the "odd" relationship with your stepgrandchildren?

"I think you always have to discuss these issues with the kids," says Brazelton. "They may have the same concerns about you. As for loving or even liking the 'new' grands as you do your own, that is not, realistically, very likely. It's best to let matters take their course. It usually works out for the best."

5. Confront Issues of Sex and Violence

Not long ago, a friend of mine had a bad argument with his son-in-law when the younger man suggested he take his grandchild to see a horror movie. This was a particularly gory film—the ads showed a crazed monster wielding a bloody knife. My friend said he'd never take a little boy to see such a movie. The son-in-law accused my friend of overreacting. They argued for an hour before finally calming down (Gramps took the child to see *Aladdin* instead). I asked Brazelton how we could handle our feelings about things like bloody horror movies aimed at kids, violent toys and sexual images rife in all the media.

"In times like these," he said, "parents have a huge responsibility to provide guidance. To begin with, parents ought to share questions about violence and so forth with their children—be straightforward in talking about it with them. And the same is true for grandparents. Discuss with them your feelings and opinions. Of course, there is a danger that you might sound overly critical about the society the kids must adjust to and live with. Don't simply complain, because they won't hear you. Ask them how they feel about what they see and hear. Ask them, 'Does this scare you? Does this upset you? Does this confuse you?'

"Remember, you can't be a critic of the world they've got to go into, but you can be a model for them. You can balance the harsh music, violent scenes and toys with things you'd prefer for them. With your example, they'll be better able to handle the violence and perhaps someday do something about it." ■

Sey Chassler, former editor in chief of Redbook, *is a consulting editor of* Parade *magazine and a board member of the Child Care Action Campaign.*

How to Be a Better Grandparent

By Myrna Lewis

A recent study of college students reveals the important roles grandparents play in their grandchildren's lives and suggests ways Grandma and Grandpa can improve their ties with the younger ones.

In interviews conducted by Lucinda Franks, gerontologist and assistant professor at Bellevue University in Bellevue, Nebraska, and her colleagues at the University of Nebraska, a majority of students felt that grandparents had had a strong influence on their lives, giving them a sense of self, family history, tradition and roots. They also reported that grandparent contact greatly counteracted the many negative stereotypes that the young tend to hold about later life.

The interviews revealed four major roles for today's grandparents: surrogate parent (when parents are deceased or absent), buddy (sharing in sports and other leisure activities or acting as coach or teacher), storyteller (passing on family history or social lore) and confidant (acting as safe havens for grandchildren's secrets, troubles and dreams).

In the face of strong evidence in this study and others that grandchildren want and need contact with their elders, Franks offers the following advice to grandparents:

- Reach out to your grandchildren—don't wait for them to come to you. Find ways to explore together the roles that best suit you and them.
- Remember that most of the time you don't have to parent the children. You can enjoy the luxury of leaving the disciplining up to the parents and concentrate instead on loving.
- Never forget that you hold the key to an important part of the secret that makes grandchildren feel secure in the world—a sense of the community of the generations and of being that "special child" in the eyes of Grandma and Grandpa.

Overcoming Fear of Grandparenting

Not everyone looks forward to becoming a grandparent. More of us than might care to admit it have probably had some negative feelings about taking on the role. "But that should not be cause for guilt or self-recrimination," says Joan E. Norris, Ph.D., associate professor in the department of family studies at the University of Guelph, Ontario. "There are ways to confront those feelings and feel more comfortable about grandparenthood."

Norris, a co-author of *Among Generations: The Cycle of Adult Relationships* (W. H. Freeman), finds three main issues here. First, there's the time-of-life factor. "You may be an active person in your 50s for whom 'grandparent' might connote an unwelcome, premature sign of aging. Or you might be older and feel you don't have the energy to deal with a grandchild." Most people get through grandparenthood quite nicely. Keep a positive attitude and talk to friends who have gone through it.

The second issue also involves time—its scarcity. Most of us become grandparents when we're still working, women as well as men. These busy people worry that they won't have much time to give to their grandchildren, or they fear being burdened with baby-sitting responsibilities along with everything else. Communicate such feelings honestly to your adult children. "Establish firm rules regarding baby-sitting and other care situations. Most of us are happy to help out in an emergency, but grandparents' own needs must be respected."

Finally, there's the complicated range of emotions to deal with when marrying into a step-family. "There can be a sense of divided loyalties and love. Keep an open mind, communicate and develop the role that feels most comfortable." —M.L.

BETTER BEDTIME STORIES

Creative ways to spin a tale

By Brendan and William Kennedy

William Kennedy has made his name—and his living—telling stories to adults: His novel Ironweed*—the third in a trilogy about life among the down-and-out in his hometown of Albany, New York—was awarded the Pulitzer Prize for literature in 1984. After hours, he put his imagination to work telling bedtime stories about the less seamy side of life to his three children. One of these stories,* Charlie Malarkey and the Belly-Button Machine*—a collaboration with his 4-year-old son Brendan—was published by the Atlantic Monthly Press in 1986.*

Here, William and Brendan, who is now 23 years old and a writer himself, recall the creative process that went into the making of the Charlie Malarkey story. Grandparents, godparents, aunts, uncles—anyone who's ever been confronted with an urgent request from a wide-eyed youngster, "Tell me a story!"—are sure to glean useful advice about how to nurture the fertile imagination of a child from the Kennedys' tale.

WILLIAM:
My son Brendan, almost four, was in bed and, as usual, expecting a bedtime story. I'd read him *Huckleberry Finn* and stories by Damon Runyon and Hemingway's *The Old Man and the Sea* and limericks and poems by Edward Lear and *Winnie the Pooh* and much more. But on this night, I had no book at hand, which didn't matter to Brendan. He wanted a story. There was a gap between his pajama top and bottom, and his belly button was peeking out.

"Once upon a time, there was a guy named Charlie Malarkey," I began, "and once he went to sleep, and when he woke up, there was no belly button on him."

Brendan quickly checked out his own belly button and then, reassured, asked me, "Where did it go?" Indeed, that was the question, and I had no easy answer.

But I moved ahead, even so, finding a certain logic in what came next: Everybody looks for the missing belly button. Where do they look? In all the logical places: in the bookcase, in the peanut-butter jar, under the porch, under Charlie's pillow. But no button. Then, in the book on lost buttons and baby teeth, an ominous fact is reported: "When a belly button is lost, it is usually stolen. Very few people ever lose their belly buttons accidentally." Uh-oh.

The story evolved as I told Brendan small fragments of the tale each night, repeating it all from the beginning, of course, and thinking after a few nights, "Hey, this isn't half bad; I should write it down." And so I did, and it became a point of interest to Brendan as well. "Tell the Charlie story," he would say.

It became a test of my ingenuity to move the story forward every night, but after a time I hit a blank wall. I didn't know what should happen next. So instead of writing another page or two of my novel-in-progress, I spent the day trying to finish Charlie's story. Alas, I could not advance even a line. Something was missing, and the something was Brendan.

So I called Brendan up to my office, sat him in the platform rocker and put a serious claim on his attention: No drawing Picasso pictures, no random talk, never mind about Keepy Loop—his imaginary pal about whom he told me stories, usually as soon as he woke up in the morning. This was a story conference, and the focus was on Charlie Malarkey and what happens next. And what did happen next? I'll let him tell you.

BRENDAN:

When my father and I first got into the bedtime-story business in 1974, many of my close friends were imaginary. Charlie Malarkey, the poor guy who'd had his belly button stolen, was but one of the many pals with whom I spent my days. Whether swinging on swings, cutting snowflakes out of construction paper, or discovering the unlimited uses of Elmer's glue, I was always thinking about my invisible buddies who accompanied me wherever I went.

What I remember most about the creation of the Charlie Malarkey saga are the bits and pieces of my father's storytelling. Nightly stories consisted of a beginning sentence or idea, as he has mentioned, and then a chain of questions.

Facing the problem of Charlie's disappearing belly button, I grappled with such mysteries as: Holy cow! Where did it go? Who could be responsible for this? Why did this happen?

Being the clever lad that I was at age four, I suggested that the ill-fated Charlie ask his mother where his button went, for I was aware that mothers always seem to know these things. However, I was informed that, contrary to the usual maternal wisdom, Mrs. Malarkey did not know where the missing button was.

"So what did Charlie do then?" asked my father.

"He went back to sleep."

"Did he dream?"

"Yes," I said.

"What did he dream about?"

"Hmmmmm. He dreamed that he had his belly button back but that all his toys were gone," I replied.

"Then what happened?"

"His friend came over?"

"What's his friend's name?"

This bedtime improvisation went on until I grew tired, ran out of answers, or reached the limit of my attention span and demanded either a cookie or a good dose of Maurice Sendak.

WILLIAM:

When you are telling a story to your child and he or she falls asleep or says, "Okay, Dad, I can't take any more tonight," the storyteller flattens with chagrin and the wind goes out of his tales. But one gets over this, for the next day the child's interest quotient is resurrected at dawn. Brendan always remembered the story line better than I did, and he usually also arrived in his parents' bed with hot news about Keepy Loop.

The authors, father and son, in 1976.

"What did Keepy do today?" I'd ask him.

"He climbed a building and then ate a banana with the peel on it. He likes peels. Then he found a book and fell on it. And there was a train. That got flat because Keepy brought a toy ax and chopped it right in pieces. But the electricity didn't kill him because it was just his imagination."

"What's imagination?"

"It's just like real things, right, 'cept you dream about it, right? And when he fell on his back on the book, he didn't hurt himself because he had two hands on his back. Have you seen any Keepys around?"

I said I hadn't.

"You don't see them around too often," Brendan said.

"How does Keepy make money?"

"He sits on it."

This was such a good answer that I put $10 in Brendan's bank account.

BRENDAN:
As our story about Charlie progressed, it was decided that a machine owned by the evil Ben Bubie had stolen not only Charlie's belly button but also Iggy Gowalowicz's (Charlie's pal). Why would anyone steal belly buttons? To get rich, of course. I may have been four, but I was wise about many things.

Ben Bubie's machine, as we described it, "was made of broken glass and plastic . . . and very serious wires going in and out . . . two unpleasant-looking prongs . . . and the middle was a big tank with eight sides, and rollers and gears and bolts and wing nuts and rivets and springs and several things that looked like lemon doughnuts."

Anything was usable when it came to designing a diabolical device — including breakfast doughnuts and a 1936 16-millimeter movie projector owned by my father since he was a child. Imagining a roomful of giants cracking their knuckles, or the belly-button machine's odor of Vicks VapoRub and cod liver oil and broccoli pie with smoked oysters — imagining anything that did not exist — was always a pleasure.

Grandparents, baby-sitting, have been known to extract spellbinding stories from children . . .

My father and I had often imagined breakfast in bed with many courses: clock juice, goat bread, telephone soup, hippopotamus cookies, french-fried socks, and a side order of scrambled shoelaces with lizard sauce.

WILLIAM:
Charlie Malarkey and his pal Iggy were two intrepid adventurers, plunging into the fantastic workshop of Ben Bubie, where the belly-button machine was pulsating. They braved the forces of evil, penetrated the sinister secrets of the machine and reinstalled their stolen buttons, sort of. (It would not be fair to the authors to reveal, outside the pages of the book, exactly how this was done.)

To tell the boys' story, however, I needed help. I had to penetrate the world that children inhabit, the world that adults have left behind and often find difficult to revisit.

How is this done? It helps to have a responsive child as inspiration, as was the case with Lewis Carroll, who was so splendidly inspired by his friend's daughter, Alice Liddell, when he imagined for her a world on the other side of the looking glass. In my own case, I had Brendan's ongoing curiosity as a goad, and as method I fell back on one of the tools of my former trade, journalism: the interview. But you don't have to be a journalist, or even a parent, for this tool to work. Grandparents baby-sitting for the week have been known to extract spellbinding stories from children by using this interview method.

Mrs. Malarkey called the doctor for Charlie, and so

I wondered: "What's the doctor's name?"

"Doctor Mamoluka," said Brendan.

"What did the doctor say when he got to the place where Charlie's belly button used to be?"

"Moop."

"Moop?"

Yes, moop. Exactly. What else would a doctor say? One might ask what *moop* means. One might ask what the belly-button machine means. In all the books we love, answers to such questions reside in the experience of the people in the story. Children will understand what a story means without any gratuitous explanation or moralizing by the author. Lewis Carroll's books are enduring favorites with children in large part because they aren't easily explained and point up no bromidic morality. They are mysterious stories, and children know the meaning of mystery. Brendan knows about houses that talk, about penguins in the sky, about the lamppost that is faster than penguins, about foxes that cut down trees and a moose that sings.

A singing moose?

Well, that's another story. And get your mittens off it, kids—and you, too, Grandpa. Brendan and I already wrote it.

Charlie Malarkey and the Singing Moose, *another story written by William and Brendan Kennedy was published by Viking Children's Books in 1994.*

Reinventing the American Grandparent

By Deborah Mason

According to the latest numbers, grandparents will increasingly face two realities in the new millennium: fewer grandchildren and more stepgrandchildren.

Who will these grandparents be? Many of us, it turns out—boomers now circling 50 who opted to have fewer children (and thus fewer grandchildren) and who divorced and remarried in record numbers, many acquiring stepchildren along the way.

With Grandma's traditional flock of grandkids fading and Americans' mobility further diluting family bonds, could grandparents as we've known them turn into cultural artifacts? "I don't see grandparenthood as an endangered institution," says Frank Furstenberg, 55, University of Pennsylvania sociologist and co-author of *The New American Grandparent* (Basic Books). With fewer children, he adds, grandparents may even take their roles more seriously.

"I don't see grandparenthood as an endangered institution," says Frank Furstenberg.

Furstenberg is just as sanguine about the stepgrandchildren bond: "There are no cultural rules about this relationship; we're making them up now. But I think people inherit all kinds of relationships by marriage that can become meaningful over time. What it really depends upon is the degree to which you invest in it—this is an 'earned' relationship."

GOOD-BYE, DAD... AND THANKS

A daughter salutes her father's organized, caring approach to his death

By Mary Alice Kellogg

Looking back with love, I know that my father was never what you'd call a role model. A peripatetic safety engineer, for much of his life he was a very self-centered man, loud and gruff, with a wide circle of acquaintances, an impressive number of professional accomplishments, but few close friends. Four times divorced, he lived his life on his own terms, for the most part excluding his four children until we were adults ourselves. His relationship with his two sons and two daughters was marked by periods of closeness and estrangement, not an uncommon story in a country where family members often live hundreds of miles from one another, where family ties are unfortunately easier to break than to strengthen.

What makes our story different is what happened when this flawed man found out that he had only three months to live. It would have been easy for my father to be selfish in the last days allotted to him. Instead, he met his death with courage, spirit and—perhaps most amazing of all—a thoughtfulness for those he would leave behind that he had rarely demonstrated throughout his life. He set the tone for dealing with our fear and his own, and in doing so he forged a new and enduring family bond.

In many ways, we were prepared for the news. My father had been in declining health for several years; in fact, he had undergone a sextuple bypass operation three years earlier. Being a robust man, he had bounced back with more energy than ever, continuing to do consulting work in his field and embarking on an exhausting leisure-travel schedule. At age 70, he was enjoying life and ignoring his doctor's orders to slow down, all perfectly in character for him. But when cancer was diagnosed in October 1992 and the second and third opinions came in—when the doctors said that the disease had spread irreversibly throughout his body—he could no longer deny that his time was limited.

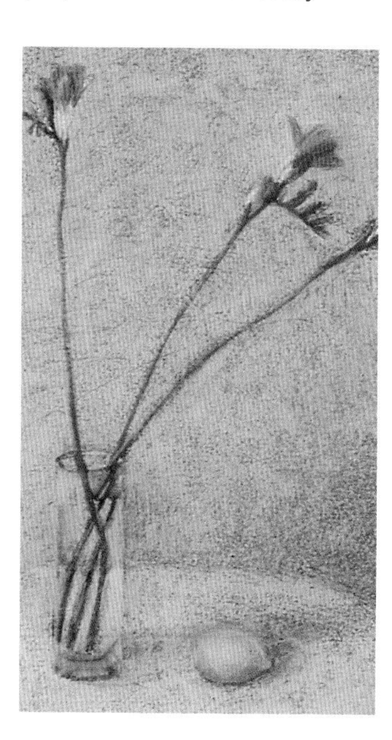

Because I was his firstborn, he often called me during difficult periods just to talk. But when he phoned from the hospital to say that he had little time left, the bravado in his voice was replaced by fear. "It doesn't look good, hon," he said, the words catching in his throat. "I've never had to deal with anything like this before. I've got to face it, and I'd be lying if I said I wasn't afraid ... I am." He began to cry, and all I could do was tell him that I loved him and that we would all be there for him—that we would help him to be strong when his strength failed him.

As he had throughout his life when problems presented

themselves, he met his fear head-on by getting organized. My father was always a master list maker. His home and business ran like clockwork; when any of us came to visit, there were lists of duties on the refrigerator, lists of things to pick up at the grocery store, lists of activities to fill the time. If list making is hereditary—and, being someone who makes lists of lists herself, I'm convinced that it is—my father made this trait work for him in his last months. He turned his talents not only to facing down his fears but also to making ordered sense of the emotional and spiritual duties of being a father.

"I know I haven't been the best father, and I've made so many mistakes," he told me. "I just want to make sure that everything is taken care of for my children. I want you to know exactly what is going on and exactly what will happen. And I want you all to know that you will be taken care of after I'm gone. Thinking about that helps me to get through this."

Two weeks after he heard the final diagnosis, he sent a four-page, single-spaced letter to each of us. In it, he listed the addresses and phone numbers of his attorney, estate administrator and accountant. He detailed the location, addresses and account numbers of all his files and legal documents, financial accounts, records and certificates, mutual funds and bonds, insurance, Social Security and pension plans, and direct bank-deposit records of investments. To make sure that his children would not be given an undue burden in his last days, he specified that he was not to be kept alive by extraordinary means, designating my brother Dennis, who had brought his laptop computer to the hospital to help him with the letter, as the one who would make the decision in consultation with the rest of us when the time came.

He also made provisions for Dennis to use his address book to notify family and friends upon his death. My sister, Debbie, was to take care of the safety-deposit box and cashier's checks to cover travel and other family expenses incurred while attending his memorial service in Sacramento and his funeral in Anchorage, where he would be laid to rest in the family plot next to his mother.

He had thought of everything: all the funeral arrangements, where the services were to be held, donations to his church, transfer to his birthplace in Anchorage for burial, services and donations there. And attached to the letter was a copy of his last will and testament, with bequests equally divided among his children—equal shares of the sale of his car and home, distribution of undesignated personal belongings equally shared (we'd pick what we wanted in birth-order rotation; unclaimed property to be donated to his church store).

Each detail of the will was carefully thought out to ensure that there would be no questions, complaints or jealousy, no squabbling about heirlooms or money. He—and we—knew well that death can often divide a family. The raw emotions surrounding the death of a parent can set the stage for bickering, selfishness and greed; grief can make fighting over a picture frame or an estate share in reality a battle for survivor territory and memory.

Very much in character, he told me, "I know you're going to use the money for paying bills and stuff like rent, but you've got to promise me that you'll take a chunk of it and have fun with it. That's what I'd do. Take a trip, buy an expensive dress, whatever. Promise me that." I did.

Although his letter dealt primarily with practical considerations, it had the effect of making me face the inevitable—as it probably had for him. I, too, had been denying that his death was so near. His matter-of-fact listing of his possessions and assets masked a tremendous effort of taking personal and emotional stock. But this was only the first step in a deeper campaign of emotional growth and reconciliation. By making sure that all the dollars—and sense—would be taken care of, he was setting the stage for a caring, loving exit, perhaps the finest gift that a parent could give to his children.

My father's mission was to bring our far-flung family—I live in New York, my siblings all over California—closer to him and to one another. In his last soul-searching months, he replaced his selfishness with a burning desire to tie up emotional loose ends with his children—the offspring from three different marriages. (He had long ago burned his bridges with his four ex-wives and did not try to contact them now.) He wanted to understand more about the effects of his behavior on his children, and he sought counseling to deal with his unresolved conflicts with each of us.

Perhaps the greatest gift he gave to us, and we to him, was the family reunion. He picked a date in early January —a month after some of his doctors predicted he'd be dead (they had told him he had two to three months, and he chose to believe the longer span)—and arranged for us to be together for four days in California for a last visit. At one point in early December he began to fail and panicked, wanting to move up the date. But the four of us consulted over the phone and decided that we'd stand firm if he'd fight to stay alive for one more Christmas, to beat the odds for a few more weeks. He rallied.

The week before the reunion, my father called each of us. "Now, I want you to think of any question that you might have about our family or me or my life," he said. "I'll tell you anything you want to know." He wanted us to understand, to be fearless in our curiosity, as he was trying to be fearless with his answers.

When I arrived in Sacramento, Dennis picked me up at the airport and we went out for a drink before visiting my father. "I want to prepare you for what you will see," he said. I'm glad that he did. For the robust man I had seen a year before was no more. In his place was a painfully thin, frail man who seemed to have aged a hundred years, someone who could sit up for only a few minutes at a time, whose mobility was hampered by an oxygen tank and who seemed to be just hanging on with every ounce of his failing energy.

His spirit was still there—there were lists on the refrigerator, a schedule of events, dinners and private time allotted for each of us. But the look in his eyes was different from the untrammeled bravado I remembered, replaced by a vulnerability, an acceptance and a painful desire to right all the wrongs in the time left. He was seeking redemption and our understanding, and his near-heroic efforts to beat back the weakness and physical ruin of his present circumstances touched each of us deeply.

Perhaps the greatest gift he gave to us, and we to him, was the family reunion.

The four days went by in a numbing haze. We'd visit with Dad until he had to go back to bed, then the four of us would go out together, sampling restaurants, taking long walks, pitching in together to help around the house, fielding phone calls from Dad's friends, monitoring one another's spirits—for we each, in our own ways, were afraid, too. We not only grew closer with our father, we also became closer as siblings, sharing our feelings every step of the way.

On our first night together, after Dad had gone to sleep, we went to a local bar for margaritas—a tradition whenever we were together. Practically at the same time, we all voiced what we had individually been worrying about: When Dad dies, what does it mean? Does it mean we won't be a family anymore? We laughed that we all had come to Sacramento with the same worry, then vowed to be even closer—geography be damned—after Dad died.

I had brought my tape recorder and several blank tapes for my private sessions with Dad. True to his nature of thinking of everything, he had borrowed a better one, with blank tapes and extra batteries for all. Each of us went in alone to talk to Dad in those last days—an hour here, an hour there. We took turns and made sure each person had equal time, adhering to Dad's schedule as much as possible.

I took my father at his word, asking him the questions I had been too angry or shy or self-centered to ask through all the years. Drinking whiskey and soda and chain-smoking — he knew he was dying, so why shouldn't he enjoy his last days? — he laughed and cried with me, reaching out in a frank and loving way that I had wanted but that it took impending death to accomplish.

At times I could see his fear, and I hugged him, trying to be a source of strength. Then he'd pick up the thread of our talk and plunge in with as much detail as he could remember. Family history, genealogy, his relationship with his mother and father, his experiences in the war — we covered them all: his divorce from my mother, the guilt he felt at not being around in my formative years, how he had wanted to change, how badly he felt about not being the kind of father the textbooks say he should have been.

At the end of our sessions, my father would fall asleep and I'd go into the living room. My sister and brothers were there and would buck me up. When they each had their turns, I and the other two would do the same. (I have three hours of my father's voice on tape still, as does each of my siblings.)

On the last day, in the living room, jokes and smiles reigned; we wanted to keep these last precious moments of normalcy as bright as possible. When the sadness hit, we would go into a corner Dad couldn't see to hug one another until it passed. We brought out the cameras for pictures: Dad with his children, Dad with his grandchildren, Dad with his sons and with his daughters, a group shot of everyone crowded on the couch. Every possible combination.

Too soon it was time for me to leave. "You're going on a wonderful adventure," I said as I hugged my father for the last time. We were both crying, and he thanked me over and over for coming. I thought of the first thing that might cheer him up: "Just think, you'll meet Thomas Jefferson and finally discover what really happened to Judge Crater. And when you do, I want you to come back and tell me all about it." He hugged me tighter. "I will" — he smiled — "I will."

"You're going on a wonderful adventure," I said as I hugged my father for the last time.

A week after my departure, Dennis called with the news that Dad had passed away. Everything was proceeding without a hitch, just as he had planned. No squabbles. No surprises. I was to leave for Paris on an important business trip, and we agreed that it would be foolish to cancel it just to fly to California for the memorial service. I had already said my good-byes. Instead, I would hold a private service of my own.

Three days later, I was in Paris. In California, my brothers and sister were attending the memorial service, which Dad had arranged — down to the Scripture readings and music. At that very moment, halfway around the world, I walked into a florist shop and bought four stalks of white freesia — white being the color of mourning in France — one for me and one each for my brothers and sister, tied together in a white family bow. I walked two blocks to my favorite bridge, the Pont Alexandre III, said a prayer for the dead and for the living, and threw the flowers into the Seine.

I watched until I lost sight of them, floating past the Eiffel Tower on their journey to the sea. My voyage of mourning had just begun. Thanks to my father's last gift, I knew his children would stay afloat, too. Geographically separated yet together. As a family.

Postscript: My father was buried according to his wishes in Anchorage on Father's Day, 1993, five months after his death. Because of the weather, it was necessary to store his body until the ground thawed. Yes, he had written the storage fees into his will: a master list maker until the end ... and after it, too. ■

Mary Alice Kellogg is a writer and editor who currently lives in New York City.

WITH YOU I AM NOT ALONE

A renowned author's touching reflections on friendship after 50 and the delicate art of keeping old pals and making new ones

By Bel Kaufman

On my recent birthday my husband gave me a party; he invited 214 of my friends. That is a lot of friends. My address book is bulging with names of fine, interesting people. Some are warm acquaintances, fun to invite to a party. Some are good friends to laugh with, to cry with, to lean on, to confide in, to need and be needed.

But my special intimate friends number three. Maybe four. We have seen each other through many ups and downs, and our friendship has withstood the test of time. That's important.

For me, the ultimate test is: To whom do I turn in an emergency? With whom do I share joy, grief? Whom do I call for comfort or advice? Not dictated by family obligations, nor motivated by sex, friendship is pure caring.

I was ill with the flu, my husband was away, and I lay in bed alone, sneezing and coughing, grateful for the telephone calls and flowers from my friends. But my special friend is the one who came, unbidden, brought me a dinner she had cooked for me and a book of crossword puzzles, cleaned the kitchen, threw me a hygienic kiss and left.

My other special friend is Russian; we've known each other since our teens, when we first came to this country. We speak Russian; that in itself is a nostalgic bond. We have read the same books, quote the same poetry, like the same things. We don't need to explain anything to each other; we are familiar with each other's history. And we can be comfortably silent together.

Another is like the sister I never had. We've known each other only a dozen years, she is 30 years younger than I, she lives 2,000 miles away, yet we try to communicate almost daily. She calls me; I write to her to bridge the miles between us. Although on occasion the telephone has been my lifeline to friends, I find myself taking to the pen more readily. A letter remains, can be read and reread; it is a permanent witness to friendship. Across the distance it tells me: "With you I am not alone." A friend is the other "I," as Aristotle said, an alter ego.

The need for friendship starts early. One child approaches another: "Wanna be friends?"—"OK." And they are, for minutes or years.

Later on, children begin to make friends on the basis of secrecy or status. My daughter, when she was six, had written out two lists of names: MY BEST FRIENDS and MY WORSTEST FRIENDS. They were frequently interchangeable.

I missed that phase, having spent my childhood in the adult world of the Russian Revolution, coming to this country speaking no English, awed by the American girls, envious of their cliques of friends, not daring to approach them. If a girl liked me, I liked her back, out of gratitude.

In adolescence, friendships are intense, based on competition, admiration, a need to conform or rebel. In high school, I had one girlfriend who was as shy as I was. We were in the same classes, ate the same lunch together every school day and joined the same school clubs. Loneliness and propinquity drew us to each other. I have not seen her since.

Some early friendships endure; some do not. When they've been outgrown, it's all right to let them fade away into memories.

Young married women with babies on park benches make friends with other mothers, exchanging recipes and advice, discussing children and husbands: "Does yours? . . ." "Mine always . . ." I was one of them. Two of my park-bench friendships developed into lifelong relationships.

Women over 50 have different needs for friendship. But why draw an arbitrary line at 50? Age has little to do with numbers. I've known old people of 30 and young ones of 80. Older women—no, I don't like that, either. Older than whom? Older than what? Why not elderly? Why not *old*? An honorable word.

Well, let's say *mature* women. Some, way over 50, have already lived through major life changes: marriage, children, careers. Most are established in a way of life that is more or less permanent and busy. They have little time for casual friendships; they are more selective. The breezy "We must do lunch one day" or "Call me" usually leads to nothing, but real friendship grows, develops and remains a constant in this uncertain world.

A great number are divorced or widowed, with children grown and away. Living alone, they tend to turn to other women for companionship and support. They bond together to travel, to go to movies, theaters, concerts—especially these days, when they fear to go out alone at night.

I say "they," but I can speak only for myself. People who meet me may have the advantage: They may know about me; perhaps they have read me or heard me speak, and they offer friendship.

For many it is difficult to make new friends late in life. Yet I have made new friends, good friends, in recent years. I no longer have a fear of rejection, of taking that first step. Sometimes, with a contemporary, there is instant rapport: "Then you, too,...?" Most of my new friends are younger than I, and we learn much from each other.

Some of my younger friends are my former students, grown now with children of their own. These relationships are not profound but mutually flattering.

Others are fans. A quarter of a century ago, a troubled 15-year-old girl wrote me a fan letter when she was given my book *Up the Down Staircase* at Christmas. I answered. Although we have never met, throughout the years we have developed a friendship on paper, exchanged photographs, gifts, confidences; at first as adult and child, then as friend and friend. I have watched her grow up in her letters, marry, divorce, adopt a child, experience tragedy, start a new career.

In a room full of strangers, I sometimes feel an affinity for one person. I always intend to call, to send a note, an invitation, but seldom do. In my desk drawer lie many visiting cards with names I can no longer recognize, which once, at a party, were enthusiastically exchanged with assurances of getting in touch. So many potential friends turned into faceless cards . . .

Whether old or new, friendship must be kept in constant repair, lest it die of neglect.

Should auld acquaintance be forgot? For me, the richest, most fulfilling, most comforting are old friends. Even if we don't see each other for months or years, whenever we do meet, it's as if we parted the day before.

The other evening, I was at a dinner party of 10 close friends: five couples who have known one another for some 30 to 40 years, some even longer. We have gone through triumph and tragedy, illness and recovery; we have common experiences and memories; we delight in each other's company. We no longer have to prove ourselves—we are friends.

To quote Emerson, "The only way to have a friend is to be one."

I try. I keep dates of my friends' birthdays and anniversaries on my calendar. I remember their special interests, their favorite flowers, authors, food, music. I send little cards or gifts on special occasions.

I make up funny rhymes for them. I clip from newspapers or magazine articles pertaining to their interests. Sometimes I just write a note saying, "I love you; I miss you."

When possible, my friend's need is my priority. I listen, really listen, without prejudgment, with empathy and patience.

When possible, my friend's need is my priority. I listen, really listen, without prejudgment, with empathy and patience. I try to be truthful, not necessarily candid, for candor sometimes masks hostility. I give advice only when I'm asked but avoid the fallacy of "if I were you," which, of course, I am not.

And my friends reciprocate. Some are foul-weather friends. They were there for me when I was desperate, devastated by a personal blow. They made me come to their villa in Italy, took me out every day to divert me, and gave me a beautiful summer. My gratitude to them remains as great today, though in fair weather I don't see them as often.

Sometimes there is a rift in friendship, inevitable and unmendable betrayals, misunderstandings, disappointments. A close friend remarried, left the city and erased everyone from her previous life. Failed friendships are sad.

And as I grow older, friends die. I recently had to deliver four eulogies in seven weeks for people who had been my friends for years. That is a deep loss, and the older one gets, the fewer old friends remain; a part of one's life goes with them.

I mourn lost friends, I depend on old friends, I am grateful for new ones. It's never too late to make a new friend.

At a party, when I hear an interesting voice or a funny comment, or see a sympathetic smile, I feel like walking over and saying, "Wanna be friends?" ■

Bel Kaufman is a lecturer and writer, best known as the author of Up the Down Staircase. *First published in 1964, this novel has been translated into 16 languages, made into a movie and performed in schools across the U.S.*

Ways to Make—and Keep—Friends

By Eleanor Foa Dienstag

As my friends know, I'm a "city girl," residing in Manhattan, where 48 percent of the households "consist of people living alone," according to the *New York Times Magazine*, "twice the national average." We urban singles aren't all chubby-cheeked, either. A growing number of us are older; tired of shoveling sidewalks and driving at night or in bad weather. Our priorities have become such amenities as apartment supers who fix leaks, and buses and taxis that provide easy access to services, friends, shops and entertainment.

Yet other single people wouldn't dream of giving up rural or suburban life, and we can learn from the ways they make and keep friends. "In the country," says Laurie Mercer, who lives in a rural community, "family and neighbors look out for each other. All you really need in this neck of the woods is a good truck." Does she ever worry about getting ill? Never. Country folks are fearless and independent, and the happy ones don't have time to be lonely. Take 63-year-old Edward Kohler, divorced since 1976. He gardens, hunts, traps, harvests maple syrup, and raises trees for Christmas and firewood. "I don't have a dull minute," says Kohler.

Mary von Kampen, 69, has lived alone for 21 years. Her secret is to "practice healthy methods"—eating well, staying active and getting regular checkups. Recently retired, she raises peacocks (how's that for imaginative?). "Good neighbors and a positive attitude are also a must," she says. She and a neighbor call each other if one doesn't see the other about.

"You don't move to the country unless you enjoy solitude," says Lois Fields, 62, who moved from Columbus, Ohio,

to rural Wisconsin in 1982. She adds that companionship is available when you want it: "If you are positive and cheerful, people will come." One divorcée she knew was skilled at meeting newcomers and "making you feel like a friend." This woman, in her 90s, knew everyone, belonged to every organization in town, and always volunteered her services, even if she had to hire someone else to bake cookies or make sandwiches. In a wheelchair the last five years of her life, she spoke to a friend on the telephone every day at 7 A.M. and 7 P.M. Two people stocked her woodstove morning and night. Another cleaned, cooked and assisted her.

"Letter writing is a big thing for country people," says Fields. She now runs Rural Network, a unique national organization. Founded in 1980 by Arlene Caldwell, a divorced mother of three grown childen, this letter-based group fosters mutual support among rural residents. Members receive a list of other networkers and exchange personal profiles. Best of all, they receive a monthly eight-page publication full of chat, information and pictures from members introducing themselves and sharing their adventures.

Passionate letter writers can also join The Letter Exchange: A Magazine for Letter Writers. The goal of this international pen-pal organization is to share "the diversity of political, religious and social viewpoints."

Recently, more country and suburban singles have banished isolation and loneliness by sending computer E-mail messages over the Internet. One forum, SeniorNet, has created an international on-line community. SeniorNet teaches computer skills at more than 55 Learning Centers it runs around the country. Perhaps one is near you.

Eleanor Foa Dienstag writes the "Living Alone" column for New Choices *magazine and is author of* In Good Company: 125 Years at the Heinz Table *(Warner Books).*

HE WAS THE PERFECT CATCH, BUT

...now the author had to decide whether her fling should turn more serious

By Isabel Davis

I think my third husband is advertising in *The New York Review* personals," I say to my friend Carol. "Just listen: DWM and—don't pay attention to the next part—70." Even over the phone I can feel her getting uptight. My younger friends always think I should be with someone no older than my own age, preferably younger. I'm 62, a young 62, if that's not an oxymoron.

"Don't think 70," I say. "Think Paul Newman. Wait till you hear the rest." She sighs. "Professor in medical school, active practice. Wait. Here it comes: Old farmhouse on a hilltop in Vermont, and . . ." I pause dramatically, then practically shout, "house on a Caribbean island. That already makes him 55 or less, right?" Small laugh. "There's more," I continue. "Omnivorous reader, loves classical music and jazz, considerable travel. Plus, he bicycles, skis and snorkels. He's gotta be in great shape."

"Well," Carol says, "you might as well find out. Write to him."

It took him a couple of weeks to call. I thought maybe I had blown my letter by mentioning that I liked physicians, which I realized too late he might not be. Turned out he's a psychoanalyst. Even better. We arranged to meet.

He looked a little older than men I've dated, but attractive—high cheekbones, blue eyes—and he ordered oysters. Things were going along very smoothly, so imagine my surprise when he confessed.

He was not 70.

He was 80.

He couldn't say 80 in the ad, he explained; he wasn't interested in meeting women who would want to meet the average 80-year-old. Okay, I could understand that. Average he wasn't. But 80 he was.

Eighty! My mother is 83. Eighty? My brother, Richard, and I were once analyzing personal ads, and he zeroed in on a guy who described himself as 5 feet 7 inches in his tennis socks. "Five feet 6, if you're lucky," Richard warned me. "Probably, 5 feet 5." Brothers understand these things—he was 5 feet 5. Well, I'm not as tall as I used to be, either. Or as young. Still, 80? By that measure, the guy in the socks would be 4 feet 10.

But.

I had found the man unusually interesting before he dropped his bombshell. He'd spent a year in Africa in the Peace Corps. He was going to Santa Fe to visit his kids for the weekend and to Turkey in the fall. And he was still seeing patients. He even sounded honest about his ex-wives. (I prefer men with a couple of ex-wives. They make me feel less like a failure at the big M.) All this with oysters.

So when the meal ended and he asked, "Well, what do you think?" I had to say that I'd enjoyed myself. I did not add, "Eighty? What kind of a person is 80?" I mean, the man was clearly exceptional, and I didn't want to make him feel bad about something he couldn't change. Besides, you can never tell if they're going to call again, anyway. (Blind dates, that is, not 80-year-olds. With the latter, you'd wonder if he'd died.)

When he called to invite me to his hilltop ("I have three bedrooms," he said. "You don't have to be nervous"), I figured, what the hell, and started humming Sondheim's "A Weekend in the Country," da-da-da-da. But when I mentioned my plans to my children, my son said, "Are you crazy? You're going to visit some old man you don't know on a farm in Vermont? It's like a Hitchcock movie. What if you're never heard from again?" I said I'd leave the address so they could come for the body.

Well, I'd kill for the farmhouse—old, comfortable, acres of land, a pond to swim in, wonderful paintings and books. And he cooks. As for conversation, he was a shrink, remember? I was almost seduced when he said, most kindly, "Do you want to talk about your anxiety?" No fee. I was having a great weekend.

Except.

Except I wasn't attracted to him. These things, always peculiar, get even more peculiar when you're older. A wise friend once told me, "It's not like when we were kids. The attraction part takes a little time; it has to grow on you." So to speak. Well, it didn't grow, and he wasn't looking for just a companion, bless his Freudian soul.

I did like the man, though. And, oh, by the way, did I mention the island house is in Anguilla? Another thing I've noticed with age is that these tidbits—like houses—become more alluring, maybe in direct proportion to the waning libido. In my earlier lives, I always managed to fall for men who were not going to make my golden years very golden.

So, I thought, since this was my first experience with someone much older (at an age when it does matter more than, say, if we'd met when I was 42 and he, 60), I had to give it a little more time. Maybe he didn't always go to sleep so early. And people much younger can be hard of hearing. I did say rather wistfully as I was leaving, "I do wish you weren't 80. I guess you probably do also." He laughed. More points for him. He said I'd know what to do by the time I got home.

Driving over the Triboro Bridge in bumper-to-bumper traffic, I knew I wanted to go back to Vermont soon. Maybe the next time would be different.

During the next two weeks, I had dreams of Ronald Colman in *Lost Horizon*, watching Margo's face wither instantly in the snow. On the other hand, I remembered *Cocoon*, one of those fountain-of-youth fantasies where Hume Cronyn and Jessica Tandy turn young. According to every other Tuesday's science section of *The New York Times*, perpetual youth is coming any day now.

Besides, how superficial was I? He was bright; he was kind. My older friends began to kick in: "Age is irrelevant. What are you so hung up on?" I'd never have to worry about wrinkles or age spots again. And to hell with those 10 extra pounds. My youngest friend went right to the point: "How's his body?" she asked. "Good for a man half his age," I had to admit.

So, back to the house on the hilltop, I decided. Think Picasso. Think Casals. Think Alfred Eisenstaedt.

But when he picked me up at the airport, I thought, "He looks old. What am I doing with someone so old?"

And through a most delightful weekend of good food and conversation, even kayaking, I just couldn't get past that thought. I felt ashamed. I felt shallow. Really awful. Till finally, a little wisdom began to seep through. (You do learn something in six decades.) It wasn't his age, I realized. That certainly didn't help. It was even a little scary. But guess what? I would have forgotten it if that old black magic had kicked in.

Oh, well. He'll probably end up with a gorgeous woman 10 years younger than I am. He's definitely smart enough to get one who won't be in it just for the houses. ■

Isabel Davis, who lives in New York City, is working on a book of essays titled A Woman of a Certain Age.

YOUNG FRIENDS ARE A MUST

Lessons in new approaches to old situations

By Dan Wakefield

"Have you read this?" the student asked. She handed me a large paperback volume with the title *Generation X.* The cover said it was "a novel," but it didn't look like a novel. It was too long and wide, more like the size of a children's coloring book, and when I flipped inside, I saw there were drawings in the margins, rather like cartoons.

I held the thing gingerly, like a sick cat, and confessed I hadn't heard of it before.

"You can borrow it," the student said. "It's really good — about my generation? Sort of '20-something' people?" (Twenty-something people sometimes speak in a queer way that makes statements sound like questions.)

I stuffed the odd thing in my briefcase and dutifully got it out a few days later, thinking I would leaf through it just to be polite. I read the first page and became absorbed. Douglas Coupland's characters — drifting young people of the '80s — seemed like post-baby-boomer versions of the dropout protesters of the '60s generation described by my young old friend of those days, Ray Mungo, who wrote of his Vermont commune in *Total Loss Farm.*

I had met Ray Mungo as a journalist when he was making a name for himself as the radical editor of Boston University's *BU News* in 1967. I was impressed by Ray's powerful writing and fresh ideas, and we got to be friends despite the almost 20-year difference in our ages. Along with Kurt Vonnegut and our mutual publisher, Seymour Lawrence, I was made an "honorary uncle" of Mungo's commune at their May Day celebration of 1970, where we represented the Older Generation as honored guests, imbibing wine but abstaining from hallucinatory brownies (not all young ideas are good ideas).

I've gotten in touch with a sense of youthful freshness from the tips I've shared with young people, as well as from ones they've given me.

When I finished *Generation X,* filled with the pleasure of coming onto a fresh and artful new literary voice reminiscent of Ray Mungo's, I thought of how many times students — as well as young people I've met through church or involvement in civic or political causes or in my neighborhood — have led me to make worthwhile discoveries. Young people have introduced me to authors, movies, music, food, restaurants, even recipes I might never have tried had I restricted my circle of acquaintances to people my own age. More important, these young people and their enthusiasms have given me new injections of energy and insight and kept my life fresh, lively and surprising.

When I taught at the University of Illinois journalism school in 1968, one of my students pressed on me a record album he thought I'd enjoy. It was *Wildflowers,* by a popular new folksinger named Judy Collins, and it soon became an old favorite. Her haunting renditions of songs like "Both Sides Now" and "Albatross" served as inspiration when I took time out from laboring over my first novel, *Going All the Way*.

While teaching at the Writers' Workshop at the University of Iowa, I learned something from those graduate students that has nourished me ever since and gotten me through many a cold winter—how to make chili (the secret ingredient is ground cloves). A big pot of chili is easy and cheap to cook, goes a long way and can serve as the focus of an impromptu feast.

There were many such feasts that second semester of 1972 in Iowa City. From the grad students there, I learned not only the recipe for chili but the recipe for hospitality—come as you are, get something to eat, sit on the floor and listen to the music. (Faculty dinners with people my own age were, of course, more formal and less fun.) The hot singer that winter was Nilsson, whose "Without You" boomed plaintively from every stereo speaker and still evokes in my mind light falling on the plain board floors of Iowa farmhouses, red wine and falling snow.

My eating pleasure has been enhanced not only by the home cooking I've picked up from young people but also by their tips for dining out. If older means wiser, one piece of wisdom I'll swear to after just turning 60 is that people who are 20-something know the best restaurants. I don't mean the four-star places with the red leather banquettes and tip-receiving captains—you can learn about those from successful peers—but rather the off-the-beaten-path, hole-in-the-wall, ethnic or diner-revival-style eateries that are heavy on the portions and light on the pocketbook (bring cash—they don't usually accept credit cards).

I recently returned to Manhattan to live while writing a novel about my own 20-something years here, only to find that the restaurants I had frequented as a budding author in New York in the '50s (if they are still around) now have prices that match the '90s. But I felt transported back to my time of youthful dining out the other night, when a 20-something friend took me to Caribe, a Caribbean restaurant in Greenwich Village, where I ate more good food for less money than at any other place I've been since moving back here.

I've gotten in touch with a sense of youthful freshness from the tips I've shared with young people, as well as from ones they've given me. I introduced a student in my novel-writing course at Boston's Emerson College to Ernest Hemingway's *The Sun Also Rises* and *A Moveable Feast*, and consequently he made a pilgrimage to France and Spain to visit the shrines of my generation's literary "Papa" and to go to the bullfights. He sent me postcards from Paris and Pamplona in 1991, which reminded me of my own pilgrimage to the same sites in 1958, when I was in my 20s—just about the age of this young novelist. Through his discovery, I was able to relive my own and appreciate it more fully.

It snowed the last night of the novel-writing workshop. I was teaching at Emerson, and when we went to leave the building, we found that the front door had been locked. The class had run late, and no one else was there. We were trapped. Disgusted and resigned, I was about to call the department chairperson at home for help when a student excitedly shouted down from the second floor that he'd discovered a way out. We could open the window of the room where our class was held and climb down a fire escape!

Breath came out in frosty clouds as we made our way carefully down the two flights of stairs, giggling, calling out, balancing books and briefcases. Clutching the cold iron railing, we reveled in the fresh, falling snow and the sense of adventure. We'd have missed all that if I'd made my official call for help, if the student hadn't seen the more challenging way to go—the way I'd probably have seen myself at his age.

Sharing the students' exhilaration at taking the unofficial way, the one less traveled and seldom seen by older, more conventional wisdom, I stomped through the snow with gusto that night, feeling more alive—and young. ■

Dan Wakefield is a novelist, journalist and screenwriter whose latest book is Creating from the Spirit *(Ballantine).*

CALL YOUR OLD FRIENDS NOW

Losing two childhood buddies brought home to this writer the irreplaceable nature of lifelong bonds.

By Laurence I. Barrett

My friends Dick Critchfield and Sol Rubinstein never met, which is a shame. I wonder whether these two—starkly different in background, personality, professional interests—would have recognized that they also had a strong bond. Lately, I've mused about the three of us having a long dinner, during which I'd explain how each of them, over many years, provided critical stitches in the human networks that enrich my life, networks whose full value became clear only after they'd begun to fray seriously.

Too late for that dinner. Shortly before Christmas, Dick, 63, suffered a fatal stroke in Washington just as dozens of us were gathering to celebrate publication of his latest book. The following weekend, I learned that Sol had recently died at 60 in Seattle, where he used his genius in mathematics to design computer programs.

By late middle age, you're bruised by such bad news but no longer astonished. You've already lost some contemporaries. And you've become all too familiar with the feelings of diminishment, anger and, yes, anxiety: They were roughly your age (too young!), it was so sudden, it isn't fair. And, of course, who's next?

For me, the sense of loss this time was even deeper. As we hurtle through our lives, changing towns, jobs and occasionally spouses, most of us move through several networks of relationships. Sometimes this passes for upward mobility. Often we forget, almost intentionally, those early associations, comfy in the illusion that new is automatically better. But new is frequently ephemeral, based on your professional

Three musketeers: from left, Jay Ebinger, author Laurence Barrett and Leon Golovner at Barrett's bar mitzvah in 1948

standing or other swampy factors.

Dick and Sol somehow caught on to all that at the start. Through instinct or life experiences or both, they understood the value of those early human connections, the need to maintain ties with where you came from, literally and metaphorically. When you lose people like them, saying good-bye is particularly challenging. You need not only to appreciate their contribution but to ask yourself what to do about the sudden vacuum.

You start by remembering what doesn't appear in conventional obituaries. Dick Critchfield had his share of those printed obits because, after his early work as a journalist in the U.S., Asia and Europe, he wrote 10 books that won wide recognition. One recounted his family's roots in the Midwest from the 1880s onward. Four of his other books dealt with peasant life and culture in developing countries. Dick's fieldwork had him living for months on end in hamlets near the Nile, the Ganges and other waters in which most of us will never bathe. Our class at Columbia Graduate School of Journalism produced many careers, but none so exotic as Dick's.

The class was intimate—only 68 diplomas that year—and we promptly scattered. An annual newsletter kept us informed of one another's progress or lack of it. Dick, the true vagabond among us, provided another kind of glue. When I bumped into him in Saigon 30 years ago, he had been covering the war for months, while I was passing through. Yet it was he who bubbled with news about classmates and former teachers because he kept in touch with a lot of them. Later, his rare appearances in Washington or New York became occasions for reunions either to mark his latest book or to gather for a nostalgic schmooze.

I last saw him a few years ago at a party he'd organized at the Cosmos Club, where he stayed while visiting Washington. The handful of us from the class of '57 made up the smallest subset. When I complimented him on his fealty to old pals, he replied by asking if we realized how many of our classmates were already gone. To my embarrassment, I did not. Five, he noted, naming them in a tone of affectionate remembrance one might use for close relatives. He was staying at the Cosmos Club the night before another Critchfield party when he collapsed. Now the number is eight, and I hope Dick would be pleased to know that I can name them.

Sol Rubinstein didn't write books or host parties in venerable venues like the Cosmos Club. Or anywhere else, as far as I know. Sol was something of a loner. His original ambition for a university life in the field of pure mathematics foundered on some obscure reef of academic politics. Boeing, which drew him to the Northwest, was too big for his tastes, so he often worked as a consultant. There would be four marriages. Despite all that change over the decades, Sol would often be in touch.

His voice had a staccato, crackling quality, and in one memorable late-night call there was even more urgency than usual. Sad news about our old friend Leon Golovner. Diagnosis: terrible. Prognosis: Don't ask. "Leon knows the score," Sol told me. "He wants to hear from you. Better do it soon."

By this time, he had my full attention. Usually when he called from the West Coast, tracking me down in New York or Washington at odd hours, he ignored the time difference. I might doze off in retaliation. This time was different. "You sure Leon wants to talk to me?" It hadn't been merely years but decades since we'd been in touch. "Sure I'm sure," Sol said. "He wants to say good-bye to everybody."

"Everybody" meant the handful of guys who spent their childhood and adolescence together on the north end of Knox Place, the Bronx, in the '40s and early '50s. In that time and place, geography and ethnicity dictated the makeup of your first little tribe. Tenement families stayed put in that era of war-induced housing shortages. Turnover in our kid clique was rare. Together we moved from kindergarten to high school, from Chinese handball to baseball, from hating girls to lusting after them. We hung out in one another's apartments, sneaked cigarettes from parents' packs, competed for part-time jobs, learned more than was decent about one another's family secrets.

Sol was the only pious one among us, a virtue that excluded him from some of our games and mischief. Never a fighter or much of an athlete, he was an easy target for childish pranks and unkind jokes.

Yet he chose a special role: As we all grew apart, he commissioned himself town crier for a hamlet that no longer existed except when he willed it to. Around the time we all turned 30 — a symmetrical 30 years ago — Sol began to check in with those of us he could find. He seemed to enjoy spreading word about our adult adventures and misadventures.

At the time, his widowed mother still lived on Knox Place. So a call from Sol or a note or an occasional drop-in when he was back east brought an update on the old neighborhood's changing ethos as well as word about someone's job change, new baby or whatever. In his apprenticeship years as town crier for the Knox Place that once was, Sol simply assumed that the position was necessary. I didn't, not decades ago.

My present and future were my agenda, thank you. The past was, well, boring — and a bit déclassé. I was bouncing between New York and Washington, changing assignments in journalism every few years, coaxing my first book into print, not to mention coping with three children. Friends? Of course, platoons of them, drawn almost entirely from the PTA or Little League bleachers in the 'burbs and from work-related activities in the city.

But relationships often dissolve when the circumstances that bred them change. The kids go off to college and beyond; parenthood isn't a social status any longer. Your fast-track career inevitably slows. You reach a time when new networks don't form automatically. You don't notice the exact moment, but somehow the worth of your older friendships rises, like that of a once-devalued bond you tucked away in the vault years ago.

. . . somehow the worth of your older friendships rises, like that of a once-devalued bond tucked in the vault.

Perhaps I was approaching that point nine years ago when Sol, still clanging his crier's bell, called with the news about Leon. Of course I intended to get in touch with Leon. But I procrastinated for a day or two, then had trouble with the hospital switchboard, then discovered that it was too late.

Ouch. Failing an old pal at a moment of great need causes painful remorse. So does the realization that you had failed yourself for many years. It would have been interesting, perhaps enriching, to know Leon as an adult. As men moving in very different orbits, we would have laughed at our juvenile rivalry for the role of alpha wolf. It would have been fascinating to learn whether he handled the challenges of fatherhood any better than I did.

Sol and I mused about that later and found that we shared a keen yen to know what had become of another of the old crowd, Bob Fisch, and why he had snipped his connection even with me, his best buddy. Sol would make inquiries among cousins who might still be in touch with cousins. Hold on, I said, I'm the reporter, I'm supposed to be able to find out things. But neither of us got very far. Finding Bob remained on the To Do list.

But it seemed as if Providence wanted to give Sol's general mission an assist a while ago, when an unfamiliar voice on the phone turned out to belong to Jay Ebinger, who had followed his father into the plumbing trade and today nurses the heating-cooling system of a large New York hospital. Years before, we had shouted to each other from our kitchen windows, separated by a courtyard, when it was time to meet for our daily walk to P.S. 80. Now, with not much more ceremony, he was calling to ask a favor. His son, close in age to my eldest, was living in Washington and needed some career counseling.

Of course. With genuine pleasure. One thing led to another, and now the Ebingers and the Barretts see each other over dinner from time to time. My wife says that watching Jay and me is a stitch. Apparently, we convey a great deal in body language and abbreviations, eliciting agreement or a laugh from each other with little need for elaboration. The lack of contact over three dozen years seems irrelevant.

During one of these cheerful dinners last fall, we realized that neither of us had heard from Sol for a long time. His bell ringing was irregular, but he rarely remained silent for more than six months. Jay would check into it. That's how we learned that Sol had died some weeks earlier. He never let us know that he was gravely ill—an odd omission for someone who had brought the news from Knox Place so faithfully for so many years. Maybe he grew tired of doing the job alone. He'd be entitled. Or maybe he figured we wouldn't care to know. He'd be very wrong.

He might have wondered, when illness engulfed him, why we didn't reach out. The easy excuse is that we didn't know. Of course, we should have, but we always relied on him to start the conversation. As a youngster, Sol studied the Old Testament as closely as he did his math lessons. Maybe that was how he began to understand the value of lifelong bonds.

"Forsake not an old friend," the authors of Ecclesiasticus admonish us from antiquity, "for the new is not comparable to him: A new friend is as new wine; when it is old, thou shalt drink it with pleasure."

It took a lot of years for me to learn that ancient lesson, restated in one way or another by sages over many centuries. It hurts to think that perhaps Sol, in his final days, did not know that I had finally gotten the point. I should have told him that. Thomas Jefferson once wrote that he saw "no comfort in outliving one's friends, and remaining a mere monument of the times which are past." Yet it is human nature to attempt to come to terms with loss.

One way to do that is to be more than a "mere monument." Dick Critchfield and Sol Rubinstein, two special people, two conservators of the spirit of villages that formed me, deserve more than that. So do the people who played similar roles in your life. You mourn them, of course. But do you owe them anything else? Yes, and yourself, too. If you came to value—however belatedly—what they did, you inherit an obligation to take on some of their mission. The old networks inevitably shrink, but they can endure for a long time if survivors make an effort.

This is satisfying rather than onerous. In my own case, Dick's death prompted me to think about a full-blown class reunion. We had already talked about a 40th-anniversary gathering, but that would have meant waiting till 1997. Given the attrition rate, it seems a long time off. So I've begun phoning around to test interest in an event sooner rather than later. We may not bring it off, given how scattered the group is, but it's fun learning that people at least like the idea.

Knox Place is a more interesting challenge. Jay and I talk regularly, and in a conversation just before I began writing this piece, he brought me up to date on Dina, Leon's younger sister, who now has a grown son just starting a journalism career on a small newspaper. Talk about delicious coincidence. A lifetime ago, Jay, Leon and I put out a few issues of our own little Knox Place sheet. We thought that getting shopkeepers to buy ads was easier work than delivering grocery orders.

Now, Jay tells me, Dina wonders if I can keep her son in mind if I hear of any job openings. That raises a marvelous prospect. Jay's son and one of mine both work for news organizations in Washington. Adding Leon's nephew to that list would, at least metaphorically, extend the Knox Place network to a new generation. When that idea crossed my mind, I imagined how enjoyable it would be to share it with Sol. He would surely get a kick out of that notion. He'd also want to know that if I ever do find Bob Fisch, I'll tell him as much as I can about Sol's life. ■

Laurence I. Barrett is a contributor to Time *and teaches journalism at American University in Wash., D.C.*

THE GREENPOINT GIRLS

Whether it's games or trouble, these friends have stuck together.

By Joanmarie Kalter

Rose and Theresa play bingo together at the church hall twice a week. They bake sausage pies and fruit pies together at holidays: Rose mixes the ingredients while Theresa rolls the dough. Every month or two, they dye each other's hair, favoring champagne blondes just a shade or two apart. Although they don't really look alike, people who meet them think they must be sisters. But Rose and Theresa are not sisters; they're friends. They've been friends since childhood, so long, in fact, that neither can remember a time when she did not know the other.

Rose Hasiak and Theresa Chojnowski are two of a larger group of friends who, if it had a name, might be called the Greenpoint Girls. There's Lucy Smith and Marie Franzese and Mary Martello and Tessie Mangone and Mary Dellocono and Julie Bonomo. Most of them, like Rose and Theresa, still live a few blocks from where they were born, in Greenpoint, Brooklyn. The neighborhood is an unremarkable collection of attached two- and three-story buildings on treeless blocks that stand in the shadow of an elevated, broken-down highway. But even those who have moved, like Marie, still make these streets the center of their social life. After 23 years in another neighborhood in Queens, Marie says, "I never really made friends where I am because I had my friends here. When you have good friends, you have to keep them."

Is it a Monday or a Friday night? You'll find the Greenpoint Girls playing cards. "Be there!" says Lucy, slapping the deck in a game of rummy before drawing the card she hopes will complete her hand. This night in December, the Girls sit around Theresa's kitchen table, munching her homemade cookies with anisette icing and colored sprinkles. They talk in thick Noo Yawk accents that would make Archie Bunker feel right at home. "Ya godda dollah?" Tessie asks, trading change. Smoke from their cigarettes fills the room like a dust cloud.

The Greenpoint Girls, who never get enough bingo, gather to play at the local church hall.

While they range in age from 60 to 70, there's a sweet girlishness to their ritual: When the Greenpoint Girls play poker, they never bluff. "Oh, no, we would never trick anyone," says Marie. "We play a friendly game." When someone admits to having put too much baking powder in her cookies, so that they expanded wildly in size, the friends energetically smooth over the mistake: "Oh, yeah," says Theresa, quite seriously. "I bet there's more to eat when they're big."

The Greenpoint Girls began playing cards some 25 years ago — "Oh, yeah, 25 at least," they say, matter-of-factly — when most of them had children in school together. Their husbands would gather a few evenings a week at the local Knights of Columbus hall, and the men became fast friends, too. In the group's younger days, they'd all pile into a few cars for weekend trips together; they'd visit family resorts in Pennsylvania or borscht-belt hotels in upstate New York.

As time went on, of course, their lives changed: Marie divorced, and Julie's and Theresa's husbands died. Somehow, though, the spirit of the group remained the same. "Usually, single women are not welcome with couples," says Marie. "But they have been very good about it."

Today, the group heads down to the casinos of Atlantic City about every other week. The ladies love the slot machines, the gentlemen play dice. Theresa, who never drove until after her husband's death three years ago, now drives only to Atlantic City. "My car knows the way," she says with a wink. The friends, who, with their husbands can number about a dozen, go so often and have such noisy fun that regulars at Trump Plaza know just where to find them. "It's called the 'Brooklyn aisle,' " says Marie, "near the bathroom."

There are, of course, closer friendships within the friendship of the group. Years ago, Lucy wangled a job at Yankee Stadium just so she could wave to the pope when he came; Mary Martello and Tessie later joined her in running the gift shop there. The mention of those years brings gales of giggles — about the fried meatballs Lucy would bring them every Sunday, about the celebrities, like Reggie Jackson, they'd meet there. Marie says that Tessie helped end her solitude after a heartbreaking divorce. "I didn't want to do anything or go anywhere, but Tessie dragged me out. I'd finally go, not because I wanted to but so I didn't have to hear her nag me anymore. I think she saved my life."

No alliance, though, is as deep and lasting as that between Theresa and Rose. They have been together — "best friends" — through every significant moment in life. As children they grew up next door to each other. When Theresa lost her mother at age four, she attached herself to Rose's family. The two friends were inseparable all through their school years. As young women, they took jobs together — they were salesgirls at Woolworth's and worked in a defense plant during the war. Together they'd ride the subway into Manhattan, the glittering Big City, where they'd see one stage show, then come out and immediately see another. And when they married, they married two friends.

In fact, Rose and Theresa were about 13 when they first went to watch Benny and Marion play sports in the schoolyard. Their friends soon just paired them off. In those days, girls were expected to stay with "their own kind," and their Italian fathers vigorously forbade their dating Polish boys. Rose and Theresa persisted, though, and when the time came, they were each other's maid of honor.

Theresa and her boyfriend, Marion — with Rose in tow — stole off to be married at city hall when he came home on leave from the service in March 1943. But Theresa was six months shy of her 21st birthday, and so the couple was turned away.

Theresa had to return home, though her father, seeing her leave to be married that day, had told her never to darken his door again. "My father was so strict," Theresa says laughing, and she was scared he would give her a beating. So she begged her friend Rose to accompany her upstairs: Her father wouldn't hit her while Rose was there. Sure enough, the ploy worked. "I got a cockeyed look, and that was all," she says. And Theresa married her sweetheart — without her father's consent — in church the next day.

Four years later, when Rose and Benny married, it was Theresa's turn to save her friend. Rose had thin and stringy hair then, and she'd gone to the beauty parlor the day of her wedding to have it done. By the time she walked home in the humid heat of August, though, it had lost its curl and fallen flat. "I ran to Theresa's house, crying!" she says. Her friend soothed her and promised to fix it. She did, rolling it, in the style of the day, in "rats."

Telling the story over coffee in her kitchen some 46 years later, Rose rushes to find her wedding photo and soon displays two smiling, broad and dimpled faces, with a young, dewy Rose clutching a bouquet and sporting a triumphantly terraced hairdo.

A few years after their wedding, Rose and Benny (who worked as a school custodian) moved a few blocks away to the apartment on Leonard Street, where they live today. As soon as another apartment in their building was free, Theresa and her husband (who was a warrant officer in the Army Reserve) moved in, too —directly upstairs.

Rose and Benny had two children. Theresa and Marion had none. "I had three miscarriages," says Theresa. "I just wasn't fortunate enough. It just didn't happen." So "Aunt Theresa" helped raise Rose's two boys and loved them like her own. "I couldn't yell at them [when Theresa was around]," Rose remembers. "I couldn't hit them."

When Marion died three years ago, at three o'clock in the morning, Rose was the first person Theresa called. And it was Benny who, loving Marion "like my own brother," accompanied Theresa to the hospital to claim her husband's body.

Today, Theresa pops down to Rose's apartment before going out and pops back in when she returns. They bicker gently, like any long-entwined and loving couple. "She doesn't eat," says Rose, exaggeratedly annoyed. "She's picky, picky, like a bird. I mean, she lost six pounds."

"You never feel alone here. The place could be falling down . . . but we would still love it."

"Since July," Theresa counters. "That ain't bad."

"That's a lot! You can't afford to lose weight," says her friend. "I oughta put a little meat on you."

Every Monday and Wednesday morning, the two walk the streets of Greenpoint—past the beauty parlors and bakeries, the potholes and pounding jackhammers—to the church hall of Our Lady of Mount Carmel for bingo. Even here, Rose and Theresa are partners, sharing what they earn. "If I win it's ours, if she wins it's ours," Rose declares as she meticulously lines up a stack of bingo boards in four neat rows. This way she can scan the columns quickly and play 28 games at once. "Coming to bingo, we don't have to worry about senility," Rose jokes. "There's too much to keep track of." Soon the number she's been waiting for, B-7, is called. Rose receives $5 and immediately holds out the crisp new bill for Theresa to touch: "It's good luck," she says.

Rose and Theresa, Marie, Tessie, Lucy, Julie, Mary M. and Mary D. stayed friends because, in this most mobile of cultures, they stayed so tied to the neighborhood in which they grew up. Then again, perhaps they stayed tied to the neighborhood because they were friends. They themselves are hard put to explain it. "We started out in school," Lucy says, "and there was the bowling alley, we had the league in church.... You never feel alone here. The place could be falling down around us, but we'd still love it."

All of their children have moved, and those who used to be friends in the younger generation have drifted apart. Nor have they maintained their mothers' tradition of gathering regularly with friends over cards or bingo or mah-jongg. Today's young families earn two incomes: The women juggle jobs and children and mortgages, and they are far too busy. "In our generation, we didn't work that much," Theresa muses, "and we were satisfied with what little we had. Nowadays everybody wants a little more. And they have no time."

Rose and Benny's sons would like their parents to finally leave the four-room walk-up in Greenpoint and join them in New Jersey or upstate New York. But Rose and Benny will have none of it. "All my friends are here," says Benny. "Why look for trouble?" And tonight, as the Greenpoint Girls gather for cards, and Tessie insists that when her husband retires they're moving to Las Vegas, her friends just laugh. "You yourself don't know that you don't want to go," says Marie. "You'll never leave us!"

Soon the Girls settle back down to their cards. Most of their conversation ceases, and it's quiet in Theresa's kitchen except for the drumming of their fingers on the table and the flicking of the deck. They do not drink on these evenings. They do not tell wild jokes. And while they are friendly and supportive, they don't share deep confidences or bare their souls to each other. But they do show up, twice a week, week after week, year after year, to play May I?, rummy and poker, in just that order.

"Be there!" says Lucy, slapping the deck. ■

Joanmarie Kalter has written for The New York Times, Columbia Journalism Review *and* TV Guide.

Too Lonely? By Myrna Lewis

Middle age often brings a renewed interest in developing social ties, but family and work pressures can leave us little time to cultivate such relationships. An unhealthy feeling of loneliness can be the net result. To determine how lonely you might be, take the following quiz.

For each statement below, check the option that you feel applies to you. A scoring guide with advice follows.

	Often	Sometimes	Rarely	Never
1. I lack companionship.				
2. I am not emotionally close to anyone.				
3. My interests and ideas are not shared by those around me.				
4. My social relations are superficial.				
5. No one really knows me well.				
6. I am unhappy being so withdrawn.				
7. People are around me but not with me.				
8. There is no one I can turn to.				
9. There are times when I have nothing to do.				
10. I wish I had a soul mate.				

Scoring Guide

Assign the following values to each of your answers: Often — 3. Sometimes — 2. Rarely — 1. Never — 0. Add up your score. A total of 0 to 12 means you are less lonely than average; 13 to 23 means average; 24 and above signifies that you are substantially more lonely than average.

If you scored 24 or above, you're probably ready to do something about your predicament. According to Nancy Showers, Ph.D., assistant director of social work at the Mount Sinai Medical Center in New York, "If being with friends is more important than what you actually do with them, you are probably an extrovert. In this case, you would do well to nurture the friendships you already have by keeping in better touch and to broaden your social contacts by joining groups in your community."

On the other hand, introverts, who tend to keep to themselves, may be more comfortable doing something interesting with others than focusing primarily on friendship per se. For these people, Showers advises finding an interest group in which they can pursue an activity they're passionate about and that offers interaction with others but does not depend on it.

"For both introverts and extroverts, midlife is a time to build bridges with others," notes Showers. "These friendships will sustain you in the years to come."

Quiz adapted from the UCLA Loneliness Scale.

SINGLES DATING:

Finding happiness in the minefield

By Cyra McFadden

Some things you grow out of gracefully; others you don't. After I was widowed years ago, in my early 40s, I began to go out on dates. Dating made me feel young again—15, to be precise, and a panicky mess. Although I was only going to a concert or dinner with some personable man, I felt as if I were venturing into a minefield.

I was sure that the man had asked me out in a weak-minded moment. By now no doubt he was thinking, "She's too thin/fat/passive/aggressive/dumb/smart/frivolous/serious." Or "I'll bet she spends the whole evening talking about her late husband. What fun for me." It didn't occur to me that my date, too, was an imperfect human being or that because he was more or less the same age I was, he came with his own complex personal history. Either that, or he'd lived a dull life indeed.

My skin broke out; for the first time in 25 years, I found myself buying a tube of Clearasil. Life became an endless bad-hair day, and clothes (never a big concern of mine) became a major preoccupation. What should I wear to a movie and coffee somewhere afterward? If I wore my black pumps with the ankle straps to an art opening, would I be coming on as a merry widow, and if I wore more sensible shoes, would I look drab?

During the countdown before the doorbell rang, I'd try on everything in my closet, then rip the offending garments off again. That dress made me look anorexic, those palazzo pants made me look like a palazzo. I felt like a border collie in the moments before a field trial. By the time my date arrived, I was exhausted and would have liked to bag the evening and go to bed with a video—maybe that classic training film for single women, *Valley of the Dolls*.

Even the word *dating* made me self-conscious, with its overtones of wrist corsages and the junior prom. But I couldn't come up with a euphemism that I liked better, although I went to ridiculous lengths; "It's not a date. We're just going to grab a bite to eat together."

All this insecurity came out of nowhere. I wasn't in love with the man at the door and didn't need him to make my life worth living. I wasn't seeking another life partner or even a romance. Nonetheless, inside the adult woman was a teenager desperate for her date's approval and certain that she'd commit some gaffe—a self-fulfilling prophecy.

Permanently imprinted on my psyche is the Night of the Snail Tongs. I've never liked bland, slimy escargots, but when my dinner companion suggested we share them as a first course, I lied and said that I loved them. He probably thinks that I don't know how to use snail tongs, I thought. Well, I'll show him. And I did: I picked up the implement and promptly fired a buttery mollusk across the room. We got through the rest of the evening, but it wasn't easy.

Another night I argued stubbornly over a check, insisting on paying "my half," although I could see that I was making my date uncomfortable. I knew that men were no longer expected to pick up the tab every time and that they welcomed the change as fair. But I didn't know when to back off and just say "Thank you."

I also recall a high-speed U-turn that I made across oncoming traffic, while the blood drained out of another man's face. I was showing off my lightning reflexes when an urban parking place was at stake. He was imagining how it would feel to spend the rest of his life in a body cast. At the end of the evening, spent at a friend's party, he called a cab.

It was somewhat comforting to see otherwise sensible friends behave strangely under like circumstances. Deprived of a partner by death or divorce, stripped of the comforts of coupledom, they were as insecure about dating again as I was. One female acquaintance who was newly divorced wouldn't date at all. She had already decided that the situation was hopeless because the men in her age group were all sexists, interested only in perfect young centerfolds. Anything but face the R word—rejection.

We're all old enough to know that no one dies of embarrassment, but we're sure that there's always a first time. My artist friend Leon told me about his first date with Flannery. She suggested that they take her car, "a new top-of-the-line, biggest, most powerful, silver Porsche," and that he drive. Leon, who owned an old Volkswagen, knew his manhood was on the line. So he faked an expertise in luxury automobiles. Things went smoothly until they got to their destination, when Leon, who'd "managed to park and turn the beast off and flip the seat belt off with an experienced shrug," fumbled at length with the door latch.

"Flannery wanted to know if I was having a problem," he recalls, "but I said no because at that moment I put my fingers into this most exotic car's exotic latch and gave a mighty wrench. The whole damn thing came away, spraying parts and loose change all over. My fingers were stuck in the remains of a coin bank."

If Leon really was being tested, he passed. Flannery later married him. He didn't have to prove that her high-performance car didn't faze him. Like me, however, he was a dating dinosaur, slow to adapt to the changed landscape of male-female relationships. We know that gender roles aren't as rigid anymore, and that dating is far more casual, but we're still the products of our conditioning. As psychotherapist Harville Hendrix put it in his book, *Keeping the Love You Find: A Guide for Singles* (Pocket Books), we're people "brought up by the old rules but playing by the new."

There's really only one new rule, my adult daughter kept trying to convince me, when I described my latest mini-debacle to her. "Mom, relax." She also instructed me by example, traversing the dating minefield lightly herself. When Caroline stopped seeing a man who'd been important to her for many months, a turn of events that I knew was painful, she told her friends with resolute good humor, "I fired him."

Close women friends who'd "been there" held my hand as I

survived a disastrous entanglement with Mr. Wrong and commiserated when I complained that all the men in my age group belonged in Jurassic Park. (On more than one occasion, a date asked what I thought about feminism, told me what I ought to think and added that we had lived in a better world when men ran it.)

I soldiered on. I met men whom I found attractive but who weren't as attracted to me. I met men who were both aggressive and needy, looking for a full-time female support system who also did windows. After many an evening, I called a friend and wailed that dating was for masochists. Why bother, when I could simply set fire to my feet?

Relax, relax, those around me soothed, and I gradually did. I stopped trying so hard to please, stopped thinking of every date as a test, stopped feeling apologetic because I was no longer 18 and dewy-eyed. That's when I began to meet men who were at ease with themselves and the times and who put me at ease as well.

Some were my age, some younger. Our dates led to no-fault romances, with no stewing about whether or not they'd turn into enduring commitments. Or they led to something much rarer—indissoluble friendships. Today, at 56, I have more close male friends than I ever had when I was younger and sexual parrying always came first.

"I stopped thinking of every date as a test . . ."

We talk intimately about our lives. We see each other often without calling it dating or giving our relationship any label at all. Sexual attraction may be a factor between us, but it's far from the most important. My friend Herb and I joke that we've skipped the courtship, the love affair, the marriage and, maybe, the divorce. We've cut right to the best part of a long intimacy—total trust.

I can enjoy these friendships because, in midlife, dating need no longer be a courtship ritual only. It can be a chance to discover new facets of oneself, through new and rewarding kinds of connections. So, as much as I wish that my late husband and I could have had more years together, dating doesn't scare me anymore.

Recently, a man I liked dropped out of my life after we'd met a few times for coffee. By reflex, I wondered what I'd done wrong. Then I had a bout of mental health. "Oh, well," I thought, "his loss." ■

Cyra McFadden is author of the best-selling The Serial, *and is currently finishing her second novel, a look at urban life, San Francisco-style. McFadden is a frequent contributor to* New Choices *magazine.*

Sexuality: "Used Up"? By Myrna Lewis

Question

My husband is having some sexual difficulties. He's convinced it's because he was too sexually active when he was young and now in later life has already spent his sexual reserves. Can this be true?

Answer

The only men I know who have this notion were youngsters during the 1940s, when boys were warned through playground channels of misinformation against "wasting vital fluids." Reassure your husband that there is no basis for his belief since semen is produced by the body until the end of life, unless surgery or severe illness interferes. Get him to see a good urologist or at least his internist to discuss the matter. If there is no physical reason for his problem, then it might help to have him consult with a therapist familiar with the emotional and sexual issues of later life.

Turning Former Lovers Into Friends

by Eleanor Foa Dienstag

This year an ex-boyfriend took me out to dinner on my birthday. Our friendship has gone on for years; our romance lasted about an hour and a half. He still remembers the birthday when I turned up with a single rose and treated him to an "all you can eat" sushi dinner. I fondly recall the time when he arranged for a mini-chocolate cake to be served with a single candle by a singing waitress.

It happened gradually, as do so many things in midlife, but one day I noticed how many of my relationships with men—launched as romances or with the expectation of romance—had turned into important and sustaining friendships.

As we age and our hormones quiet down, the superficiality of physical allure is replaced by an appreciation of more profound charms, such as intelligence, caring, wit, a good heart, selflessness and honesty. Once masculinity and femininity are no longer linked to sexual success and prowess, we are able to enjoy what each person has to offer as a companion even if the romance fades — or never ignites.

One woman I know spends every New Year's Eve (and most of that holiday week) with the same man, even though they are no longer lovers.

What a lovely idea. Each lives alone—she in New York, he in California—and eagerly looks forward to their annual visit, which often includes a jaunt to a country inn or nearby destination.

"Traveling with a man, even if there's no romance, still carries with it a male-female glow," says Betsy (not her real name). "But when the week's over, I'm glad to resume my normal life."

Even a platonic male-female evening feels different from an evening out with a friend of the same sex. Men enjoy having a woman on their arm. It makes them feel more masculine. In addition, as my ex-boyfriend put it, "Women are more caring, more nurturing and more emotionally aware than men. Men compete. Women cooperate. With women, I can show more of my sensitive side."

Women enjoy having the appearance of a dinner or movie date and giving advice to male friends. Cross-sex friendships keep us in touch with different points of view. It's fascinating to hear men and women talk about, say, relationships with children and grandchildren. Women relish the baby years; men mostly become pals with grandchildren as they get older.

What are the secrets of turning former lovers into companions?

First, be tactful and diplomatic. For example, on two occasions last year, I knew after three or four dates that the man was not for me romantically. But both men had qualities I enjoyed. Instead of ending the relationships (as I used to do), I expressed the hope that we could see each other as friends. Then I followed up.

This is probably the second secret to success. Both times I called within a week, inviting one man to join me at a tennis match and the other at an art exhibit. One of them has become a pal, while the other has disappeared—some men aren't interested in or can't handle "just a friendship."

My third secret: When you've just ended a long romance, don't expect to transform it into a friendship instantly. Wounds take time to heal. But try a "How are you doing?" call a few months later.

Ironically, friendships with the opposite sex are easier to maintain if you're single. Perhaps it's because we don't have to deal with a suspicious or sensitive spouse, or because we need each other more. Whatever the reason, enjoy the benefits.

SEEKING MR. RIGHT

—and finding something better

By Jane Adams

A year ago, I went to the wedding of a friend who met her second husband through the personals. I was to offer a toast at the champagne reception. I said all the right things, but I wanted to blurt out Samuel Johnson's maxim that remarriage represents the triumph of hope over experience. The same could be said of romance through the classifieds, I suppose. My one attempt to locate love in the want ads, many years ago, still rankled enough that I mostly used that part of the newspaper to line the bottom of the birdcage.

Nevertheless, a few weeks ago, I sat scanning the crowded cocktail lounge, looking for Keith, whose letter had promised, among other things, that he'd never tell anyone how we'd met. There I was, checking the foot passengers in line at the ferry dock, wondering if the red-faced, anxious-looking fellow with the *Seattle Times* under his arm was Leo. His response to my personals ad had been a funny checklist suggesting possible scenarios, including "No, this guy sounds like a total jerk and I wouldn't be caught dead in his company."

And that was me at a Scrabble board in a neighborhood café, across the table from Grant, the scientist. During our one phone conversation, he had told me he was interested in how things worked and I told him my anxiety dream. It involves a post-apocalypse world in which all the survivors except me have something to contribute to recreating civilization—like knowing the principles of the turbine engine or how to make paper from trees or where microchips come from. Since all I can offer is a few lines from Emily Dickinson, the plots of almost every mystery novel written in the past 10 years and the lyrics of the Beatles' *White Album*, I am cast adrift on an ice floe somewhere near where Santa Barbara used to be. Upon hearing this, Grant suggested that perhaps one right brain and one left brain might make for an interesting evening, so here we were.

And thank heaven for the Scrabble board between us, because two halves of a brain, in two separate people, do not make for an interesting evening after all. If they had, I might have let him win. The last time I placed an ad, I would have let him do so under any circumstances. But that was another time, and I was a different woman. Then, I risked (or

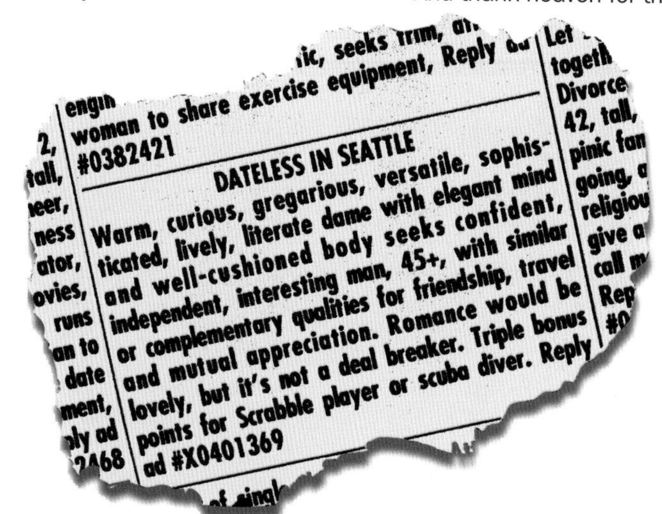

woman to share exercise equipment, Reply ad #0382421

DATELESS IN SEATTLE

Warm, curious, gregarious, versatile, sophisticated, lively, literate dame with elegant mind and well-cushioned body seeks confident, independent, interesting man, 45+, with similar or complementary qualities for friendship, travel and mutual appreciation. Romance would be lovely, but it's not a deal breaker. Triple bonus points for Scrabble player or scuba diver. Reply ad #X0401369 believed I risked) rejection, ridicule and a fatal blow to my self-esteem. This time rejection and ridicule are still possible — consider that I am older and the field of possible friends, let alone lovers, is narrower — but my self-esteem feels secure enough to withstand most challenges.

What led me to this café was a plethora of conversations held recently with people who, on notable birthdays — their 40th, 50th or even 60th — undertook some physical risk they described as "challenging death": bungee jumping, mountain climbing, scuba diving. I understand the impulse — 10 years ago, I dived off my first undersea wall, faced the abyss of a bottomless sea and surfaced with a gleeful sense of daring I've rarely felt since. But I'm more interested in challenging life than death; inertia, busyness and fear have kept love at bay for far too long.

One thing is clear: Meeting someone in this artificial way hasn't changed much in 15 years. Listening to someone's life story reminds me of why a male friend dates only much younger women — not because their bodies are more beautiful but because their stories are shorter. It's awkward to make small talk without a shared history.

No wonder these men seem as if they're interviewing for jobs. Very few ask me more than one cursory question about myself before they launch into their spiels. One, in fact, sat down, ordered a coffee, excused himself to make a phone call and never came back. I had entertained fleeting notions of doing the same thing, so it only bothered me for a minute. Another sent me his credit report after one get-together. A third has called me several times without making plans to meet, but I think he's the stranger who's been hanging around my building this week. And a couple of guys who want to make dates for February 2001 or December 1999 have given me the box numbers and zip code of a nearby prison.

Still, at least three times a week for the past month, I have gone somewhere to meet a man who responded to the following ad, which I placed in the local newspaper personals:

"Dateless in Seattle: Warm, curious, gregarious, versatile, sophisticated, lively, literate dame with elegant mind and well-cushioned body seeks confident, independent, interesting man, 45+, with similar or complementary qualities for friendship, travel and mutual appreciation. Romance would be lovely, but it's not a deal breaker. Triple bonus points for Scrabble player or scuba diver."

My first personals ad, more than 15 years ago, described the man of my dreams but said almost nothing about me. Back then I thought that if I found Mr. Right and he gave me the specs, I could be whomever he wanted me to be. This time I knew better. Since the postdivorce frenzy, of which that first personal ad was a symbol, I'd created a life and furnished it with too much I value to make myself over to fit someone else's fantasy. I have an identity — independent, self-sufficient, successful. Over the years there have been men I loved and some who loved me, but the same bad timing that made being a wife and mother out of style just when that was all I knew how to be has rarely arranged for love to happen to both of us simultaneously. And almost without realizing it, I'd given up the expectation that it ever would.

With enough men in my life for those social or professional occasions when an escort is de rigueur, for an occasional hug or help buying a used car or even an explanation of how things work, I've generally kept a tight rein on my heart. Listening to my friends complain about their relationships has been enough for me — remembering the pain in my own relationships convinced me that I was finished with love and glad of it. Done with the fantasies, immune to the expectations, secure against rejection. And too old, too set in my ways and too unwilling to remake myself for some man's dream.

And then, damn it, it happened again. Circumstance placed me in close daily contact with a wonderful if wholly inappropriate and much younger man who stirred feelings in me that swelled like a brook in spring. Even though he didn't return all of those feelings, I reveled in his attention, his caring, his tenderness. I felt rejuvenated and slightly ridiculous, silly as a teenager with a crush on the football captain. I didn't lose myself in him—I lost myself in love. I'm not a teenager, though, and I could see the end at the beginning, and when it came, I might pine, but I wouldn't whine.

I didn't, either. What I took from that second springtime was the realization that because life is short and connections are often imperfect, I could not wait for fate or circumstance to put me in love's way again. I put another ad in the personals, despite what had happened the last time.

Fifteen years ago, I got a lot more responses, either because I was younger, less self-defined or less choosy. This time it took me a longer time to answer any of them. On solitary Saturday nights, I read and reread them and felt empowered but oddly uninterested ... like having a refrigerator full of food but not being hungry. It was enough to know that I could have a date—hell, I could have 20. But so what? Did I really want someone so unappealing or unattractive that he could only find a woman in the newspaper? And if I did, and if due to some fantastic and unique circumstances he turned out to be fabulous (say, he'd been in a coma for 20 years, and when he woke up, he had amnesia and didn't remember any woman's phone number; or a well-meaning friend, without his knowledge, had written to me on his behalf), what could he possibly think about me except that I was desperate enough to declare my availability in such a, well, needy way?

Finally, back then, I stilled the cynic in my soul and answered one letter, a friendly, funny note. We met for lunch, and by the time dessert arrived, I was crazy about him. By the next day, I was ready to remodel my house, my career, my kids and myself to suit him. By the day after that, I was anxious, and by the time it was clear that he wasn't going to call me back, let alone live up to my fantasies, I had ripped up all the other letters and resolved never to put myself in such a position or suffer such callous rejection again.

"Despite the mixed results, I've become accustomed once again to the company of men and remember how much I like them."

And I didn't—not intentionally, anyway. Until love sneaked up on me recently to remind me that I've lived through it before and survived, I have felt about it the way a prominent politician once described his feelings about his presidential aspirations—certain that he had put them away but aware that if he needed them again, he could probably dig them out.

I had a reason, so I placed the ad, and this time I answered all the letters and calls. Well, almost all. I passed on the survivalist, the Hell's Angel, the illegal alien looking for a way to stay in the country and the leather fetishist. I challenged myself to leave my cynicism, rather than my romanticism, at home. To assume that whoever answered my ad was quite possibly as worthwhile, interesting and honest as I was. To realize that I was a long way from needy or desperate, and if I simply managed to have a pleasant and lively evening, let alone add a new friend to my life, I'd be delighted.

My first date was a rather stiff, awkward hour over cocktails, during which both of us tried to pretend we weren't sizing each other up. My second was the man who excused himself to make a phone call and didn't come back. For my third outing, I suggested something a little more active, less structured—we went for a bicycle ride and brought our own picnic lunches, and even though no sparks were struck, we both got some exercise and have biked together a couple of times since. Subsequent meetings with others have involved similar activities—even if the men were hapless or hopeless, I did something that was enjoyable.

Some men were taken aback when I suggested a bike

ride, art exhibit, street fair, even a brief trip on a ferry instead of coffee or cocktail dates; when they said, "Let's get to know each other first," I understood that they would risk only a few minutes to size me up, and, not wanting to be judged on my looks or their fantasies, I passed them by. But most men seemed relieved that I had something specific to offer. "It's not that I have anything against 'relating,' it's just hard to do that with a stranger," one said, and I couldn't have agreed with him more.

The results aren't all in, but so far I've made a couple of new friends, seen several baseball games and art exhibits, learned a few new bike paths and ridden the ferry a lot. At least twice I've been told "I'll call you" by men who haven't, but worse things have happened and I'm still here. I'm accustomed once again to the company of men and remember how much I like them—enough to take some risks but not enough to be that younger me who was so desperate to be relieved of the burden of self.

What was missing in my life was not love but the possibility of it. There hasn't been anyone, yet, who stirs those old feelings in me. But at least the possibility is not wholly foreclosed. ■

Jane Adams is a Seattle-based writer who's latest book is I'm Still Your Mother *(Dell). Adams is a frequent contributor to* New Choices.

Update Your Lovemaking

By Myrna Lewis

Is your love life getting stale? If so, perhaps you need to develop a sexual style more suited to who you are today, according to one expert. "As we grow older, our sexual sensibilities shift," says sex therapist Sandra Scantling, Ph.D., who is an assistant professor of psychiatry at the University of Connecticut. "This can be traced to hormonal and other physical changes, as well as a maturing in our personalities."

Continuing to express love and affection just as we did when we were younger simply may no longer work—for ourselves or our partners. To get in tune with our evolved sexuality and to recapture some of the passion that may be missing in our relationships, Scantling says that we should try any or all of these steps:

1. Ask your partner whether he or she still likes the same aspects of lovemaking as before. "Don't make assumptions," Scantling warns. "Make it a habit to ask each other about preferences in touch or any other area of sex that may have changed."

2. Be aware that age changes can have unforeseen consequences. For example, some people's sense of smell tends to become less keen with age. To compensate, an older woman might use too much perfume or a man too much aftershave lotion, leaving a partner reeling from fragrance overload.

3. Instead of relying on the same old habits, try something new, spontaneous and romantic. An example might be a shift in timing, location or atmosphere for lovemaking.

4. Practice becoming "pleasure experts" by discovering what you like and telling each other, rather than focusing on what you don't like.

5. Put aside bad times from past lovemaking. Leave old complaints behind and deal with the present pleasure that you and your partner can create.

6. Be less goal-oriented and more involved in the moment together. This especially takes the pressure off men to perform. Scantling observes that one does not have to "do soup to nuts" in every encounter. "Appetizers can be great, too!"

FRIENDS FOREVER? NOT ALWAYS

As values and relationships change at midlife, here's how to keep friendships healthy and honest.

By Deborah Mason

There are no rules, no 'oughts' or 'shoulds.' There are no constraints, but there are deep ties. She's there when I need her. I'm there when she needs me."
— Judy Waterman on Vicki, her friend of 25 years

Your friends: Over the years, they have comforted you, irked you and, more than a few times, saved your skin — middle-of-the-night friends you know you can call and they'll be there in a minute, friends you have known for decades but still can't wait to see next week for lunch.

But what about the friends you have known just as long who suddenly exit your life with a bang, amid allegations as soul-wrenching as betrayal or as silly as a perceived "snub." Or friends who disappear with barely a whimper or a word between you as to what went wrong? Or friends with whom meetings have come to feel as stale and dutiful as a waning marriage? All you share now is history, and no one wants to be the first to call it quits.

The changes that come with midlife can't help but throw friendships into sharp relief. It is, after all, a time when you are shifting gears in your work, waving good-bye to your children, maybe moving to a new home, perhaps taking on a new partner and often creating a firmer, more freewheeling sense of self as you peel off values and people who no longer ring true. Some friendships thrive on the changes, others wobble. Why?

For a culture that has a ceremony or an FTD bouquet for every life passage, we are left curiously adrift when it comes to certifying the crucial role of friendship in our lives. Purely elective, friendships have no conventions to follow when they falter, no formalities that allow us to celebrate the ones that make it or to mourn the ones that don't. In an effort to fill these gaps, *New Choices* magazine interviewed 50-plusers across the country. Respondents offered guidelines as to what glues friendships together and pries them apart — and what rules and rituals can be improvised to negotiate the tricky transitions of midlife and keep 50-plus friendships healthy and honest. The key: acknowledging and coping with change.

HOW INNER CHANGE AFFECTS FRIENDSHIPS

"I'm growing all the time; my friends are growing all the time. So you expect that your friendships are going to change."
— Pearl Rosenberg (below)

One of the most powerful forces reshaping 50-plus friendships comes from inside us. Buoyed by the know-how

and confidence we have gained in working out a life, we feel bolder in letting people know who we are and who we aren't. Age often has a way of nudging us to reconnect with our core self, the self that existed before work and family obligations dictated our days, before we came to believe that getting into some club was our ticket to "the good life."

As we sort out our values,

we find ourselves becoming more selective about our friends or taking a second look at what one woman I know calls "situational friends," people who shared a particularly intense period of our life—the birth of our children, an anguished divorce. "They're like the people you go through a blackout with," she says. "You're so sure the intensity you share will bind you forever. Sometimes it does, sometimes it doesn't."

So what course of action can we take when we realize that our bedrock values are no longer in sync with the people we count as friends. "My husband and I know a couple with whom we still exchange Christmas cards and call when we're in their town," says Judy Waterman, 60, of Hillsborough, California. "But we just don't think the same as they do. So when we're together, we've started to avoid certain subjects, such as abortion or whether a woman can be the primary breadwinner in a family. The friendship just isn't the same—they realize it, we realize it."

Pearl Rosenberg, 64, a retired college education and psychological counselor who lives in Great Neck, New York, has a friend she treasures, but she says she has run out of patience with the woman's husband, who routinely spouts judgmental views of minorities and the disadvantaged. What she has done is to judiciously reshape the friendship: "I now meet her for lunch or dinner when her husband is out of town. I've never discussed it with her, but she's a bright woman; she knows what's going on here. By not saying it, I feel as if I'm doing a service."

Rosenberg has been able to keep old friendships alive by adjusting them, but some people find this an uphill battle. Denver attorney Jerry Conover, 63, sees a dwindling common ground with a friend of 35 years. "We've shared our kids growing up," he says. "We've shared some investments, but now it's really getting hard for me. We go to lunch, and our talk is filled with clichés. He's still a sweet guy, but he has this one-dimensional view of world problems; and it all relates to the fact that it's not like it was when he grew up. I have to rely on a sense of duty to see him from time to time. I guess something about the sheer length of the friendship keeps it going."

There are instances when old friendships are beyond sustaining altogether. Arlene Klein, 56, of Sarasota, Florida, tells of one couple, longtime friends, who pressured her and her husband to join them in their newfound lifestyle. "He happened to be drinking a little bit; she had become real 'swinging.' I think they thought that we were very square. And I, in turn, felt they were just not where I wanted to be," says Klein. "We never had words, but now we rarely see them. I equate the end of a friendship with the way you experience a death: You have to go through every emotion, every stage of loss. Then you come out the other side."

SHIFTING WORK ROLES

"Just when he's beginning to spend some time smelling the roses, she's left the garden club and gotten a job."
—overheard in a Denver grocery store

The many women who shift into high gear at midlife and start back to work face a radical reshaping of their friendships, too. "You take a job that's very demanding, and, yes, at first you don't pay as much attention to your friends," says Waterman, who owns her own career-counseling company. "When I started back to work, some of my friends just kind of disappeared. And a few who weren't working asked some nasty things about me, like was I having marital problems, and why was it so important for me to fulfill myself?"

Such sniping can reveal a rarely acknowledged element in women's relationships: competition. Former therapist Carmen Renee Berry, M.S.W., who wrote *Girlfriends: Invisible Bonds, Enduring Ties* (Wildcat Canyon Press) with Tamara Traeder, says most middle-aged women don't know how to manage their competitive or envious feelings with friends—or co-workers—because they have never had a chance to learn. "We weren't raised to beat our friends in games like men were," she notes. "We always did things together, and usually the activities weren't competitive. It takes a lot of courage for an older woman to acknowledge her competitive feelings; but if she doesn't, they will become an unconscious barrier, and they will not help the friendship."

On the other hand, many men have trouble making social adjustments as their careers wind down.

"Without the structure of work and team sports they had when they were younger, middle-aged men seem to need a new framework for their friendships," says therapist Matthew McKay, Ph.D., of San Francisco, California, who wrote *Being a Man* (New Harbinger) with Patrick Fanning, his friend of 27 years. "But men often don't make contact to set something up because initiating means needing, wanting to be close to another man, and that doesn't fit with the John Wayne stereotype they were raised with." McKay's advice: "Set up small bits of structure — lunch every Wednesday or a basketball game every third Friday. Then the relationship is not something you have to think about."

Conover, who jokingly refers to himself as a "recovering trial lawyer," is making more room for friends as he has scaled back his work hours and changed his focus to the art of business mediation. "I really do think I'm developing a gentler side," he says. "And as I think more about relationships and the meaning of life, I've found that now most of my friends are teachers or psychoanalysts."

NEW PSYCHOLOGICAL NEEDS

"I was the kind of person who was always there for everyone. I'd twist myself like a pretzel trying to accommodate them, but no longer."
—Arlene Klein (below)

Many women said that moving into midlife has felt like waking up, clearing their heads and starting a fresh new day. Freed from time constraints like child rearing, they also have begun to challenge stereotypes of "womanly" behavior that seem out of sync with the new straightforwardness of their lives. And their friendships have been the winners.

Klein now travels the country, speaking and fund-raising on behalf of the Morris Animal Foundation. But her description of her former self as a pretzel sums up the caretaker reflex many older women bring to a relationship, a role for which they had been groomed and rewarded since birth. When they detect any nuances of need in conversations with friends, they instantly move in to make things right; when they do nothing, they feel guilty.

"Taking care of other people is a way of bolstering your own self-esteem," says Berry. "But when you need something, you're up the creek because you don't know how to ask for it." Her advice for women as well as men in one-sided relationships: "You can tell a friend overtly that you feel you are doing all the work. Or you can just not give as much; allow the other person to pick up the slack. Because sometimes, without realizing it, we don't allow people to give to us, to let them be the ones to make the phone call. If the other person is really capable of a mutual relationship, this provides the opportunity."

Also trained from girlhood to "make nice," many women gloss over any conflict in a friendship with a "No, everything's fine" smile. "Yes, I do tend to hold things in; I don't say when things are bothering me," says Jane Riesenberger, 67, of Yardley, Pennsylvania. "I guess the reason is that I don't like confrontations. I like to keep things pleasant."

"Women are good at talking about their feelings," says Berry, "but often not when those feelings involve the person in the room. When it comes to, 'I don't like the way you did that yesterday,' they have a hard time saying it. And the anger builds. Then later they say, 'I don't know what happened to the friendship. She's just not talking to me anymore.' You have to be willing to get in there and take a little risk and say to your friend, 'This really doesn't work for me; can we talk this through?' This is a friendship that will last."

SEARCHING FOR THE SOLID GROUND

"A sense of irony—that's what I share with friends. We're able to see the different dimensions of the human condition and laugh at our frailties."
—Jerry Conover

For men and women who have always taken for granted that it is all onward and upward, life over 50 can introduce an unnerving new twist: a sense of limits. And by acknowledging this and building on it, we can forge the best friendships of our lives. Facing the early rumblings of mortality, 50-plusers are often nudged into a mellowed acceptance of themselves and a keener perspective on what is important to bring to a relationship.

"Men are so used to being in competitive situations at work that it often takes getting to middle age before they feel they can trust other men and talk openly," says therapist McKay. "Now they don't have to do so much image management or protect some fragile sense of self-worth; they don't have to keep their flaws hidden from other men."

Chastened by time and troubles, 50-plus men often reach out to one another and deepen their friendships in the process. "I have an associate for whom intensity is a middle name," says one Iowa insurance man. "I used to have a hard time with him, but in the last year he's experienced a bitter, painful divorce, and I've been through my wife's illness. This has made me more tolerant of his failings. As a result, we've become close. These kinds of experiences change your perspective."

Berry sees two qualities leading to solid friendship: "Commitment and flexibility. These are the key elements of a friendship being able to last a lifetime, so to speak—the same things that are true for an enduring marriage. Without both of these, it just doesn't fly."

Small rituals help, too. Berry knows two midlife women who, every Christmas for 15 years, have sent the same plastic poinsettia back and forth. "It's a reminder that they are important to each other," she says. "Opening up the poinsettia, you can laugh; you don't have to get all mushy about it. But what you know is, 'My friend really cares about me. I matter to her. I'm in her life.' " ■

Deborah Mason, a contributing editor to New Choices *magazine, has also written for* The New York Times *and* Mirabella.

Men Need Hugs, Too By Myrna Lewis

We are so used to hearing that women are better than men at maintaining close relationships, it's easy to forget that men want and need closeness, too. A recent study reminds us that the need for intimacy is genderless.

Researchers at the Hunter Holmes McGuire Veterans Affairs Medical Center in Richmond, Virginia, interviewed men ages 42 to 100 who resided at an affiliated nursing home. The men placed a great value on social intimacy—such as visits with family and friends—as well as nonsexual affection, including touching and hugging.

"Such intimacy is beneficial even to the most awareness-impaired people living in nursing homes because it increases quality of life," says Thomas Mulligan, M.D., chief of geriatric medicine at the VA center and head of the study. He adds that family members should visit often and remain in physical contact with the patient during the visit. "Just being there is not enough; hug the person when you come in, hold his hand while you talk, and hug him when you leave.

"The bottom line is that to feel loved is a basic requirement for well-being," Mulligan notes. "And that goes for men as much as for women."

WHEN THEY HAD GIVEN UP ON LOVE

Tom Casapulla, 83, and Matilda Vaccaro, 73, found each other and a future they never imagined possible.

By Joanmarie Kalter

No, Venus did not shine brightly in the sky that night. There was no full moon. In fact, if there had been anything remotely compelling on TV, neither Tom nor Matilda would have even gone. It was, after all, just the regular Friday dance at Parents Without Partners on the last wintry night of January, and they were two lonely people, widowed in the twilight of life.

And yet it happened. Matilda Vaccaro was at the Rustic Lodge in Elmwood Park, New Jersey, when a few of her friends spied Tom Casapulla sitting at another table and whispered, "Go get 'im!" He was single, a new member and, with the dearth of widowed men, she says, "already surrounded by eight other girls. My girlfriends warned me, 'If you don't grab him . . .' " So when women's choice was called, Matilda gamely asked Tom to dance and felt something spark immediately. "I think you can spot a gentleman," she says. His hands didn't wander in the sleazy way so common to the dark rooms at singles nights, and even in that initial chitchat, he seemed to genuinely admire his children. What first attracted Tom? "To tell you the truth—her looks," he says. "She was tops in my eyes."

"She took me right out of my slump," Tom says of Matilda.

By the end of the evening, they were holding hands, and six weeks later they were engaged. For Tom, whose wife of 60 years had died just months before, it was the end of a grief so keen that walking into his house had felt like a sentence of "solitary confinement." For Matilda, it was the start of something she'd never known. After 42 years of a troubled marriage and another 9 as a widow, this 73-year-old woman has been given what she never expected: "I finally met the man of my dreams."

On the surface they seem to have very different styles. She's talkative, warm and gregarious, heartily urging a visitor who suppresses a sneeze to "go on, let it out!" He's precise, soft-spoken and sweet. Asked about his health, he pulls from his pocket a neatly printed list of every medical condition he's had since 1951—from "removed large toenail on right foot" to two open-heart surgeries. Yet despite such differences, it's clear they're deeply in love.

Since the moment they met, they've been in a whirlwind of dinners and dances and shows; they spent five days in the Catskills and plan a cruise to Bermuda. As Tom proudly puts it, "We've been stepping around." His daughters say his eyes are alight and he walks — no, dances! — with a faster gait. "Oh, boy," says Matilda, "We're like two big kids. We walk into places hand in hand. If nobody's looking, I get an extra smooch. And an amazing thing is happening. Tom's hair is growing back in the center of his head." Sure enough, new shoots of silvery white now cover what once was bald.

For Matilda, being so showered with kisses and hugs is a totally new experience. "I never got the affection I get from you, Tom," she says as he drives, one hand on the steering wheel, the other clasped in hers. "I never had a mother's love . . . or anyone else's."

Within days of her birth, Matilda's mother died, swept away in the flu epidemic of 1918. Her father, frantic, sent Matilda and her two older sisters to live with three separate aunts until he remarried nine years later. When they were reunited in their new home, she remembers racing to greet him with her new baby stepsister and seeing him pick up the baby — not her — to kiss and hug. His love was lavished on his new family, but she was part of the old.

And then there was her marriage. Her husband, it soon turned out, was jealous and demanding. She learned not to speak to other men or even to go out for long with friends. Because he made a meager living as a chauffeur for an order of nuns, Matilda worked as well in several electronics factories. "He drove me to work, he picked me up, he drove me home. I cooked, I cleaned, we went to bed and got up, and that was my life for 42 years," she says.

Both had wanted children, and she had been trying for years to conceive when, at age 42, Matilda had a routine internal exam — and was diagnosed with cancer. She speaks of radium burns and of having her "insides taken out." She emerged with her life but lost the chance to ever have those children. Nor, without a larger income, could they adopt. It was the death of a dream for them both.

Looking back, Matilda now sees her husband's jealousy as "a disease." Perhaps because he was slightly lame, she muses, he feared that a man with two good legs would take her away. Perhaps because she catered to him, he came to expect her obedience. If she'd been born to today's generation, she says, she'd never have taken what she took from him. But he did have his good points, and she was raised to honor the marriage vow. She honored it through seven years of her husband's final illnesses — emphysema and liver cancer — when she fed him, walked him and washed him. Then right before he died, he whispered something. "I said, 'What?' I couldn't hear him. He said it again, he almost shouted it: 'I LOVE YOU.' He had never said it before; he'd always said, 'You know I love you, I don't have to tell you.' But he said it at the end and that's when I cried."

"Memories," says Tom, sitting at the kitchen table in the small apartment Matilda has rented for 45 years. "We both have memories." His own marriage was a good one, reaching back 60 years — 64, he's quick to point out, if you count the years his wife waited for him, pledged to him, while he was attending college. When he graduated with an engineering degree in the depth of the Depression, class of 1931, Tom was one of only four lucky enough to land a job. Through the years, he helped design the George Washington Bridge and the Lincoln Tunnel, spanning the Hudson River between New Jersey and New York. And when he retired two years ago at age 81, he was his company's oldest male employee.

But that was only his day job. At night, Tom played the trumpet. He played in bands on radio, in nightclubs, in marathons and walkathons on the New Jersey shore, in burlesque and in vaudeville. He backed up Kate Smith and remembers when an unknown teen asked to sing a few bars with the band—he turned out to be Frank Sinatra.

It was tough on his wife to be left alone to raise their four children while he worked two jobs—days, nights and weekends. But theirs was an old-fashioned marriage, and she was devoted to him. Together, they suffered the death of their first-born son at 27 months; they lost him from an infection that penicillin—introduced the following year—might have healed. They endured the Depression and prospered so in the postwar years that Tom now owns three houses, mortgage-free. They had two more sons and two daughters, all thriving now at the ages of 43 to 53. "Mom was the only girl Dad ever went out with, and he was the only man she ever went out with," says their older daughter, Terry. "They were destined for each other. That was his life."

What haunts Tom still is how she woke him up one night in May 1991 to say that she no longer could stand the pain. What pain? And why hadn't she said anything sooner? "She would worry that he would worry," says Terry. By the time she did speak up, the cancer had spread so far that she died, suffering horribly, some three months later. Tom wouldn't leave her hospital bedside. Says daughter Irene, if she and Terry hadn't brought him food, he would not have eaten.

When Matilda was widowed at the age of 64, she threw out all but two of her pots and kept only a set of Christmas napkins: She swore she would never cook and clean for a man again. She traveled to Mexico and Florida and Europe and "had a real fling." But the men she met would want to jump into bed, "and I'd say, 'If that's what you're looking for, you'll just have to look for somebody else.' " After nine years, she'd grown discouraged. "It gets lonely as the years go by, believe me."

Tom's grief was so deep that Irene feared it would kill him. He was lost. He had never cooked for himself. (In his kitchen, a granddaughter left a sign in bold letters, "OVEN INSTRUCTIONS: Set middle knob to bake or broil, whichever is preferred. . . . ") And his children had to coax him to even leave the house. Yet during dinners at his daughters' homes, he would hardly talk. Says Terry, "It's rough seeing your father in such a state. We didn't know what to do."

Before Tom proposed, he asked for his children's blessing. "They told me, 'Go to it, Pop. We're with you.'"

Five months later, Tom met Matilda at that Friday-night dance, and "she took me right out of my slump," he says. He worried at first that his mourning had been too short. But a priest advised him that "the moment you lose a spouse, you're single." Matilda chimes in, "That's right. If you walk out of the cemetery and meet someone . . ." "There's no harm in it," Tom says, completing her sentence.

Still, it's hard to leave behind a mate with whom you shared a lifetime. When Tom first told Matilda he loved her, she hurt him by saying that yes, she "liked" him, too. "I knew it was more than a 'like,' but I was afraid," she says, "afraid to get involved again." Together they visited their spouses' crypts; the coffins lie very near each other in the same mausoleum. They both explained to their dead lovers that they'd met someone new, someone who'd take care of them, and they asked to be released. Tom began to cry, and Matilda encouraged him. "Get it out," she said. "You must." But as the two proceeded with their wedding plans, Matilda had a nightmare that her husband had come back and was raping her. The dream was so terrifying that she fled to the bathroom and vomited.

Before Tom proposed, he called his four children to seek their blessing. "They told me, 'Go to it, Pop. We're with you,'" he says. His two sons, who live on the West Coast, have just recently met Matilda, but his daughters, who live nearby in

New Jersey, have embraced her. Yet because their mother's death is so recent, their welcome is tinged with pain. "In no way would I want to begrudge my father any happiness, and Matilda is a wonderful person," says Irene. "But it is weird. It's strange to think, after all these years, of my dad being with someone else." She says that it was rough at first for her two children, 14 and 20, to see their grandfather as love-struck as a teen. But she remembers how despondent he was, how aching and crushed, and concludes, "I think my mother saw that and sent Matilda. She would want him to be happy."

Both Tom and Matilda know friends who date but don't marry. Some fear that a new spouse will eat up assets meant for their children. Others worry that they'll soon be tied down to another sick mate. For her part, Matilda has made it a point that Tom not change his will and that he be ready to help his children should they need it. He'll leave them his real estate ("That's the way I want it! Absolutely," she says), although he's offered to set up a trust in her name. And both have pledged to nurse each other when illness comes. "If I love somebody, it's no problem," says Matilda. "Till the day he dies, I will take care of him." "And vice versa," says Tom.

But what Matilda does want, what she dreams of, what she never had before, is a big wedding. Her father didn't approve of her first husband, so he refused to pay for a party. Only her brother-in-law and his girlfriend attended, and her husband dropped the ring on the floor; he had to get down on his hands and knees to find it. This time, she wants to walk down the aisle past 100-plus guests and have flowers and flower girls and music. Last spring, on a visit to a bridal shop, she sampled the look of a wedding dress. She was led onto a pedestal surrounded by mirrors while a saleswoman fussed around her. And when Matilda looked down, she realized it was the first time she'd ever seen herself in a gown: "Even my knees were tingling!"

With some misgivings, they've decided they'll live in the three-bedroom house that Tom shared with his wife and children. "It's hard for a woman to move into someone else's home," says Matilda. "I am always seeing his wife there. But as we're together more and more, it's me and him, and the house . . . it's ours."

Before they began renovations, they gave a guest a tour. Tom's wife's clothes had been removed to basement closets, and her belongings were either packed in boxes or thrown out. The clutter and the general disrepair bespoke a depressed and lonely man.

"I told him, I don't want to sleep in your wife's bed," Matilda said, leading the way into the master bedroom. "That would really curl me inside out." So not only will they buy all new furniture, but, Matilda added as she poked through his dresser drawers, she'll also insist on a brand-new batch of underwear. "Out with the old," she said. "Every stitch!"

Already, Tom notices that Matilda has taken on some of his wife's tender habits. At meals, she makes sure he eats not only his portion but half of hers as well, slipping a piece of sole onto his plate while muttering distractedly how she couldn't possibly eat all this. Matilda, for her part, is happy just to stare at him. "Sometimes his eyes are blue, and sometimes they're brown," she says dreamily. "He's got such beautiful eyes. And you know something? I couldn't tell you what color eyes my husband had. There you are, isn't that something? It fades."

Both are aware of the toll that time has taken. Matilda has lost her parents, her husband, and two of three sisters. Tom has buried his parents, his wife, a son and all four siblings. Still, on this spring afternoon, with forsythia in bloom and a wedding gown to choose, they laugh and joke, and he nuzzles her neck like an eager schoolboy at the senior prom. "We're making the most we can out of life," Tom says, "whatever we have left."

Matilda and Tom were married on September 20, 1992. ■

JOANMARIE KALTER has written for The New York Times, Columbia Journalism Review *and* TV Guide. *She is also a contributing editor for* New Choices *magazine.*

THE TRUTH ABOUT LIFE AFTER 50

An eminent novelist offers his perspective on the shocks and satisfactions at midlife.

By John Updike

My dear boomer, I'm afraid we can't really call you "baby" any longer. Yours is the most famous demographic group in America, and it has been your youthfulness that has characterized you at every stage. In infancy, you popped into being in unprecedented numbers on the great wave of postwar fertility and prosperity between 1946 and 1964. In childhood, you filled the new Levittowns with your tricycles and backyard wading pools, and you imbibed the newly concocted milk and honey of television in such giant drafts that child psychologists feared your brains would be washed away; you were carpooled everywhere by an army of moms, and you hid under your school desks in drills designed to mitigate the effects of atomic war. In your adolescence, you learned to rock and roll, and you waitressed on roller skates at the drive-in on the edge of town. In your youth, you went to Woodstock, experienced altered states of consciousness, protested Vietnam, or fought in it, or both. In your adulthood, you invented Yuppieness, health-consciousness and corporate greed. You thought that, whatever happened, you would never grow old. You went from left-wing revolution under Johnson to right-wing revolution under Reagan without losing your waistlines and fine brown musculature. Now the first of

Welcome to the ranks of "the unspeakable pod people, the thick-waisted, indisputably middle-aged," says Updike.

you are passing 50, and henceforth at the rate of one every seven seconds, you will be joining the unspeakable pod people, the indisputably middle-aged, the over-the-hill, the thick-waisted and presbyopic. I write to welcome you, immigrants to life's second half century, and to offer what guidance I can.

In my own experience, the 50th birthday is less traumatic than the 30th, which says good-bye to youth, or the 60th, which says hello to old age. But my experience is that of another generation, the Silent, or Almost Absent, Generation. We thinly straggled onto the stage during the Depression and World War II — a baby bust. Yet in our quiet, wary way, we were fortunate, stepping into adulthood as America bestrode the world; our modest expectations were often exceeded. Your expectations, nurtured by all those postwar upward trends, were sanguine, but your world began to come apart in 1963, when John Kennedy was shot. Other assassinations and dislocations followed, climaxing in 1968, when your generation, from Chicago to Paris, kindly offered to relieve the world's corrupt and doddery leaders of their responsibilities and run things along the utopian lines of love (not war), racial harmony, pot, rock, bell-bottoms, LSD, tie-dyed T-shirts, a cozy communal anarchy and plenty of risk-free sex to go around. While not all points of this ambitious program were instantly adopted, boomer thinking infiltrated the mainstream, and now one of you sits in the White House. The Silent Generation never had a president. We had Michael Dukakis, Jesse Jackson and Gary Hart instead.

Turning 50 for us, perhaps, was no big deal, since we had been born old, or at least meek. But for you — a rude shock, no doubt. Your first big bite of obsolescence; your first clear mathematical indication that, unless you haggle and stagger your way to a hundred, the larger part of your life is over. What can I tell you about this territory of the downward slope, of thickening twilight? Well, there is the matter of the winking-out neurons. On your brisk way to perform a minor errand, you forget what the errand was. You stand in the center of the room, inwardly waltzing with the ghost of your good intention. About to greet a neighbor at the supermarket, you confidently reach down into a mental pocket that has only a hole in it. But let's not forget that forgetfulness is the safeguard of sanity. If we remembered everything all the time, our brains would be clogged and clamorous. The neighbor's name will come to you in the car driving home, and the errand (taking the car to get its inspection sticker, say) will come to you in the middle of the night, when the garage is closed. Neurons die painlessly, and ignorance is bliss. What I didn't realize until after I turned 50 was how little information one needs to get by — all those once-memorized baseball stats and stanzas by Henry Wadsworth Longfellow, the sun still comes up without them.

Physical deterioration: You boomers have jogged and bench-pressed and done yoga until you are somatically as gods. Nevertheless, after 50 the air conditioner gets heavier every year you lift it out of the window. Running up five flights of steps, you will feel on the final landing as if your knees are made of liquid detergent. Sexually (and I know this was important to you), there is a new force of gravity dragging at your angel wings; bed becomes more and more a place to fall asleep in. Indeed, all the old enemies of sleep — a voracious lover, a hilarious party, a fascinating book, a sheer excitement at being alive — slowly lose their puissance and pale beside the majestic attractions of oblivion. These lessenings are not entirely debits; the remission of romantic fury allows more time for, say, crossword puzzles, and the need to cut a dynamic figure at every weekend party and tennis scramble no longer shoulders aside those household and gardening chores that once appeared so contemptibly marginal.

A quaint tidiness creeps over the later decades, along with a long-dormant interest in the songs of birds and the names of plants. The annual return of barn swallows to our carport, for instance, and their subsequent rearing of three or four swallowettes, have become principal topics of excited conversation between my wife and myself—little natural miracles relieving the level quiet of our days. Over 50, you shall find, one makes more of less. The muscles of empathy and curiosity strengthen while those of youthful egocentricity weaken. As the familiar old biological missions—mating and begetting, mostly—slacken in urgency, the world itself, in its multifarious and ceaselessly shifting nonhuman detail, sifts into awareness, imparting an innocent sense of witness like that of childhood.

These surrenders take place inch by inch. A 50-year-old is still a fierce being—potent, competitive, prone to surges of animal energy. For men and women in the workforce, the decade of the 50s should be a prime time of vigor fortified by experience, of grave responsibility and maximum salary. But a time tinged, it may be, with an undercurrent of ebbing creativity, of magnetism and savvy passing to a younger generation who have the new technology in their veins and effortlessly speak the language of the up-and-coming consumer. One is, after 50, no longer up-and-coming, not even in the sluggish realm of the arts, which allows youthful promise to 40-something performers who, if athletes, would be already retired. It will be hard for you boomers, for so long the bearers and consumers of the new thing—be it Bob Dylan and the Beatles, miniskirts and safari jackets, or PCs and videos—to yield fashion to generations yet younger. Like the flapper generation of the 1920s, you were made much of in your youth, envied and analyzed, deplored and deferred to. But history did not halt its self-consuming progress for even you, and, although some few of you will ascend in the next decade or two to summits of political and corporate power, most of you have had the bulk of your fun.

Well, but what is fun? It comes in many flavors, and there is, believe it or not, an over-50 flavor. Most of your

Fun comes in many flavors, and there is, believe it or not, an over-50 flavor.

decisions, willy-nilly, for good or bad, are behind you. You have rough-hewn your fates; now self-preservation and a certain sweet, blameless self-solicitude move to the top of the agenda. The quality of life—a side issue in the thick of the battle—becomes a matter of careful consideration and numerous discriminations. New choices arise. Pressing obligations suddenly loom as imaginary. The charms of saying no, of not-doing, for the first time exercise a significant appeal.

There are, if you don't panic, terminal satisfactions. Now that your future is no longer infinite, your entire life can be, for the first time, contemplated in its achieved shape, susceptible to a few finishing touches, applied with the feathery touch of an artist rather than with a warrior's heavy hand. There is, believe it or not, a certain relief in knowing how little remains in your control, how little remains to be proved. In the meantime, that inestimable treasure, that perpetual present in which life is lived, that motionless split second of awareness around which all else moves, remains in your possession, along with, if you are lucky, health and sanity.

You boomers have pushed in a herd down this half century, swelling the chorus in each decade. Now you are on your way, collectively, to bankrupt Medicare and the Social Security system. But I address this letter in the singular. After 50, the essential solitude of being a human being can scarcely be hidden; trust me that the chill rather clears the air. Shakespeare's Prospero, upon taking his retirement, promised that "every third thought shall be my grave." That leaves two thoughts, however, to entertain above the ground, and you have in your colorful pilgrimage long rehearsed what these thoughts might be: (1) love one another, and (2) seize the day. ■

John Updike's latest books are the novel In the Beauty of the Lilies *(Knopf) and* Golf Dreams: Writings on Golf. *He has won two Pulitzer Prizes, the first in 1982 for* Rabbit Is Rich, *the second in 1991 for* Rabbit at Rest.

CONFESSIONS OF A BOOMER

Life for a lot of boomers has been a soft and pleasant ribbon, unspooling more or less smoothly, each day.

By Peggy Noonan

When you write about a large group, you have to generalize, so here goes. In general, it seems to me that this is true of a number of the members of the baby boom generation: They are hitting or have hit middle age, yet they have not fully found themselves.

Which is amazing. After all, we have been nothing if not forceful in terms of our impact. We are and have been the most significant demographic fact of American life in all of American history: We changed, in our youth, the culture of a great nation, sweeping it with our music, our movies, our art and styles and tastes in entertainment. Our assumptions about sex changed the sexual landscape. We altered our country's political climate when we decided to oppose a war, changing American attitudes about our government in the process.

Before Vietnam, we all pretty much felt that if our leaders concluded that war was necessary, then it probably was. Now our leaders cannot wage war unless they first guarantee that it will be short, relatively painless and triumphant. This is not all bad: War is hell, and nations should be dragged, not jump, into the pit. Then again, down the road, some stern, dark military action that is truly justified in terms of national defense or clear morality will be up for discussion, and at that time we will perhaps not be able to do what we must, and tragedy may result. Bad guys, whether street muggers or Third World dictators with tertiary syphilis, calculate; and if the bad guys of the near future calculate that Americans will always do nothing, then American deterrence will not be credible; and if it is not credible, well, world, watch out. We enter interesting times.

But the point stands that for all our power to change our world—and we changed it when we were young—a lot of us might say that as a generation, we haven't fully become what we were supposed to become, haven't done the job history meant us to do. We are in our 40s and 50s; we have wed, chosen professions, borne children, bought homes. We pay taxes, support families, run marathons, give to good causes. Some of us have assumed responsibility for and buried parents; some have buried children. We are full-fledged adults, enmeshed in life and at its generational center. So this feeling of mild failure is odd.

I'll tell you what I think is at the heart of it: We have not had our trauma yet. We haven't had to face the building of a nation, civil war, depression or world war. We grew up in the great age of affluence. Life for a lot of boomers has been a soft and pleasant ribbon, unspooling more or less smoothly each day. History has not cold-cocked us, and so we haven't had a chance to impress the world, and ourselves, by getting up off the canvas.

There have been other American generations that weren't handed a supreme challenge. People born after the Civil War had a pretty great ride, a lot of them, until 1917. But they didn't have to watch documentaries about the valor of their parents on *The History Channel*. We compare ourselves to our parents and wonder if we could do it. Could I leave home for four years and fight like Dad in '41? Could I endure poverty as Mom did during the Depression? We think so, but we don't know. Deep down, below consciousness, we wonder

We compare ourselves to our parents and wonder if we could do it . . . if we're tough enough, brave enough.

if we're tough enough, brave enough, good enough.

We were told we had come into our own as a generation when Bill Clinton, the first boomer president, was elected. But that good-natured, handsome man has been, to my mind, ambivalent and confused. In my opinion, he's like a man walking around wearing a sign that says, "The Boomers Aren't Ready."

In politics, Clinton took his cue from John Kennedy; in literature it was previous generations, too, that influenced us, and here we were lucky, indeed. The generation before the boomers produced great novelists like Walker Percy and Flannery O'Connor, John Updike and the great postwar he-men James Jones and Irwin Shaw. We were novel readers; as a matter of fact, we may have been the last generation of novel readers, and the messages of those novels still shape our assumptions. We like China—thank you, Pearl Buck. Whatever our judgments on policy, we are emotionally pro-immigrant—thank you, Betty Smith, for *A Tree Grows in Brooklyn*. We experienced a wave of romantic approval of drugs, alcohol, late nights and what might be called illicit romance—thank you, American expatriates in France. Thank you, Lost Generation.

On TV, it was Johnny Carson, the master. And later Dick Cavett. Uncle Walter. Carol Burnett. Mar', Lou and Ted. The first few years of *Saturday Night Live*. Actually, what we may remember most from television are simple phrases: "A fine young man named Elvis Presley...." "Here they are—the Beatles!" "Mission Control, Tranquility Base here. The *Eagle* has landed." And finally, "The Associated Press reports shots were fired...." At JFK, RFK, Wallace and King. For a long time, television bulletins were horrible things that made us anxious—until CNN came along, and everything became a bulletin.

As for the movies, nothing

impressed us more than the ones we watched on *The Early Show*, *The Late Show* and *The Million Dollar Movie*, all of which featured classics starring good-hearted guys and gals like Jimmy Cagney, Pat O'Brien, Virginia Mayo and Ann Sheridan. Those old movies from the '30s, '40s and '50s gave us, in our little sequestered suburban houses, a sense of our country. It's how those of my generation who became screenwriters learned, unconsciously, how to write a movie. We memorized the dialogue. (My own specialty as a child was Ida Lupino's courtroom breakdown scene in *They Drive by Night*: "The doors made me do it! Yes, the doors made me do it.") We absorbed, unconsciously, pacing and rhythm and camera angle.

You know what was really ours? Music. We grew up listening to old soundtracks of Ruby Keeler singing "A Latin from Manhattan" and hearing the big band sound our parents would lindy to. And for an amazing lot of us, the first music we really emotionally responded to was recordings of Broadway musicals — *West Side Story*, *My Fair Lady*, *South Pacific*, *Gypsy*.

But really our creation — the thing we invented by supporting it and following it and then becoming part of it — was rock and roll: our own great barbaric yawp, for almost half a century the authentic sound of the American continent. And we can be proud of it because rock and roll is great and always was, from Chuck Berry to Elvis to Smashing Pumpkins. We can lay claim to it not only because there was never a more American American than Elvis but because even the imports were ours. The Beatles didn't become the Beatles until America decided they were the Beatles. They knew it — they sang, from their Liverpool beginnings, with American accents.

The boomers, for well or ill, really were shaped by previous generations. And, like every generation, they were shaped most by their parents. Concerning whom, a thought: Our parents, who survived a Depression and a world war, were too busy fighting Germans, finding jobs and inventing Levittown to spend time pondering whether they had found their inner core, their historical reason for being. But maybe they should have been a little more thoughtful. I continue to generalize, but they were not only a stoic and heroic generation, they were a confused generation. They thought that history had taught them one thing: Security is all. They started with nothing and wound up with a split-level and a gratefully subsidized old age. They worked to help us through college so that we could become professionals and know a professional's security. They suggested to us by the way they lived, by what they worked for and what they did without, that there is joy in material things. And, for all our caterwauling about rebellion, we took their lead and got material things.

We have them now; they surround us. But we were misled. We have more possessions, we have more success and status and style than previous generations, but we're not happier than previous generations. Depression and anxiety are epidemic. I don't know anyone of my generation who still smokes marijuana or takes cocaine, but I know three people on Prozac or other antidepressants. Our affluence has given us much, but the more we have, the hungrier we are and the more we buy. We try to assuage our hunger with the beautiful things of the world (not only watches and jackets and art but also admiration, respect, standing, power) — and with the most beautiful thing, with love. But the hunger grows.

Not all of my generation are sick from overindulgence, however; many are sick from worry and insecurity over money, the job, the house, the kids, the cost. I feel this way also sometimes, and when I do, I think of what my friend Anne's mother experienced when she lay in bed in a hospital 30 years ago with her seventh child. The baby was born at a bad time, with Anne's father newly laid off and the older kids entering high school with college coming. After the birth, Anne's mother lay in bed in the hospital weeping quietly, wondering: How would they survive? As she lay weeping, she heard these words in her head: "Be still and know that I am God." I think "one by one, from the inside out," as the social thinker Glenn Loury puts it, my generation is learning those words.

There is a Presbyterian minister named Tim Keller who gives a Sunday-night service in Manhattan. It draws quite a turnout of people in their 30s, 40s and 50s. A few weeks ago, Keller told them something that seemed tailored for boomers. He said that it is important to remember when we are thrilled by a piece of music, or a play, or a lover, or a group of friends, or a beautiful necklace, or a brilliant painting, or a brilliant person, that the thrill you are feeling is a gift from God, a gift of happiness. And its purpose is to give us a reflection of the divine. These gifts are like the moon. The moon is a lovely and wondrous thing, but it's only seen because of the sun. It has no light of its own.

The moon is our possesions, our loves—the things of which we think, "If only I can own it or merge with it I will be complete." But the sun is God. We have, all of us, "worshiped the moon" by living for art, sports, political victories, whatever. But we're ignoring the source; we're worshiping the wrong thing, and "it will not last or benefit us," says Keller.

I think that as a generation we're getting this straight. Here's one reason I think this: When we talk about our heroes, we get caught up in a media version of who they are and recite names like Jimi Hendrix or James Dean. But you know who I remember a lot of us really admired when we were kids? People who seemed to know who God was. A local minister, Albert Schweitzer, Albert Einstein. The heroes of our childhood and young adulthood, the heroes we don't talk about, the ones who form some part of our inner being that has never gone away, include Pope John XXIII, Billy Graham,

Not many generations get away unscathed, and I suspect we'll get our trauma.

Thomas Merton, Gandhi. And later, Mother Teresa and the present pope.

We don't talk about them, and the TV producers who do documentaries about us never ask. But they made a bigger impression, a quieter impression, on our generation than a lot of mere cultural figures, which has happy implications for our future. Because here's the thing: Not many generations get away unscathed, and I suspect we'll get our trauma. I don't know what it will be, but I suppose it will be either a worldwide economic crash, or something worse. What I fear is something fearsome.

I didn't fear the use of nuclear arms in the '70s and '80s—we had the bomb and the Soviets had the bomb, and neither of us was going to use it because we weren't evil and they weren't crazy. But now each year more little Saddams, more little Khrushchevs, have the bomb—and some of them are evil, some of them are crazy. A week ago I read something the poet and songwriter Leonard Cohen recently said: "I've seen the future, baby, it is murder." He is living in a Zen center now.

Like him, I think a bad shock is coming. But I think a second surprise will follow. I think whatever trauma comes, we'll be up to it. I think we boomers are tougher than we know, and if I'm right that we are finding God, we will be stronger than we know.

We will survive and build. We will endure, like pioneers. For years we have been saying of nuclear technology, "You can't get the genie back in the bottle." But once the genie causes havoc, we may finally agree, across the world, that we must find a way to push her back and close the bottle tight.

Not a pretty thought, but it may turn out to be the job history sent our generation to do. ■

Former special assistant and speechwriter for two presidents, Peggy Noonan is author of many books, essays and columns, most recently Speech! Speech! *(HarperCollins).*

Meeting the Challenge of Leaving the Workforce

By Melody L. Kollath

"I can hardly believe it's this close," Steve told me nervously when he had a little less than a year to go as section manager at a large lab. He had just moved up his departure date on his doctor's advice: Standing on concrete floors for 29 years had taken its toll. Thanks to careful planning, Steve and his wife, Roberta, were in good shape financially. His immediate concern was psychological.

Steve looked forward to his new life with great eagerness. What he hadn't thought about was what leaving his job meant. Nearly three decades ago, he had started work with a boss and three lab assistants. Now the section he headed had 31 people. Some of them had worked with him for 25 years; many were like family to him. When Steve announced his retirement, he had given little thought to how they would react, and their responses were wrenching. Some asked how they could apply for his job. Others expressed fears that a new boss wouldn't treat them as well and asked, in effect, why he was abandoning them—he was barely older than they were, in his prime, doing excellent work; how could he leave?

As Steve related this history to me, he realized that he had concentrated only on retirement, not the retiring process. I suggested that he go home and write down some thoughts: what his job meant to him, what was going to change in his life, what those changes would mean for him and his wife. Then he needed to look at the benefits of retirement and what it meant to him. On his next visit, I suggested that he talk with the co-workers he felt closest to and share his concerns and excitement. He did and later called me to say, "You know, besides helping me deal with my own feelings, talking allowed my friends to express their feelings about my retirement, and we all ended up happier." After this exchange, Steve was able to enjoy his final time at the job and retire in the warmth of good feelings.

Another client of mine was very aware that she didn't want to retire. Participating in the transition on the job helped her to feel better about it. Frances was angry that her husband, Mel, was pressing her to join him in retirement so that they could, in his words, "enjoy life." She did enjoy life. She had built her department at a small manufacturing plant out of nothing and in the process had made it a key component of the company's success. Her ambivalence about leaving ended when she decided to ensure that her work would be carried on. First, she analyzed her department and job as objectively as she could. Then she figured out what the next manager would need to maintain and expand the department. When she actually announced her retirement, she gave this assessment to her boss and asked if she could participate in the selection of her successor. He readily agreed. At her retirement party, Frances shed some tears but had no doubt that she was ready to go and was leaving her department in good hands.

Many of us derive much of our identity from our work, from being able to say, "I am an executive secretary" or "vice president" or "sheet-metal worker." We find it difficult to imagine ourselves without a title or profession and the sense of self-worth that a job provides. Saying "I'm retired" can feel a lot less impressive, until we recognize that this isn't a useful self-definition if the question is "What do you do?"—just as "I live in a house" isn't a helpful answer to the question "Where do you live?" The ways you spend your time and your zest for new ideas and experiences are the true keys to who you are and how much you enjoy life. Retirement is a means, not an end.

THE BOOMERS HAPPINESS POLL

The happiness index of boomers turned 50 — results of an exclusive poll reveal what this generation is thinking and doing.

By Myles Callum

Excuse us — got a minute? We have a few questions, if you wouldn't mind obliging. Do you look forward to retirement, or are you dreading it? Are material comforts more important to you now than they were 20 years ago? What's your favorite movie from the '60s? Do you see yourself as better or worse off than your parents were at this stage of their lives? Are you more conservative than you used to be, or perhaps more liberal? By the way, mind telling us how much money you make? And, uh, how's your sex life? Ever do drugs? Say, here's a question: Would you care to trade in your spouse?

Those are not the exact words, but they capture the gist of some of the questions *New Choices* wanted put to an important group of people — the ones born at the onset of the baby boom that started, not surprisingly, with the joyous return of veterans at the end of World War II.

Those first boomers, born in 1946, have now turned 50, and they've had quite a ride. They were young children during the button-down, white-bucks '50s who went on to grow up during the sexual revolution and the peaceful protests of the early '60s. They've lived through the Cold War and hot pants, Pet Rocks and rock and roll, assassinations, Vietnam, love-ins, television, Watergate, feminism, the civil

rights movement and, these days, the unsettling challenges of a changing economy.

What are they like now as they turn 50, and how do they feel about that milestone? What do they expect — and what do they fear — as they approach retirement? To find the answers, *New Choices* commissioned EDK Associates, a New York–based public-opinion research firm, to conduct a survey of the men and women born in 1946. It was EDK's job to randomly select 1,000 boomers who'd provide answers to a series of thought-provoking, personal, sometimes intimate quetions.

The big picture? It's nothing if not upbeat: Baby boomers have done well. They are an educated group. Their finances are sound. They say they have, on the whole, pretty good love lives. But nothing's perfect. Boomers don't have a great many regrets, but, yes, if they had it all to do over, there's an important thing or two that they would like to do differently.

So who exactly are these early baby boomers, and how do they feel about turning 50? The survey says:

They're smart.

Or at least well educated, which isn't quite the same. Almost all (96 percent) are high school graduates, and 73 percent have had some college or technical school. Four out of 10 are college graduates. Early boomer women, especially, did themselves proud here: They were the first generation of American women to enter college in such large numbers. Thirty-eight percent have a college

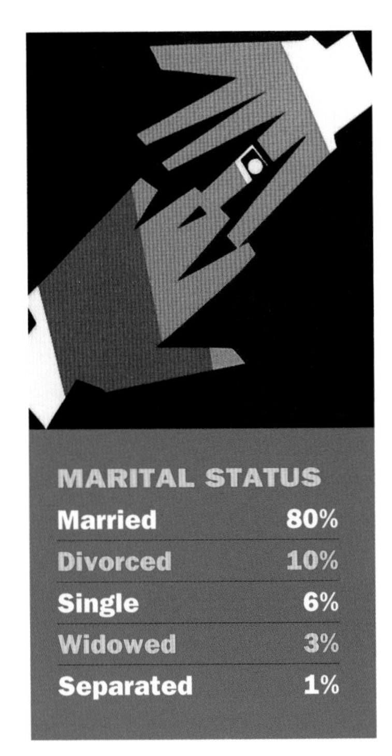

MARITAL STATUS

Married	80%
Divorced	10%
Single	6%
Widowed	3%
Separated	1%

degree, and 14 percent have advanced degrees.

They've done well financially.
More than half the men make more than $35,000 a year, and more than half of them are in two-income households with family incomes of $65,000 or more. A third have household incomes of $80,000 or more.

They're working.
Seventy percent are employed full-time, with another 10 percent working part-time and a further 10 percent self-employed. The rest are homemakers, unemployed or retired.

They're very married.
The figures (above) say that boomers are together in impressive percentages. A healthy 80 percent are married, whether for the first or fourth go-round, with only 10 percent currently divorced and 6 percent having never married.

They're lovers.
A majority of both men (69 percent) and women (62 percent) are having a pretty good time sexually, claiming either that they "have sex a lot, and it's great," or that they "have sex less often, but it's better." It's probably no accident that 66 percent answered either "very well" or "to some degree" when asked if they consider themselves "sexually very experienced."

They are family-oriented.
More than half still have children under 18 who are living at home. Many of those started their families later than did their parents or are on their second families.

Don't call them crybabies.
So much for demographics; what about the tough stuff? How do they handle stress, for instance, and all the complexities of modern life? These early boomers rate themselves fairly high on these emotional scales as well; they seem to have learned to go with the flow. Seventy-two percent say they're managing the stress in their lives, while only a few (13 percent) feel they're "living on the edge."

Sex, drugs, Vietnam and rock and roll.
How'd they get to be who they are? They're often called "children of the '60s," but the first boomers predated that era in many ways. They finished college before antiwar demonstrations were common and married before feminism raised questions about male-female roles. They were already in their 20s when drugs first became a major recreational component of the rock-and-roll lifestyle. Very few men (13 percent) and women (7 percent) admitted that experimenting with drugs was an important part of their youth or young adulthood.

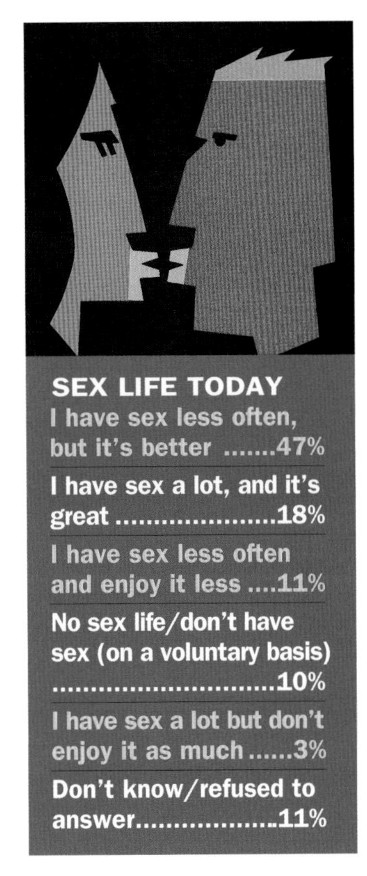

SEX LIFE TODAY

I have sex less often, but it's better	47%
I have sex a lot, and it's great	18%
I have sex less often and enjoy it less	11%
No sex life/don't have sex (on a voluntary basis)	10%
I have sex a lot but don't enjoy it as much	3%
Don't know/refused to answer	11%

Ask them about their drug of choice and these early boomers mention exercise first —with wine or beer a distant fourth (see chart next page).

What they did have was the sexual revolution. In the era of "sex, drugs and rock and roll," this group never quite made it past the first part. A big reason for that was the introduction in the early '60s of the oral contraceptive pill. Early boomers were the first group that didn't have to worry about pregnancy.

Ask them what event had the biggest impact on their lives and these boomers cite the Vietnam War (38 percent), the assassination of President John F. Kennedy (25 percent) and the social movements of the time (20 percent). These weren't the flower children or the groovin' Woodstock crowd; only 1 percent picked the fabled music festival as a major shaping event. Not surprisingly, Vietnam was cited much more often by men (49 percent) than by women (28 percent), who were more likely to point to the assassination of JFK (women: 32 percent; men: 18 percent).

Pop culture? Once again, their choices reveal that these early boomers weren't the counterculture group. For example, 31 percent say that the movie that influenced them the most was *The Graduate*, with its contemporary songs by Simon and Garfunkel and provocative sexual theme, while only 8 percent cited the more radical tale of alienated youth, *Easy Rider*. Their personal theme song from the '50s and '60s is much more likely to be "Blowin' in the Wind" (33 percent) than "Rock Around the Clock" (15 percent) or "Stop! In the Name of Love" (also 15 percent).

My, how they've changed.

As they've grown older, many boomers have found themselves turning more to religion

Early boomers look forward to having more leisure time.

as a source of community, spirituality and solace. Nearly 4 out of 10 men and women say religion has become more important to them over the course of their lives. Not surprisingly — it's a well-established phenomenon — many of them have also become more conservative. The majority (57 percent) think their values have remained fairly constant over time. But 4 in 10 see themselves as having changed, and they are almost twice as likely to report being more conservative (27 percent) now than more liberal (14 percent). They've grown attached to their cars, VCRs and microwave ovens, too: Half the people surveyed say that material success and comforts have become more important to them.

My, how they haven't changed.

Early boomers weren't the most radical group, but they were still part of an era that challenged authority and distrusted institutions. Some of that distrust lingers for both men (56 percent) and women (50 percent), even as they've grown into authority figures themselves. Their social conscience remains as well: Many people turning 50 say they still feel a personal responsibility to make the world a better place. Women (63 percent) are even more likely than men (54 percent) to say this is a central part of who they are.

So, what's the problem?

If they're well-educated, employed, in decent financial shape and sexually more or less satisfied, what's to worry about? Regardless of their current status, people turning 50 still have two major concerns: their health and their finances. Fifty-seven percent say they have at least some concerns about developing health problems. Of that 57 percent, 21 percent report that they are "very worried" about illness. Nearly half are worried about money: Some (19 percent) worry about not having enough to retire, but more (29 percent) worry about having enough funds to maintain their lifestyle. Women worry about money more than men (54 percent to 41 percent).

If they had it to do over.

Do they have any regrets? Not too many, but there are a couple of big ones. Two in three say they would like to have been better prepared for a job or career. Fewer than half are happy with their career choice, not necessarily because of money but because of job gratification: Dollars aside, 57 percent would have preferred to do something else with their professional life. Twenty percent would change their appearance if they could, and a third would change jobs. And we are pleased to report that only 3 percent would choose to trade in their spouse for someone else.

How do they feel about turning 50?

The survey's startling finding is that 73 percent of baby boomers say the half-century milestone doesn't faze them. Few hate the idea (13 percent), and the rest (13 percent) claim they haven't given it a thought. Is this possible?

A friend of mine on the Internet, Sylvia, a midwestern married mother of two who teaches English in a community college, happens to share this boomer philosophy. "Turning 30 scared and depressed me," she says. "Fifty fascinated me. I'm more comfortable with who I am and what I do than I have ever been."

Part of the reason for such a positive attitude is that boomers simply don't feel their age. Ken Dychtwald, president of a California company that tracks various lifestyle trends of older Americans, says that many boomers imagine themselves to be 15 years younger than they really are. That point is echoed in author Gail Sheehy's latest book, *New Passages* (Random House). Writing of baby boomers, she says, "...the image of themselves they carry around in their inner eye usually falls somewhere between 28 and 35."

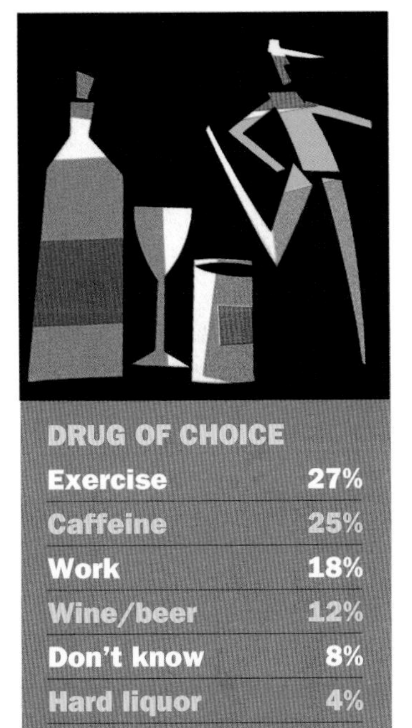

DRUG OF CHOICE	
Exercise	27%
Caffeine	25%
Work	18%
Wine/beer	12%
Don't know	8%
Hard liquor	4%
Prozac	1%
Other	5%

What's next?

Boomers' healthy attitude toward turning 50 also extends to their view of the future. By a large majority (81 percent), they see the coming years as being a time of new opportunities rather than of closed doors (14 percent). In the same vein, they envision the future as having a lot of options (62 percent) rather than being a time of hard choices (33 percent). Most (54 percent) will settle for the comforts of friendship, but a large band of happy optimists (36 percent) expect to be basking in romance. They look forward to having more leisure time (19 percent), having fewer demands placed on them by others (19 percent), spending more time with their families (16 percent) and, perhaps best of all, having the opportunity to try something new (29 percent).

They're a well-adjusted, forward-thinking, upbeat group, these early baby boomers. "Age 50?" they seem to be telling us. "Hey, let's do it." ■

Myles Callum is a New Jersey–based writer.

The EDK report is based on a national telephone survey of 1,000 men and women born in 1946, conducted in June 1995. The margin of error is 3.5 percent.

PAST 50 AND TAKING NEW RISKS

What it means when you start trying out Ferris wheels, perilous trips alone or remarriage after 20 years as a single

By Lois Gould

I can still see the wagging finger, keeping time with my father's voice. "The devil you know," he says. "Better stick with him." He winks; I get the message. The devil you know keeps you locked up tight. His key, safe inside you, is the simple terror of *What if?*

I grew up never risking anything. Clinging for dear life to my familiar devil, I developed fear of falling, climbing, throwing and catching, the dark, sliding down a banister, being called on, jumping rope. I cried if I had to learn a new piece on the piano, a new irregular verb. *What if* I can only do the one I know? *What if* I forget that one, too?

At 11½, allowed to cross my very first street alone, I crossed — to my amazement — on the diagonal: Heart in my throat, I marched down the dangerous roadway, in the dazzling teeth of onrushing traffic, for the full length of that terrifying city block. It was my first adrenalin high.

I never told anyone, and I'm sorry to say it was the only act of daredeviltry I was to commit until I reached midlife crisis — or what I still prefer to think of as second childhood.

Then, without warning, I found myself turning into a reckless adventurer. Traveling alone to unknown destinations; scaling a slippery sea cliff; falling off a horse; dangling over a chasm on a fraying rope bridge; living beside a thrashing sea at the wildest side of a rude foreign country. In short, getting to know quite a few strange devils. As we used to say, if my Dad knew what I was up to, he'd die. He did die, in fact; could that be why I was up to it? Why I quit looking — and began to leap?

I recently heard about an acrophobic lady in Haverford, Pennsylvania, who had, at 51, gone up twice in one week on an amusement-park Ferris wheel, having steered clear of "scary" rides all her life. I called to congratulate her and to ask not Why? but Why now?

Was she, too, going through a second childhood?

Carol Lee Lindner, an elegant suburban mother of three, had some delightful thoughts about "risky'" midlife behavior—generally, and in her own case. My favorite was the Mother's Day dream in which she sat nodding contentedly as her children, in their late teens and 20s, recounted their daring adventures—including the tears and the scary parts. Carol woke up angry: "I wasn't contributing to the conversation!" One of her daughters later challenged her to look up *contented* in a dictionary. "Satisfied"? "Leaving nothing to be desired"? Carol Lee Lindner woke up again.

The Ferris-wheel ride was only one of several leaps she then took. Giving up her safe, pleasant job as assistant to a school admissions director was another. "I'd stopped stretching!" she explains. She experimented with kayaking and in-line roller skating, and she took on a demanding round of volunteer work with people in hospitals and nursing homes. New friends of all ages have "something to teach me that I need to learn," she says.

I thought of a passage attributed to André Gide in a new novel I had just read. A young female character reads it aloud, with the same passion I heard in Lindner's voice: "When your surroundings have taken on your likeness, or you yourself have grown like your surroundings ... you must leave them. Take from each thing only what it teaches you." Gide saw the endless, necessary journey of the hungry spirit as a "nomad's life."

My friend Jean Valentine last year gave up her celebrated New York poet's identity for midlife remarriage—after 20 years of single contentment—and a wrenching move to another country where she was virtually unknown. She told me that she had gotten cold feet—literally, walking pneumonia—just before taking the plunge. But she remembered a Japanese artist's words: If you are famous, you must change your name at 50. It is the only way to release yourself from what you have become.

Another artist—and another lifelong acrophobe—Bob Parker of West Cornwall, Connecticut, celebrated his 64th birthday parachuting out of a plane at 6,400 feet (he says the numbers were pure coincidence). Parker's wife, son and one of six grandchildren stood on the ground, videotaping all the astonishing colors of Grandpa's terrified descending face. Like Carol Lee Lindner, Parker wasn't cured of his phobia. While talking to me, he confessed, he was gazing up into the darkness of his 20-foot-high studio ceiling and dreading the climb up the ladder to change the lightbulb. On the other hand, like many artists, he has always flown in his dreams. So what was it that drove him finally, at 64, to step out of that plane into midair, just for the sheer, longed-for hell of it? Is there, in our 50s and 60s, another kind of biological clock—a daredevil alarm that begins its insistent ticking: If not now, when? Bob Parker says simply, "It was about time."

Last Christmas, in the west of Ireland, I met a woman of 76 who had abruptly taken to her bed in a cozy guest house near her own isolated cottage. All through January and February she remained holed up in her rented room, with a fire blazing, her small, yappy terrier and a pack of cards for company. Rumor had it that she wasn't a bit sick, mad or even depressed. Just biding her time, literally playing Patience through the dark and stormy winter of her discontent. Sure enough, when the days began to get some stretch in them, as the Irish say, she got up, put on her cleated walking shoes, left her dog with the neighbors and took off—on her first tour of China.

Down the road from me lives another intrepid septuagenarian, Boston-born retired publisher Fred Zeserson, who three years ago took up skiing on sand. He skis on beaches, grass lawns and, in a pinch, on freshly paved roads. Last spring, at 75, Fred schussed off to the Swiss Alps to enter a marathon with some 11,000 competitors, nearly all many decades his junior. "If I finish," Fred mused, "it will be the beginning of something. If not, it'll be the end of something." Then he laughed, packed up his Zen philosophy texts and a supply of arnica gel for his stiff knee.

This explosive appetite for risk in what was once called the sunset years has yet to be officially diagnosed. We could name it the Ferris Wheel Syndrome, after Carol Lee Lindner, or the Flying Leap, after Bob Parker. We could—and many would—call it the midlife crazies. Fifty is old enough to know better; to know, in fact, only too well, all the things that can go wrong—and probably will.

Take travel, for instance. The mere sight of a foreign waiter brandishing a strange menu is enough to make strong men go weak in the money belt. This is why new airports, shops and hotels all tend to look more and more drearily alike. I once stayed in a new luxury hotel in Milan that actually had all its public rooms built underground. Nervous business travelers on the verge of big deals, noses buried in their hometown papers and comforting scrambled eggs, never had to look up and glimpse some magnificent cathedral or unintelligible street sign. Imagine Dorothy and Toto in the Land of Oz—without the feeling (gulp!) that they're not in Kansas anymore.

Women may worry less about being embarrassed or taken advantage of—but more about getting sick, lost, mugged or just horribly ignored. (What if I fall down and can't get anyone to help me?)

I've had disaster strike and lived to tell the tale. Once I had a car door slammed on my hand after a glorious picnic in northern Italy. It could have happened at a Cape Cod beach resort, near ambulances and English-speaking X-ray technicians. To this day I don't know how many bones were crushed. Another time, in Greece, I dove off a cliff into the glowing wine-dark sea and got stung on the face by a jellyfish. In each case, rescue came.

My father would have said he told me so, every time. But my bones did knit, my wounds did heal. As my psychiatrist husband once said, in the midst of a raging fight, "What are you crying about? You're a writer—you can always use it."

"Midlife—like all life—is a risk," says the author. But still, "go for it."

But the sad fact is that the wagging finger, the nagging *What if?* keeps coming along for the ride. The midlife fear of risk—of harm, of loss—gets stamped on our emotional passports again and again. Images of ourselves as victims-to-be—wobbling uncertainly down some dark alley, stalled in our car at the wrong red light. Mad-dog killers lurk in the slow lane, the backseat, the lurid imagination.

If you manage to get (or stay) home alive, some thoughtful, worried talk-show host will fill you in on what else you stand to lose, violently, any minute. Think about the empty nest, job insecurity, wandering spouses, dry mucosae. Midlife—like all life—is a risk.

I suppose the best defense, as always, is a good offense. In other words, go for it. I recently stumbled in a badly lit hotel lobby, missing the second of two shallow steps. My knee buckled; I went down. Suddenly, I realized what I'd done—or not done—right. I hadn't known I was falling, so I didn't tense, freeze or attempt to break the fall. Like a baby who topples out of a window and survives, miraculously unhurt, I was, for once, entirely innocent of fear.

Another trick is to get someone to give you "permission" to do something risky. It doesn't much matter who, although the odds are, it will be a new friend rather than a loving, protective mate or an old pal who knows you and your fears all too well. Katharine Hepburn, playing the immortal athlete Babe Didrikson Zaharias in *Pat and Mike*, always looked up before a tricky golf shot to meet her fiancé's encouraging, worried gaze. She missed the ball every time—until she stopped looking up at him and married the Spencer Tracy character instead. He knew she'd hit it.

When I confessed that I wanted to restore a jinxed sports car, a young male friend exclaimed, "Brilliant!" Everyone else I knew pointed out the downside: Extravagant, foolhardy, it would take a year, cost the earth and never be right. My daredevil pal agreed but lent me his silver Alfa Romeo while he helped me get it done. Brilliant!

I keep thinking of Sir Rudolf Bing, the great director of New York's Metropolitan Opera, who in his 80s met up with a somewhat young lady and went off with her for a holiday in the Caribbean. His family—all midlifers with crises of their own—shrieked in horror and hired attorneys to "rescue" him. *Incompetent* was the word the press bandied about. No fool like an old fool. Ought to be locked up in some safe place (with the devil he knew), not out there dabbling his creaky toes in that warm blue sea. No sex, please, we're, er, adults.

Well, this year, after my hot-air-balloon flight, I might be driving a Jeep across Europe, through Russia and down to India. Carol Lee Lindner is getting ready for her first roller-coaster ride. And Fred Zeserson is back from the Swiss Alps. He finished that marathon, coming in 9,603rd. Or as he put it, "There were 24 guys behind me."

Care to join us?

Lois Gould is author of eight novels, two nonfiction books and many essays. Her most recent novel is No Brakes *(Henry Holt). She has also taught at Boston University, New York University and Wesleyan University in Connecticut.*

Psyching Yourself for a Job Search

By Myrna Lewis

It's no fun to seek employment, especially at midlife. Age discrimination, competition from younger workers and fewer opportunities due to persistent corporate downsizing can leave older job seekers feeling especially vulnerable and demoralized. "But the situation is far from hopeless," says career specialist and journalist Bob Weinstein. "There are ways you can use your age to your advantage and psych yourself into improving your chances of finding a new job."

The key is to understand the new rules of the employment game, says Weinstein, author of *So What If I'm 50? Straight Talk & Proven Strategies for Getting Hired in the Toughest Job Market Ever* (McGraw-Hill). Here is some of his advice:

- First, adjust your attitude. "You must accept that the comparatively stable work world of the 1950s, '60s or even the '80s is gone," notes Weinstein. Employment will increasingly become more provisional, requiring yet additional job hunts in the future. Develop a disciplined approach to looking for work, and assume you'll have to use it repeatedly.

- Put yourself in an employer's shoes and find out what he or she is looking for. Don't kid yourself—it's a buyer's market, and profit is the bottom line in today's survival scramble. Figure out what you have that fits the employer's needs, and promote those points. Draw on your years of experience.

- Become more flexible and creative. The conventional 9-to-5 job is disappearing. Consider consulting and contract work.

- Don't go it alone. Construct a safety net using family, friends and job seekers' support groups, which are cropping up in many cities (for starters, check with your trade association for referrals). Share your feelings. Admit to disappointments. Celebrate successes. Don't be afraid to be human!

JUST IMAGINE

A guide for tapping into our creative potential at midlife

By Kathleen Fury

Move over, Grandma Moses. As a reigning symbol of creativity among the aging, you may soon be replaced by any one of us.

"Lots of people become more creative in midlife," declares Dean Keith Simonton, psychology professor at the University of California at Davis and editor of the *Journal of Creative Behavior*. "Some look back and decide their career choices didn't really suit them. Women find they're no longer so enslaved by sex-role demands. Parents don't need to focus so much energy on their children." Looking at friends and colleagues, says 48-year-old Simonton, "I find it remarkable how many people have great creative potential just waiting to burst out."

Creativity is not a special province of artists or poets, Simonton and other researchers have concluded, nor is it the same as talent or intelligence. It is a life-affirming spirit we are born with, the same quality that allows children—and fortunate adults—to be confident, playful, inventive, flexible, curious, open-minded and willing to take risks. Over-50s who reconnect with this spirit find practical as well as spiritual benefits.

"Creativity is an approach to solving problems," says Yale psychologist Robert Sternberg. "It's a frame of mind whose principles apply to every aspect of life. For example, an original and efficient filing system may not rock the world, but it can

go a long way toward improving one small corner of it. Besides, living and working more imaginatively is a joy in itself."

Two years ago, Chicago businessman Roger Gerth enrolled in a drawing workshop run by Betty Edwards, author of *Drawing on the Right Side of the Brain* (Jeremy P. Tarcher). "I had never done anything creative in the artistic sense," relates Gerth. "But after five days, I was able to draw and, more important, to see better. I'm not an art teacher, but now I've taught my daughter and son-in-law how to draw." Gerth is convinced that we can all experience the pleasures of tapping our creative potential. "It's just a question of believing in it and learning a few techniques or mechanisms that open the door," he says. "For me, it was an incredible experience, sort of like a plane taking off."

"What we've found is that creativity is almost like physical conditioning; we need to exercise it," explains Suzanne Merritt, who founded the Creativity and Innovation Laboratory at Polaroid's headquarters in Cambridge, Massachusetts. Like Dr. Edwards, she is one of a growing number of experts teaching people to be more creative in everything from dealing with a difficult colleague at work to scheduling household errands. Here are some of their suggestions:

- **Change**—for the sake of change. Routine and habit, although comfortable, can interfere with fresh approaches. "If you always do what you've always done, you'll always get what you've always gotten," says Larry Wilson, founder of the Pecos River Learning Centers near Minneapolis. If you invariably read the sports page first, force yourself to read it last. The next time you eat out, choose a dish you never order, one you think you don't like. Try to live this way for an entire day. Then try again for a whole day the following week.

Once you've tried breaking your old patterns, move on to activities that are new, strange and even scary. Try wallclimbing, scuba diving, square dancing. What matters is that the activity is new for you.

- **Take risks.** Sternberg suggests that we live in a "risk-averse" culture, a world that bombards us with cautionary maxims: Don't rock the boat. A penny saved is a penny earned. The way to go is the way you know. A bird in the hand is worth two in the bush. Yet one attribute all highly creative people share is a willingness to take risks.

At the Pecos River Learning Centers, workshop participants are sometimes asked to climb a 25-foot telephone pole. "Everybody says the same exact thing," says Hersch Wilson, son and co-worker of the center's founder, laughing. "'Oh, I could never do that.' We give them a supportive team. We tell them that whatever they do is okay; they can shake or cry or whatever. So they put on the harness and put their hands on the pole and everybody applauds—and next thing you know, they've climbed a 25-foot telephone pole. That's a learning moment."

What's the lesson? "Play to win," says Hersch Wilson. "Most people do the opposite—they play not to lose, to be safe, secure, take no risks. But living that way prevents learning. It keeps you from being who you're supposed to be."

- **Believe in yourself.** Don't be afraid to be laughed at, even by yourself. Creativity is a willingness to ignore the "wisdom" of the crowd. "Who the hell wants to hear actors talk?" asked Harry Warner of Warner Brothers in 1925, when he heard they'd found a way to add sound to movies. Two decades later, another studio mogul, Daryl F. Zanuck, supposedly dismissed the invention of television: "People will soon get tired of staring at a plywood box every night." Creative people pay more attention to their own passions than to naysayers, "experts" or voices of authority.

- **Neatness don't count.** All creative endeavor is a process that, when fully engaged, usually produces mistakes, failures and some mess on the way to success.

Scientist Alexander Fleming is said to have been an untidy man who let his cultures sit around in piles so high that some of them didn't get treated with antiseptic. One day he noticed that one of the culture plates had green mold on it and that the germ colonies around the mold had disappeared. His disorderly procedures had led to the discovery of penicillin.

- **Find the child in you.** Children are creative because the survival of our species depends on it. The human child must learn his or her survival skills from scratch, over a period of many years. Child's play, therefore, is actually the most creative work. Many of us had that early creativity drilled out of us by well-meaning adults or at best have let it rust from disuse.

Sternberg and Todd Lubart, co-authors of *Defying the Crowd: Cultivating Creativity in a Culture of Conformity*, tell a story of two boys who encounter an enormous grizzly bear in the woods. One of the boys, a straight-A student with a high IQ, quickly calculates the grizzly's speed in his head and realizes the bear will soon catch up to them. Seeing his companion removing his hiking boots and putting on jogging shoes, he exclaims, "God, you're stupid. We'll never outrun that grizzly."

"That's true," says the other boy. "But all I have to do is outrun you."

Fortunately, the innate creativity of every child is never hopelessly lost, according to Michell Cassou, co-founder of The Painting Experience near San Francisco. "In fact," she says, "once you're past a certain age, the need to contact your own soul is much more acute. You've already accomplished much and 'proved' yourself. In our workshops, I see older people who are no longer interested in impressing others. As a result, they are more open to letting the freedom out of their brush."

Watching a child lost in concentration while examining an object, an adult is apt to assume that the child is wasting time. But the very act of observing with one's full attention is creative and not nearly as easy as you might imagine.

Try this: Take an object, something that fits comfortably in the palm of your hand, such as a small stone or an apple. Set a kitchen timer for five minutes. Move the object around in your hand, and look at it from different angles and distances. If you find yourself losing concentration before the timer goes off, gently bring your attention back to the object.

Do this exercise a few times and you will discover how increased powers of observation and concentration can enrich your life immeasurably, solving a vexing problem, talking to a friend at dinner or observing a beautiful sunset.

• **Unleash your unconscious.** "We often underestimate the power of the unconscious mind," observe Daniel Goleman, Paul Kaufman and Michael Ray in *The Creative Spirit*. "But it is far more suited to a creative insight than is the conscious mind." Only a fraction of all the information that the brain takes in surfaces to the conscious level, say these experts. Underneath lie memories, feelings and the sources of those sensations we call "hunches" and scientists call intuition.

Various techniques can expand connections between your conscious mind and your unconscious. Many people find that meditation clears the busy noise. Keeping a dream journal can be helpful. So can simply giving yourself enough time—and permission—to dream.

You will discover how increased powers of observation and concentration enrich your life immeasurably.

• **Yes, another reason to exercise.** Studies have found that physical activity can spur creative thought. Some researchers think that aerobic exercise releases chemicals that promote brain activity.

In *The Listening Book* (Shambhala), author W. A. Mathieu writes about the fun walking can be—"hum, whistle, sing and shout, clap, snap, beat your body, squint your eyes, dance, jive, swing and sway." Mathieu offers another intriguing suggestion: Say (to yourself if you like) left, right, left, right as you are walking at a comfortable pace. Begin accenting every third word: left, right, *left*, right, left, *right*, etc. You will soon be waltzing down the street.

"When you get to the bottom of all human problems," declares Hersch Wilson, "it always comes to this: People need to get moving, to act." To get going, find workshops and classes at your local adult-education center or Y.

• **Lose your inner critic.** The largest obstacles to creativity are usually internal. If you're like many people, you've come to believe critical messages that you have heard or imagined over the years: I can't do that. I'm too slow. I'm an underachiever. I never finish what I start. I'm a slob. I'm boring. I don't know enough. My trouble is....

Keep repeating these refrains and you're bound to defeat yourself. But if you learn to recognize these nasty intrusions—you can begin to talk back to them and shut them up.

"Creation is never about changing yourself," note Michell Cassou and Stewart Cubley in *Life, Paint and Passion*. "It is about meeting yourself, probing deep into your own core. Creation wants only to fulfill your deepest desire: to know and accept yourself as you are." ■

Kathleen Fury is a widely published freelance writer who lives in Connecticut with her husband and their two cats, Bill and Tootsie.

The Single Life: Freedom to Change Lifestyle, Location and Jobs

By Eleanor Foa Dienstag

Our nation was built on the idea that all of us can reinvent ourselves. In the past, that dream was mostly for the young. Today, it's just as true for midlife Americans, especially singles.

We all harbor fantasies about changing our lives. Relocating is perhaps the most common, even if it's just from suburb to downtown. That's the plan of a soon-to-retire Illinois executive I know who devotes most of his free time to writing plays. He's saving aggressively so he can afford to move into Chicago, closer to the downtown theater world.

Going from city to country is another common dream. "I just crave a garden," says a 56-year-old friend who has lived and taught school part-time in Boston for 30 years. She does not have much money and has been thinking about buying a house somewhere in an inexpensive rural area. Her mother recently died, leaving her a small sum that she could use as a down payment. Born and raised in a small town, in a house with a front porch and a backyard garden, she finds that the rhythm and way of life she once fled now shape her vision of the future — "to have a place my children can visit during the summer and holidays where we can cook together and I can work during the week alone."

My friend worries about whether she can find a teaching job in a small town and whether her children will, indeed, come to visit. But one thing she doesn't have to consider is a spouse's job, schedule, health or lifestyle preferences.

It's also far easier for a single person to find ways to see the world. A twice-widowed Rochester journalist, for example, has arranged to teach English and journalism in China for a year; and a former general counsel for a New Orleans company who accepted an early-retirement package has since spent more than half of each year in Eastern Europe. Working through a U.S. government agency, she teaches aspiring capitalists how to set up public corporations, including how to sell stock and pick a board of directors.

"If I were still married, I could never have taken advantage of this opportunity," she says. "Nor would I have been inclined to."

Her comment made me think of a married friend who had to adjust to her spouse's predilections. She had hoped to live part-time in New York, near her children, once her husband retired. But he hates the city, so they're planning to retire to Cape Cod and make do with frequent visits.

Between midlife burnout and corporate downsizing, more and more single people I know have made — or plan to make — dramatic changes in their lives.

Where will I be in a decade? I have no idea. I hope new writing projects will lead me down unexpected paths. I'd like to spend more time each year visiting my adventurous friends, contemplating whether their new ways of living might one day attract me as well.

CHANGING CHANNELS AT 50

Fired by NBC, the author is trying out the career he always said he wanted.

By Lloyd Dobyns

Getting off the merry-go-round is a lot easier — and clearly more necessary — if you get a little push. I got a big push. In March 1986, NBC News sent a vice president to Tokyo, where I was assigned as bureau chief and senior Asia correspondent, to tell me that when my contract with the network ended in June it would "not be renewed." That's network-speak for "You're fired," and it meant that my $205,000 annual salary had just disappeared. It was four days short of my 50th birthday, and the vice president who told me did not understand why I was not upset. I don't think he ever understood.

Dobyns still sees his NBC *Weekend* co-anchor, Linda Ellerbee, from time to time.

He probably never read the column that Lawrence Laurent, then the TV critic for the *Washington Post*, wrote about me in 1975, when I was close to the top of the NBC News heap. In it, Laurent quoted me as stating that "when all my children are educated, I will quit and write for a while." I modified that slightly, saying that would probably be when I turned 50. He made it clear that he did not believe me. No one ever did. I'm not sure I believed me, but I wanted to believe that I would have whatever it takes to walk away from a network salary and do what I wanted. The network made the decision easy; it walked the salary away from me. I did not try to get another television job — that much of the decision I did make. I was either going to write for a living or stop saying that I was a writer.

"In this world there are only two tragedies," Oscar Wilde wrote. "One is not getting what one wants, and the other is getting it." For the next six months, I drank too much, and on too many nights I woke up in the night, soaked with sweat, wondering whether I could support my wife and myself with written words. Even if it's what you want, being out of a steady job does something to your self-esteem. I had been raised to believe that only bums did not have a steady job. I did not even want one. Had I become a bum? Suppose I was wrong about how good a writer I was. Could I go back to television? I asked myself all the questions that I could not answer, then I asked them all again. Over and over.

I still ask them sometimes, but I don't wake up sweating in the wee hours anymore.

The transition was particularly difficult because I'd never done anything except television. I went to work at a small TV station in Virginia the day I graduated from Washington and Lee University in May 1957 with a bachelor's degree in journalism. Two things you should know: First, almost no one wanted to work in television news in those days; second, the only course I ever failed in my life was titled "The Motion Picture and Television." I wanted to be a writer, not a performer, but a newspaper offered me $67.50 a week, and the television station the paper owned offered $75. My whole career went like that. People kept telling me I wasn't qualified, then someone else would pay me to do it.

I went to New York in 1968 only because I had been fired at a station in Virginia. New owners wanted their own people. When I got to NBC News in 1969, I was hired in management because, I was assured, I did not have what it took to be a network correspondent. In those days, no one said, "Your nose is broken, you have acne scars, and there are gaps between your teeth." (One reviewer described me as "thug-faced," and she liked me.) I was the Paris bureau manager when the secret Vietnam peace talks between Henry Kissinger and Le Duc Tho surfaced. With no correspondent available, I went on the air to cover the peace talks. Every day for three months I found a way to say, "I haven't a clue what's happening," and made it sound as though you should care. I became a correspondent.

Impressed by my writing, the all-but-legendary NBC News producer Reuven Frank asked me to do a documentary with him. I didn't learn until later that David Brinkley, himself a classy writer, had refused to do it. Reuven couldn't have the network's best-known correspondent, so he'd take the least-known and succeed anyway. He did, although associates warned him that I wouldn't be able to handle an hour-long documentary.

Despite the success of the documentary, Reuven had to fight to get me as his writer and anchor for a news-magazine program he was developing. I might be able to luck out on a single documentary, said associates, but I couldn't handle a regular program. The same day in 1974 that I was assigned to anchor *Weekend* for Reuven, I got a polite rejection from the news director of WNBC, the network's flagship station in New York, saying that I was not qualified to anchor his local news. He was right. You don't need a writer to anchor local news.

When circumstances conspired in 1986 to turn me into a writer full-time, my wife, Patti, and I sold our apartment in Manhattan and moved to North Carolina so that Patti could live near her sister. It suited me. I hated New York, and no one cares where a writer lives. Our children were adults; the only one who still lived with us stayed in the city.

During the days following the sleepless nights, I started working on a book about Asia. (I had begun reporting from Asia in 1975, and the last of my nine documentaries on the network was *The Japan They Don't Talk About* in April 1986 — my last appearance on NBC.) I also began rewriting the partial manuscript of an adventure-thriller novel that I'd started in 1973, when I was a European correspondent in Paris. Neither book has been published; neither has been finished. A second career has delayed them, a career into which I stumbled almost as blindly as I had stumbled into my first.

Clare Crawford-Mason had been the Washington bureau chief for *Weekend* until the show was canceled in 1979. In the summer of 1980, Reuven Frank produced a documentary on productivity and the relative standards of living in the United States and Japan. Clare and the late Ray Lockhart were the two field producers, and I was the writer and narrator. Clare located W. Edwards Deming, the American who had taught the Japanese how to produce higher-quality, lower-cost consumer goods after World War II. She and I interviewed Deming, then 79 years old, and featured him in the documentary *If Japan Can . . . Why Can't We?* It was enormously successful in terms of

Although out of the limelight, Dobyns wakes up happy more mornings than not.

documentaries, and it won the prestigious duPont-Columbia award for excellence in TV journalism.

Sometimes excellence isn't enough. Clare was "not renewed" later that year and started her own production company. She stayed in touch with Dr. Deming, and in 1987 she agreed to put his quality-management method on videocassette to reach a wider audience. She called me, and we started working together on this project.

We learned a lot about quality management. Our first book, *Quality or Else: The Revolution in World Business* (Houghton Mifflin), was published in 1991; our second, *Thinking about Quality: Progress, Wisdom, and the Deming Philosophy* (Times Books), was published in 1994. There are 28 videocassettes in *The Deming Library* so far, and they are used by industry, government, educational and health-care institutions to teach quality management. One thing leads to another. We did three hour-long documentaries for PBS on the same subject. I make speeches to business groups, and this past academic year, I lectured on communications and quality three days a month at Jacksonville State University in Alabama.

I'm as well prepared for this career as I was for my first. The Deming quality-management system is partially based on statistical analysis and requires a solid understanding of economics. While I failed my only television course, I never even took a course in economics, and Washington and Lee would not allow me to study mathematics. I had no aptitude for it and still don't, but it's amazing what you can learn when there is no steady paycheck to rely on. You grab opportunities where you find them, and if it's not quite what you know, then you learn.

". . . it's amazing what you can learn when there is no steady paycheck to rely on."

I am not doing what I thought I'd do when I said I wanted to write. I meant fiction. I still mean fiction. But writing nonfiction that sells well is a marvelous tonic. When I was a network correspondent, people would sometimes ask me to autograph my picture. Now I'm asked to sign my book. I know which I prefer.

I am still asked if I don't miss what I used to do. How could I not miss network television, a fat paycheck and the big city? I was somebody—President Reagan quoted me at a White House conference, and a member of Congress put one of my scripts in the Congressional Record. I was even a clue in a national crossword puzzle! Fame, how could I not miss it? People I knew in New York assume that I live in Washington now; those in Washington assume that I am still in New York.

No one seems willing to accept that I live in Garner, North Carolina, and that I am happy here. My wife and I have 10 acres and no lawn. It's all trees and weeds and tall wild grass, and the raccoons, possums, foxes and deer love it as much as I do. I still travel, but not nearly as much as I once did. I worked in 47 states and 47 foreign countries, and I was an expert on airports and hotels. I eventually came to hate them all.

I miss the people. I worked with some of the best at NBC, but most of them have retired or died or been "not renewed." Most of all, I miss the daily conversations with Reuven Frank (retired) and Linda

Ellerbee ("not renewed"), my co-anchor on the last year of *Weekend* and on *NBC News Overnight*, which *Time* magazine called one of the 10 best television programs of any kind in 1982. We all worked well together and liked each other, which is not usual in a highly competitive, cutthroat business. I still see them from time to time. (Linda has her own production company, and we talk on the phone, but it's not the same. The us-against-them is gone. I miss Hurley's, one of the world's great bars, but that is probably because Linda and I drank there, and she doesn't drink now.)

The challenge of work I don't miss because I still have it. I still wonder every time I start a project whether this is the one on which I will fail and expose the fact that I am a complete fraud. I still feel the thrill when I don't fail. For a while now, I have awakened happy more mornings than not. I hadn't done that since 1979, when *Weekend* was killed. Part of the reason is that since then, I've made more money on my own at times than NBC paid me. George Herbert was right: Living well is the best revenge.

But I still wonder—if I hadn't been pushed, would I have had the courage or commitment to jump? I will never know. Could I have done it in another profession? What if I were a middle-level corporate manager caught in downsizing? Would I want to go out on my own and do something else, or would I try to find another steady job? If I hadn't had a 10-room New York apartment to sell, what would I have done for money? Gauguin quit as a stockbroker and went to Tahiti to paint; his idea, I guess, of running away to join the circus, but he left his wife and four children in poverty. I never wanted to run away to the television circus. That happened by accident. I did plan to run away from the circus, but in the end, that happened by accident as well.

So far, it has worked for me, but the important words in this sentence are "so far." I still want to write fiction. Happy or sad? I don't know yet, but probably happy. I love it when I smile in the morning. ■

Since writing this essay, Lloyd Dobyns has completed his novel. He now teaches journalism at Washington and Lee University.

Job Market Hiring Practices: The Good News

By Deborah Mason

Amid corporate downsizing and plant closings, employment specialist Shirley Brussell has spotted an astounding new trend. "What I see is more companies looking for older workers," she told me. Brussell is founder and executive director of Operation ABLE ("Ability Based on Long Experience"), a Chicago nonprofit senior-employment network (with affiliates nationwide) that lists more than 5,000 jobs—from editorial assistant to nursing-home administrator—yearly. "We've even seen companies get angry if you send over younger people!" said Brussell, 73. "Just last week a department store called, wanting older workers. One of the companies running riverboats on the Mississippi did the same. Both cited reliability and loyalty as the reason."

Brussell, who herself returned to the work force after 20 years, offered these tips to job-hunting seniors:

1. "Hang loose—be flexible. It's often a matter of timing. You could be told there's nothing and five minutes later something could open up!

2. "Be willing to be retrained. People are always surprised to find out how many strengths they have and how they translate into other areas.

3. "Think about going back to school, not for a master's or Ph.D. but just to brush up on computer courses, to at least 'learn the language' of the new technology so you won't be screened out for not knowing anything about it or not being willing to try.

4. "Consider starting as a temp or a volunteer. If you think you have the skill a company needs and want to show them, do it! Volunteering is how I got started again."

GET SLY—AND LIVE BETTER

A curmudgeon's crafty tips for easing through your middle years as comfortably as your average Rockefeller

By Larry L. King

Memo to any fearful folks soon turning 50: Relax. Don't take personally those televised no-physical-exam-required insurance ads pitched to citizens in "the 50-to-80 age group" by that old dude in the bad wig. At least the old dude found work, which should encourage us all.

My sermon today, friends, is that there are many things to look forward to other than senior-citizen discounts. Take it from this youngster of 64 years: Life not only goes on, it gets better every day—provided you accentuate the positive, as the old song from 1944 advised, and maybe lie or cheat a little.

Look on the bright side: You've already lived more years than Napoleon Bonaparte, most rock stars and many of your friends. Even the latter losses may be seen as a plus once you realize that few people survive who clearly recall your youthful follies. Bet you're feeling better already, right?

Opinion surveys reveal that man's—and woman's—greatest fear about aging centers on a loss of physical attributes. Piffle! Personally, I find it restful these days not to be so often mistaken for Robert Redford or pursued by stray blondes certain to disturb my blood pressure, to say nothing of the domestic tranquility. Are you getting the hang of this mature optimism I espouse?

From my own joyful experiences, I offer this advice: Be sly. Try to become known as an eccentric. Eccentrics can get away with everything from nudity to larceny because they are expected to be weird. Consider claiming dim vision even if you can read anything as small as my paycheck. This will permit you to ignore bores and signs warning against walking

on the grass or smoking in restricted areas.

Further, a loss of hearing isn't really a handicap in this age of heavy metal, rap or other random noises sounding like bus wrecks or cat fights and masquerading as music. But even if you bear the handicap of normal hearing, it can be profitable to fake hearing difficulties. Bellowing in an old codger's quaver or wheeze does wonders in discouraging those who telephone to collect bills, beg charity or sell you unwanted bargains. For face-to-face encounters, I recommend wearing a hearing aid whether or not you need it or turn it on; when faced with words you don't want to hear, talk loudly of irrelevant matters while claiming to be victimized by dead batteries.

Here is a serious warning: Three things clearly indicate approaching old age—or even its arrival. One is short-term-memory loss. The others are, uh, ah, well, heck, they were on the tip of my tongue just a minute ago. Anyway, cultivating a reputation among kith and kin for memory loss has its advantages: The phone rings; you pick it up and say in a quavery bellow, "Say you're my grandson? I'll be dogged! What's your name, boy? Where you live? How old are you?" This exhibition is guaranteed to short-circuit the kid's plan to hit you up for a $3,000 loan to buy a used car or found yet another rock band. The senior citizen who becomes adept at this strategy may even find himself relieved of the obligation to buy birthday presents.

If you truly suffer short-term-memory loss, don't worry about it: You'll soon forget you have the problem anyway. On the positive side, you are now able to hide your own Easter eggs.

Somehow, we seniors acquire a reputation for wisdom no matter how undeserved and often against the accumulated evidence of a lifetime. It is ever-so-satisfying to utter total nonsense and then watch your descendants wrinkle their brows in an effort to understand what they mistake for exotic philosophies or deep profundities. To double the effectiveness of this charade, curse contemptuously at those unable to comprehend your myriad complexities; the human ego being what it is, they will immediately profess to "understand."

And if you aspire to be treated better than you ever dreamed—and certainly better than you deserve—work at giving the impression of great, secret wealth. One easily discovered $50 gold piece wrapped in an old sock, a couple of hundred in greenbacks loosely hidden in a shoe box, a weathered "treasure map" drawn in your own hand, and a cultivated reputation for (1) parsimony and (2) a fear of being kidnapped for ransom should go a long way to guaranteeing that those who wish to be favorably remembered in your will rush to do your every bidding. This can make your retirement years almost as comfortable as those expected by your average Rockefeller. But there are many other helpful, morale-building things to keep in mind.

For example:

- The older you get, the more your furniture is worth.
- You have reached that stage in life when you aren't required to exercise anything but caution.
- You no longer have to ask permission to use the family car.
- Nobody can make you eat your veggies.
- You can't be drafted, no matter how many wars the politicians start.
- You don't have to fret about finding greener pastures, because even if you did, you'd have trouble climbing the fence.
- If you need a little extra income, you can threaten to talk to the newspapers as a person who is forced to subsist on cat food unless your grown children agree to pay hush money. Regularly. In cash.
- No matter what the mirror tells you, you are not really old: You have just been young for a very long time. ■

Larry L. King is the author of 12 books, including The Terrible Night Santa Got Lost in the Woods *and* Confessions of a White Racist; *7 plays, among them* The Best Little Whorehouse in Texas; *and assorted screenplays, television documentaries and magazine articles.*

NEW CAREER AT 50?

With the look of a southern belle and the toughness of a marine, Tillie went to Washington.

By Joanmarie Kalter

When Tillie Fowler, at 50, tells you how excited she is to be starting the "second half" of her life, she is kidding—but only sort of. One of her grandmothers lived to be 100 years old, she says, and the other died at 87, failing then only because she suffered a bad fall. Tillie herself has been blessed with good health, and no one who sees her practically sprint to the steps of the Capitol for a last-minute vote or leave her office at 8 P.M. carrying a sheaf of papers three inches thick could doubt her stamina.

In fact, she's so buoyant about beginning a new career as a member of the U.S. Congress that when asked to cite the pros and cons of being a freshman representative from Florida at the age of 50, she ticks off "experience," "maturity," "background," and then grows uncharacteristically silent. She can't come up with a single disadvantage. It seems that Tillie Fowler embodies a certain truth about the modern age: If, in the 1990s, women still can't "have it all," or not

all at once, they can certainly "have it all" in time.

"When you've had 50 years of background in a lot of different things," she says, her dark eyes glimmering with enthusiasm behind large-framed tortoiseshell glasses, "it brings another dimension to the type of representative you can be." Although soft-spoken and slight of stature, Tillie is so purposeful and self-assured that her words rush out almost faster than they can be taken in. "I always felt that I could be anything I wanted to be," she says, "as long as I was willing to work hard. And I'm willing. People say I have more energy than my young staff. They're all collapsing, and I'm still going strong."

Consider: Tillie (named for the grandmother who lived to be 87) grew up in Milledgeville, Georgia, and attended Emory University's law school in the days when there were only five women in her first-year class. Degree in hand, she motored up in her Nash Rambler to our nation's capital in 1967 and began a government career: first as a legislative aide to a Georgia congressman and then as general counsel in the Nixon administration's Office of Consumer Affairs.

Married by then to her law-school sweetheart and having reached the ripe old age of 29, Tillie wanted a family. So she and Buck Fowler moved down to his hometown of Jacksonville, Florida, where he joined his father's small manufacturing company and she gave birth to two daughters in less than two years. With children, Tillie didn't want to work full-time and was fortunate, she says, not to have to. Instead, she took up that time-honored tradition: volunteer work.

Through the years, she was president of the Junior League in Jacksonville, a member of the county's Public Education Foundation, chair of the state's Endowment for the Humanities —the list goes on. Finally, in 1985 she took a part-time paying job: She ran for and won a seat on the Jacksonville city council and four years later was elected its first woman president.

Politics came naturally: Her father served in the Georgia state legislature for 42 years, almost the whole of Tillie's life. But it was not until 1992 that she saw her own opportunity. Charles Bennett, who had represented her congressional district in Florida for 44 years —one of the longest tenures in the House of Representatives—had been considered unbeatable. But reapportionment had recently redrawn the district's boundaries. In addition, Bennett, a conservative Democratic member of the House Armed Services Committee, had opposed Desert Storm—this in a district with three navy bases and a port that serviced the Gulf War. So behind the scenes, Tillie, a Republican, did some research.

Although the district was 60 percent Democratic, she found that its voters had chosen Ronald Reagan and George Bush throughout the 1980s; she calculated that they'd vote Republican again if the right person came along. Quietly she approached Charlie Bennett's longtime supporters in the business community of Jacksonville and asked if they'd support her instead this time around. Many of them agreed. When her list of financial backers was released, so many of them were former supporters of Bennett's that he bowed out.

With the blessings of her family (her daughters were on the verge of leaving the nest for college and prep school), Tillie was ready to begin the campaign. Her Democratic challenger was state senator Mattox Hair—a man every bit as conservative as she. Although they did differ on some issues, Tillie's greatest asset was the help she received, in a new-style twist, from a kind of Old Girls' network.

In those early years in Washington, she had struck up a friendship with Elizabeth Hanford in the Office of Consumer Affairs. When Tillie's second daughter was born, she asked her friend to be godmother and named the baby Elizabeth. That old friend went on to marry Robert Dole, to become the influential-in-her-own-right Elizabeth Dole; Tillie's father, who calls himself her unofficial campaign adviser, says those Washington ties proved very helpful.

During her race, Tillie secured a commitment

from Republican leaders in Congress that, if she won, she'd be appointed to the House Armed Services Committee. It was an appointment that went a long way in her defense-dependent district. And it meant that, even with Charlie Bennett's withdrawal from Congress, his seat on that crucial committee would not be lost. On November 3, Tillie won, 56 to 44 percent.

"I would have been happy with 51 percent," she says. "I just wanted to win! But it was very gratifying," she adds, the triumph still in her voice, "that I carried every single one of my counties, all five of them."

What is a woman like who has spent the better part of her adult life raising children and now lands, at the age of 50, in the U.S. Capitol? "She is a born leader," says her proud old pal, Elizabeth Dole. Or, as *Working Woman* magazine put it, Tillie Fowler "looks and sounds like a diminutive Southern belle but can be as tough as an old Marine."

Calm and affable, Tillie nonetheless targets her goals and heads straight for them. "Her hallmark," says fellow Jacksonville councilwoman Ginny Myrick, "is that she does all this advance work. You never see her failures because she would never go public if something didn't work." Perhaps that's why, when asked if she expected victory, Tillie says evenly, "Oh yes! I would never have run if I didn't think I would win."

There is nothing stuffy about her. She carries herself more like another mother in the carpool than like a representative in the U.S. Congress. Rather than try to blend in with the sea of dark suits in Washington, she wears bright colors like kelly green or deep red. And there's something about her that immediately compels everyone to call her Tillie.

Don't ask, though, for any self-reflection from this doer. Her style is direct, even bold.

She carries herself more like another mother in the carpool than a representative in the U.S. Congress.

She admits, with a chuckle, that the following story is true: Sporting an anti-Clinton button at the president's State of the Union speech, she nonetheless walked right up to him, stuck out her hand and introduced herself. And in her first three months as representative, she co-sponsored no fewer than 60 bills—from one to improve the accuracy of the census to one including rape on the list of international war crimes.

Fowler is, of course, a woman in a man's world, and she knows it: Of 55 members of the House Armed Services Committee, only 5 are women. She has never chosen, in such circumstances, to be confrontational.

"We had some real good ol' boys on the [Jacksonville City] Council, and they may not have liked me," she says, laughing. "But if you don't wear your feelings on your shoulder, if you're prepared and informed, and not babbling away, men respect you—maybe grudgingly, but they do respect you."

Although her position on most issues is bedrock conservative—she opposes tax increases, favors cutting the capital-gains tax, champions military spending in her district—she has joined the Congressional Caucus for Women's Issues and supports such concerns as codifying *Roe* v. *Wade*, applying sexual-harassment policies to Congress, boosting Head Start funds and increasing funding for research on breast cancer. Still, such solidarity goes just so far: At a reception last spring in honor of another female freshman, when decidedly liberal Democratic representative Pat Schroeder buzzed by, Tillie publicly smiled at her, then privately groaned, "If that thing is still running," she said, nodding at a reporter's tape recorder, "I'll be quiet!"

Moments later, she was urging her staffers to take home the uneaten remains of the fruit-and-cheese platter that she contributed to the reception. "She's not only our boss," said one aide, "she's our mother."

Of course, even motherhood was never quite this hectic. Tillie's new career keeps her busy most days from 8 A.M. to 10:30 P.M. If she gets back to her apartment earlier, she probably has a tall stack of constituents' letters to read.

She crams all her work in Washington into three days, generally flying home on Thursday night and returning to the capital on Monday night. The other days, she works from her district office in Florida. ("A day off?" she asks, trying to remember when last she had one.) With this schedule, her husband can stay home, tending to his business in Jacksonville. ("I think he enjoys the peace and quiet," she says. "He can sit and read a book, and it's just him and the dog.") She also makes sure to be home, whenever possible, for her daughters' school vacations.

What advice does Tillie have for people contemplating a career change at 50? She relishes the question and is characteristically straightforward in her response: "Go for it!" she says with delight. And then, like the very model of a good-and-tough mom, she wags her finger and adds: "If you don't challenge yourself, you know, you just don't grow."

Are You Stress-Resistant?

By Myrna Lewis

How do you manage your stress? Take this quiz to measure your ability to cope, based on your feelings about life, work and risk taking.

Score 0 if the statement is definitely not true for you; 1 if it is usually not true; 2 if it is somewhat true; 3 if it is definitely true.

1. ____ **When I work hard, it makes a difference.**
2. ____ **Getting out of bed in the morning is easy for me.**
3. ____ **I have the freedom I want and need.**
4. ____ **At times I've sacrificed for an exciting opportunity.**
5. ____ **Sticking to my routine is not important to me.**
6. ____ **I vote because I think it makes a difference.**
7. ____ **You make your own lucky breaks.**
8. ____ **I agree with the goals of my boss and my company.**
9. ____ **I've been "lucky in love" because I try to be a loving person.**
10. ____ **I believe I get what I give. But I don't "keep score."**
11. ____ **It's important for me to try new things.**
12. ____ **Free time is a gift I really enjoy.**
13. ____ **Growing older doesn't stop me from striving to reach my goals.**
14. ____ **My family is a great pleasure to me.**
15. ____ **I speak up for what I believe in.**

Add your scores for # 1, 6, 7, 9, 13. This is your stress-management score. The higher it is, the more control you feel you have over your own life, and the better you are able to manage stress. **TOTAL** _____

Add your scores for # 2, 3, 8, 10, 14. This is your commitment score. The higher it is, the more you are committed to and the more you enjoy your life. **TOTAL** _____

Add your scores for # 4, 5, 11, 12, 15. This is your risk score. The higher it is, the more willing you are to take risks. **TOTAL** _____

Add all three scores together. This is your stress-resistance score. **TOTAL** _____

If you score 35 or above: Congratulations—your attitudes make you very resistant to stress.

27 to 34: You are somewhat resistant but could be more so; look at each item and choose a few to work on.

18 to 26: You need to examine your habits and attitudes to improve your resistance to stress; go through the statements above, and pick one to improve each month.

Under 18: If stresses get serious, you could be in trouble. Take time now to change your habits and attitudes. You may want to ask a professional counselor for ways to feel more positive about yourself.

ROSY DREAMS VS. HARSH TRUTHS:

Do your values change after 50? A famed author, at 78, reflects on his lifelong battle to cling to his idealism.

By Budd Schulberg

I confess that I find myself somewhat shocked — and I am not sure whether I'm boasting or confessing — to discover near the end of these fourscore years that my values have changed little from youth to maturity. Those values may have been buffeted about by the winds of change: the Depression '30s, the postwar '40s, the stolid '50s, the rebellious '60s, the Vietnam- and Watergate-guilty '70s, the Boesky & Milken '80s, and our troubled Where-do-we-go-from-here? '90's. But, looking back, I realize that while the specific politics I once fervently believed in had to be jettisoned when harsh truths caught up with rosy dreams, still there's a core of idealism I cling to.

Even before the crash of '29, *underdog* had become a shibboleth in my family. My father, B.P. Schulberg, a pioneering Hollywood producer, was running Paramount studios when I was at L.A. High. My mother, Ad, was one of filmdom's leading hostesses, celebrated for parties that brought together the most famous stars, directors and writers of her day. But more was going on than anyone reading the fan magazines would have believed. Mother was also a women's rights advocate; she helped start a home for unwed mothers; she represented Margaret Sanger and the pioneer Planned Parenthood movement in southern California; she knew educator John Dewey and was a founder of Hollywood's first progressive school. She championed Judge Ben Lindsey when he was driven out of the judicial system for suggesting that unwed couples should cohabit before marriage — "companionate [or trial] marriage," as he called it. Theodore Dreiser, radical-minded icon of American literature, came to dinner. And so did Lincoln Steffens, whose autobiography had become an instant bestseller and whose visit to Soviet Russia inspired the clarion call "I have seen the future and it works."

Poor Steffie. Through the most beclouded of crystal balls, he found the young Communist movement on the side of the angels — somehow,

Marxist slogans were bathed in Christian piety: "And the last shall be first." Not Lubianka and gulags but a bright future for the human race is what he thought he saw. One after another they came to our dining-room table, these men of goodwill, and built their case for the dawn of the underdog. In some way, Stalin's five-year plans and FDR's New Deal, if not interchangeable, were flags flying in the same winds of change: the Common Man, throwing off the chains of Russian czars and American "economic royalists."

No one in our family had read a page of Marx's *Das Kapital*, but it didn't really matter. In the rosy if hazy, optimistic glow on the Schulberg hearth, not Doug Fairbanks or Charlie Chaplin but the underdog was the real star of the moment. My old man, a maverick in the tight little world of Hollywood tycoons and an Al Smith Democrat who voted for Roosevelt, welcomed the New Deal as a lifeline for "the little guy," an inevitable step in our forward march toward the far horizon of world peace and an end to man's inhumanity to man.

As I went off to college, underdogism became a guiding principle. At football games I rooted for the smaller "eleven" against the two-touchdown bullies. At prizefights, when beery-faced bigots were shouting racial epithets, I rooted for black boxers.

There were other family values: the work ethic my mother established, a love for books both parents inspired as an antidote to Hollywood's narcissism, and an early education in the roller coaster of American success, as seen in the constant rise and fall of great movie stars, so famous today, so forgotten tomorrow.

But even as I was coached by my father and pushed by my mother to work, write and achieve, underdogism remained a given, neither grown more intense nor slackened from 18 to 78. In my experience, one's character—the grand total of all one's values—doesn't change from youth to old age.

In my 20s I accepted the cliché that the young are more open and tolerant and that rigidity, ultraconservatism and intolerance are inevitable expressions of septuagenarians. By the time I was tapped for membership in the Old Boys' Club, I had come to realize that youth had no corner on the sweet flow of permissiveness.

It's less a question of age than of mental disposition. The years hardly dulled the sharp pen of George Bernard Shaw, who challenged sacred cows into his 90s. So, too, Upton Sinclair, who held forth on his social theories at our dining-room table and whose muckraking novel *The Jungle* (1906) raked so much muck that the Chicago meat-packing industry would never be the same. Sixty-one years later, Sinclair had the satisfaction of being invited to the White House for LBJ's signing of the Wholesale Meat Act of 1967. Old generals may fade away, but old crusaders seem to march under flags of social justice right into the grave.

Sinclair wrote his great book when he was still in his 20s. So did I when I wrote *What Makes Sammy Run?*, a novel about an amoral young hustler who claws his way to a major studio power, which made me as popular in Hollywood as Sinclair had been in Chicago. When I sent the manuscript to my father, he was greatly impressed, he wrote. But as a father, he advised me not to publish it. It would infuriate the Hollywood moguls, who would see themselves in Sammy Glick and the book as a stab in the back by a native son.

"Since this book shows you can write, I'd put it aside and start another one. Then, if that clicks, it'll be safer to publish *Sammy*. Otherwise, how will you live? You know Louie Mayer. All he has to do is pass the word along, and you'll never work in this town again."

How will I live? I had a young wife and a one-year-old daughter. I felt a responsibility to them, but I also felt a responsibility to the aesthetic values my parents had inculcated in me. Father had read out loud to us such uncompromising authors as Mark Twain, Nathaniel Hawthorne, Frank Norris and Theodore Dreiser, and in my young adulthood I had devoured John Steinbeck, James T. Farrell, Erskine Caldwell and the plays of Clifford Odets. "If I don't publish this book," I wrote back to B.P., "I'll never have the heart to write another. I've got to take my chances."

When the novel was republished on its 50th anniversary, I recalled that decision. The wrath of L. B. Mayer had come down on me, just as my father had warned. Indeed, he had actually thundered to the Motion Picture Producers Association that I "should be deported!" But I was saved by the success of the book, a runaway bestseller that paved the way for the books to come.

A handy test for the longevity of our connections is the college class reunion, which I attend every five years both for the camaraderie and because the writer in me keeps his antennae out for the effect of time on the ideas and lives of my classmates. I reminisce with hundreds of fellow Dartmouth '36ers but make it a point to seek out a particular three. They were among the brightest in the class. They also reflected intriguingly different points of view.

I was the radical editor of the daily paper. I hadn't left much room to the left of me. But Dan managed to slip in there. At the top of our class academically, he was quick minded, if somewhat rigid and politically puritanical. Joe, equally quick-minded and gifted with wit, was a pragmatist who kept his ideals in check, never abandoning them but also never wasting his time on hopeless causes, no matter how worthy. He became an influential advisor to his state's Democratic party.

The third member of the disparate foursome was Dick—handsome, earnest, ethical, a moderate Republican. As the business manager of our paper, he never questioned my editorial integrity, even when sharply disagreeing with me. We all respected one another's views, and over the years, our differences have been reflected in banter rather than in acrimony. Mutual respect is the key to our four-way bonding.

At these catch-ups, I'm astonished and reassured to find that all four of us remain essentially what we were as undergraduates. As we run down the front-page issues of our day, our reactions could have been predicted from the stands we took back in 1936.

Our 30th reunion fell on the first anniversary of the Watts riots. I had gone to Watts, and eventually I would spend more and more time there as a founder of the Watts Writers Workshop, which started with a handful of young street poets. It would grow to several hundred over the next few years, transforming a burned-out supermarket into classrooms and a theater.

It wasn't easy to explain to some of my Hollywood friends what would impel me to go to Watts when racial tension was at the top of the fever chart. But Dan, Joe and Dick only teased me about it. They said that as soon as they saw it happening on television, they expected me to show up. Not that I was a hero. Something just drove me, a craving I had to satisfy in spite of my fear.

In our undergraduate days there had been a bitter marble-workers union strike in Vermont, and I had gone there to describe it for our paper, then organized campus support for the marble workers and got myself in trouble with the state troopers. Sounds heroic, but I was scared as hell. And my classmates, knowing my nature, teased me for the counterpoint of courage and cowardice that has tug-of-warred in me from blond-haired sprinter to white-haired marathoner.

Budd, you're not trying to tell us there's been no change in your values, your ideas, your behavior in 60 years? No. Since I began this testimonial with a confession, let me close with one. Through my professional successes and failures, personal happiness and family tragedies, "good" wars, cold wars, bad wars and anxious periods of peace, I feel unchanged inside—but with this admission: In my youth a cock-eyed optimist, in my young maturity a more cautious optimist, I no longer keep the faith that a new and better day's abornin'. Scourges that were unknown a generation ago—drugs, AIDS, pollution—are added to the old sores still infecting the body politic. I bleed with the children struck down by snipers fighting their unholy war for "ethnic cleansing." A cold war mercifully ends, but a hundred hot and nasty little ones break out all over the globe.

"If you do it to the least of mine," Christ said, "you do it to Me." On the evening news I watch "them" doing it to the least without end. Having entered this world with the outbreak of World War I at Sarajevo, can you blame me for asking what all our technological progress avails us if we cannot cope with the ethnic madness of Sarajevo '92?

I no longer see rosy solutions to our problems. I see us staggering, bleeding, reeling, into the 21st century. It is farewell to utopia and the lofty dreams espoused when I was growing up in Hollywood.

But instead of surrendering to despair, I am inspired by the example of my late wife, actress Geraldine Brooks. When she knew she was dying of cancer and would not reach the age of 52, she planted a new garden. She accepted a part in a film. She got through a summer singing *Fiddler on the Roof.* Among the posters of her films on the wall of my study is a saying that expresses her passion for life: "If I knew I was going to die tomorrow, I would go out and plant trees today."

Amen. That is the antidote to my latter-day pessimism. Acknowledge it, but don't wallow in it. Since we don't *know* the world is going to die tomorrow, our choice is simply to push on and plant those trees today. ■

Budd Schulberg is the author of many books and screenplays, including On the Waterfront *and* Moving Pictures: Memories of a Hollywood Prince.

How Do Your Family Values Measure Up?

By Myrna Lewis

Ever since "family values" became a buzz phrase, politicians, religious leaders, TV pundits and people at large have been debating what Americans believe them to be and whether these same people behave accordingly. To help determine how you stand on the issue, here is a survey devised by researchers Charlotte Muller, Ph.D., and Catherine B. Silver, Ph.D., of the International Longevity Center at the Mount Sinai Medical Center in New York, and Louis Harris Associates.

Read each statement below and indicate how strongly you agree or disagree. Since this exercise is about values, there are no "right" responses. But you can compare your answers with those of 1,500 survey participants in the grid that follows to see how "mainstream" your views are.

VALUES SURVEY	AGREE	AGREE SOMEWHAT	DISAGREE SOMEWHAT	DISAGREE
1. Life without children is empty.				
2. Older people should be respected primarily because of their age.				
3. Breaking a promise to a family member is acceptable when one's job requires it.				
4. One can succeed by trying very hard and having a little bit of luck.				
5. If you have money, almost everything will go your way.				
6. You should honestly say what you think, even if it means hurting another person.				
7. One must never forget the kindness received from others.				
8. A person should not resort to a means he or she knows is wrong even though it will lead to success.				
9. I can't trust someone who does not believe in God.				
10. I am proud of being an American.				
11. One should actively participate in local activities and functions.				
12. One should actively sacrifice some of one's lifestyle for the sake of society.				

HOW 1,500 OTHERS RESPONDED

	AGREE	AGREE SOMEWHAT	DISAGREE SOMEWHAT	DISAGREE		AGREE	AGREE SOMEWHAT	DISAGREE SOMEWHAT	DISAGREE
1.	61.5%	21.2%	6.9%	5.6%	7.	82.6%	15.6%	1.0%	0.2%
2.	36.5	37.7	12.4	7.5	8.	70.5	19.2	4.5	3.2
3.	29.9	38.5	17.1	9.0	9.	3.6	7.1	24.5	56.6
4.	34.6	34.4	16.3	9.6	10.	63.6	26.2	4.3	2.0
5.	14.3	25.5	26.4	30.3	11.	34.5	48.3	8.4	3.4
6.	19.4	25.0	30.0	19.7	12.	13.2	36.1	27.5	14.3

WHAT WE BELIEVE

Over-50s express strong feelings about health care, sexual permissiveness, money problems and more.

By Jon Robert Steinberg

Call them the generation of paradox. Energetic, proud of their achievements and optimistic about their personal futures, post-50 Americans look forward to retirement and feel positive about getting older. At the same time, they're pessimistic about the future of their country. Age, income, gender and employment status make little difference in their attitudes. In this generation, the gap between personal and social outlooks runs through every issue:

- Overwhelmingly, they like their own doctors but worry about the cost of medical care.
- They're watching more television but complain that TV and movie sex is polluting the airwaves.
- They're passionately concerned about current events, volunteer in their community and help relatives in need but think the country as a whole has grown hard, crime-ridden and prejudiced against older Americans.

These are some of the findings that emerged in a survey of 750 people, a representative national sample of 50- to 70-year-olds, conducted for *New Choices* by National Family Opinion, Inc. This group of 45 million Americans represents a potent commercial and political force. Here's more about what they believe and want.

Health Care.
Respondents have more confidence in their doctors than in hospitals. Eighty-one percent agree that their doctors provide excellent care, while only 69 percent say the same about hospitals. Nearly all say that the cost of care is excessive: 86 percent say that doctors' bills are too high, and 92 percent fault hospitals for overcharging. Only 66 percent agree that their "medical coverage is satisfactory."

They're also worried about long-term care. Fewer than half believe that nursing homes provide adequate accommodations and service. When asked what the federal government should do about nursing homes, "Provide more funding and set standards for enforcement" was their typical response.

Even when confronting increased debilitation or final exits, this generation remains practical and independent. For example, 81 percent agree with the statement "I should have the right to decide when to die" if confronting an existence dependent on life-support equipment.

Employment.
Although only 23 percent plan to go on working for as long as they can, our respondents don't want to be told when to retire. Fifty-five percent oppose a mandatory retirement age set by employers. Three-quarters agree that "people over 50 are discriminated against in the workplace." And they want something done about it: Four in five agree that "laws should be stronger to prevent age discrimination." Women advocate stronger laws more often than men, perhaps because they started (or returned to) work later or because they have experienced both age and sex discrimination.

Finances.
More than half (56 percent) say they have more money now that their children are out of the house. That same percentage travels more than ever before. But slightly less than half (47 percent) feel they are

better off financially than at any other time in their lives. Even fewer (40 percent) expect to maintain their current standard of living after retiring. More than a third feel less secure about their personal economic prospects. And only 20 percent think that Social Security gives them "satisfactory protection." (Among people with household incomes of $25,000 or less—those who rely on Social Security the most—satisfaction with the system is highest. That confidence is also higher among people in their 60s.)

These 50- to 70-year-olds look forward to retirement. About 7 in 10 agree that "[I have] worked hard all my life, so I deserve to retire." Their pragmatism and eagerness to reap delayed rewards show up in their response to the statement: "Parents have an obligation to leave as much money as they can to their children to give them a better start in life." Six out of 10 disagree. Those in their 50s are more reluctant to finance their offspring to the limit of their ability than those in their 60s, perhaps because they feel more financial burdens and uncertainties. People in the middle-income level, ($25,000–$49,999) are least willing to help their offspring by leaving as large an estate as possible.

Social Values.

Are Americans "kinder and gentler" than they were a decade ago? Almost 7 out of 10 respondents say no. The same proportion thinks our overall values have been going

downhill. When asked whether workers in America have become lazier, 60 percent agreed.

They're also concerned about sexual mores: Only 12 percent are happy with the more open treatment of sex on television and in movies. (Disapproval is greatest in smaller towns.) More than half (52 percent) say their attitudes about sex are not more permissive than 10 years ago. Specifically, 63 percent don't believe in premarital sex, and 83 percent say that they don't believe in sex outside of marriage. Slightly more than one in three never-marrieds, both women and men, believe in premarital sex, as compared to one in six married individuals.

Religion is important or very important in the lives of 90 percent of the post-50 generation. As we will see, this spiritual outlook is reflected in a strict sexual morality and a sense of responsibility for relatives and neighbors.

Media.
Keeping up with current events is almost an obsession with this age group: Ninety percent say the daily news is important in their lives; nearly half credit TV as their primary source. Many (47 percent) are also reading more books.

Although half report watching more TV than ever, the 50-plus generation is critical of what media moguls are feeding it. These people weren't born yesterday and know a stereotype when they see it. Sixty-three percent say that the media do not "give an honest picture of over-50s today."

The Environment.
People in the 50 to 70 age group are not usually identified with environmentalism, but our respondents prove otherwise. More than four out of five are convinced that Americans aren't doing enough to protect nature, and three out of four favor stronger environmental legislation. Seventy-two percent say they are recycling more than they were 10 years ago, and 10 percent have stepped up their participation in environmental groups or causes.

Crime.
We aren't as safe from lawbreakers as we used to be, say 9 out of 10 respondents. In keeping with their belief that Americans have grown harder, half say that we're less likely to look after the safety of neighbors. But this sense of heightened callousness does not dampen their own concern. About 12 percent say they are taking a more active part in local civic issues, and 17 percent are voting in more elections.

Self-image.
Most of these 50-plus Americans are happier now than they've ever been and say that their lives are turning out pretty much as they had planned. This is particularly the case among older respondents, who are saddled with fewer work and family responsibilities.

More than half reject the notion that they're lonelier now that they're older. (Not surprisingly, married people are less likely to feel lonely.) And when asked whether life was easier when they were younger, our respondents are about evenly split.

They know their limitations, more often disagreeing than agreeing with the statement "Physically I feel I can do just as many things now as I did when I was younger." Yet the members of this generation, born and toughened in the Great Depression and World War II, know how to get the most out of their lives. For 66 percent, personal satisfaction includes having meaningful goals, while 73 percent say they go out of their way to learn new things.

Families.
How do they rate the quality of their family life? Good or excellent, say four out of five respondents. Only 2 percent rate it as poor. Married people and those in the higher income brackets (over $50,000) are most likely to say they have a happy home.

A positive outlook about their family situation coexists with our respondents' continuing involvement in the physical and/or financial care of close relatives. Sixteen percent report that they are caring for a parent, another 16 percent are providing care for a child over age 18, and 12 percent care for a grandchild.

Shouldering this responsibility isn't easy. Among those providing physical care for elderly parents, 47 percent consider their efforts a major burden.

The Community.
This is a generation with a passion for following current events, and knowing what's going on isn't just a matter of idle curiosity. These people act on what they learn. An impressive 48 percent write to elected officials about issues; an extraordinary 58 percent do volunteer work. Half are members of at least one fraternal, religious, civic or other group.

From the time when Puritan leader John Winthrop envisioned founding a "city upon a hill," belief in God and a sense of community responsibility have gone hand in hand. More than 150 years ago, Alexis de Tocqueville observed that the chief bulwark of American democracy was our enthusiasm for participating in myriad groups and associations. Our respondents' generation continues these traditions. And when a group of people constituting almost one-third of all voters and collectively worth more than $500 billion wants something done, chances are they will eventually be heard.

Self-reliant yet open to government intervention, independent yet community-minded, Americans between 50 and 70 years old could be the great untapped force in national politics. Candidates, take note!

Jon Robert Steinberg is a senior editor at New Choices *magazine.*

Do You Make a Difference in Your Community?

By Myrna Lewis

The desire to pass on knowledge or skills to the next generation; trying to better one's community; being concerned about having an impact on others and leaving an enduring legacy — taken together, these impulses are known as "generativity." According to some researchers, people in midlife are more strongly guided by a desire to achieve so-called generative ends than any other age group.

"Generativity motivates us to make commitments to the community and help to improve the environment in which we live," says Dan P. McAdams, Ph.D, professor of human development, social policy and psychology at Northwestern University in Evanston, Illinois. "But it also makes us feel good about ourselves."

The quiz that follows, adapted from the Loyola Generativity Scale, can measure your generativity. Indicate how often each statement applies to you by using the point scale below.

0 = never; 1 = sometimes; 2 = usually; 3 = always.

1. **I try to pass along the knowledge I have gained through my experience. ____**
2. **I feel as though I have made a difference to many people. ____**
3. **I have made an impact and have created things that have had an impact on other people. ____**
4. **Others say that I make unique contributions to society. ____**
5. **I have important skills that I try to teach others. ____**
6. **I have made commitments to many different kinds of people, groups and activities in my life. ____**
7. **I am responsible for improving my neighborhood. ____**
8. **People come to me for advice. ____**

SCORING GUIDE: Add the numbers of your responses.
0 to 7 = low; 8 to 15 = average;
16 to 24 = high generativity.

If you scored high, congratulations! On the other hand, if you scored low on the generativity scale, here are a few reasons why:

You may score low if you feel stuck in life or preoccupied with yourself or your problems. In addition, many of us have a tendency to underestimate our own value, feeling that contributions need to be grand to be worth something. In fact, even humble actions — the little things you do each day to help others out — are worthy acts of generativity.

McAdams says that two basic ingredients are needed to improve your generativity: "One, you need to believe that humankind is worth contributing to, and two, you need to believe that if you do your own part, you will help make the world better."

Five things (almost)

MORE IMPORTANT THAN SEX

By Dr. Ruth Westheimer

For more than 10 years she has been one of America's most popular authorities on intimate relations, but there's much more to Dr. Ruth Westheimer than sex.

Her most recent books, The Value of Family *(Warner Books) and* Dr. Ruth Talks About Grandparents: Advice for Kids on Making the Most of a Special Relationship *(Farrar, Straus & Giroux), tackle some of the issues affecting people today. In the following article, Dr. Ruth admits that sometimes even sex can take a backseat to other concerns.*

I'm not obsessed with sex. Yet when people hear about my new show, which deals with a variety of topics, they ask me, "But Dr. Ruth, isn't sex the most important thing in life? If it's not, what is more important than sex?"

As a student of human beings and what makes us feel good, I find it difficult to make comparisons among life's activities. For one person, a walk in the woods may be more important than good sex; for another, it may be something else. But I *can* tell you five things that are right up there with sex—and for many people they may be more important. For me, they have been so important that I think I could not have become the person I am without them, nor can I do without them now.

My parents died in the Holocaust; I lived for the time when I would grow up and be able to help others.

1. Energy

This may be the most important thing in my life. From the time I lived in an orphanage in Switzerland, beginning when I was 10 years old and on through my late teens, my teachers were always impressed with my energy. They said I was smart and fast and talked a lot. Especially that I talked a lot. I'm still the same way.

I don't know where my energy comes from. Maybe my genes. Maybe because my body is so small and compact, it can provide me with the extra energy that other people need just to keep their bigger bodies going. I don't know. But my energy, and the *joie de vivre* that energy gives me, has carried me from a poor and lonely childhood to success beyond even my wildest dreams.

The other night I was in a very famous, very expensive restaurant in New York City—me, little Karola Siegel (my old German name), sitting right next to former secretary of state Henry Kissinger! But even though I had to sit on a pillow to bring him to my level, I was looking him straight in the eye and talking with him. And I didn't even have to pay for the meal. I like that, not because I can't afford to pay for anything I want but because it tells me that my energy and my gift for talking are working to give me influence with the people around me. That's very important because of my next point.

2. Helping Others

I have mentioned that I grew up in a Swiss orphanage. My parents died in the Holocaust, you see, and as soon as I got to the orphanage, I lived for the time when I would grow up and be able to help other people.

My ambition for much of my early life was to be a kindergarten teacher. I did some teaching in Switzerland, then later in a kibbutz in Israel and eventually in the United States as well. Indeed, many of us refugees from World War II went into the helping professions.

Today I do a great deal of community work and fund-raising for dozens of organizations. My activities range from the presidency of my local YW/YMHA in New York City's Washington Heights to being on the board of directors of a new employees' child-care center at John F. Kennedy Airport. I like to tell people, "If you help me on any of my projects, you will have a good sex life!" They laugh, but they also respond.

The Y is a special favorite. It was there for me when I needed it years ago—both my children went to this one. It was cheap and good and well supervised. My daughter Miriam says that going there helped inspire her to go into education. And now I can give back something of what I got to the community—all the new Russian Jews, Dominicans, Chinese and African-Americans who are my neighbors.

3. Making Friends, Keeping Friends, Using Friends

You can't get anywhere or accomplish anything in life without friends. I learned that, too, in the orphanage, and I'm still in touch with many of the people I met there. They helped me, and I have helped them.

When I first came to the United States, I had to make new friends, so even with a tiny apartment and very little money I threw parties and served potato chips and coffee. With the friends I made, I got help with babysitting, learning English, getting work and so on. I was not exploiting them—we did for each other. But even if you exploit friends, as long as you're willing to help them in return, that is not bad. I always attend parties, family affairs, any occasion where my friends—even from 30 or 35 years ago—want me to be. And making friends is not just for the young. It's important for all of us.

4. A Place to Be

Today we are all very much concerned with shelter, when so many people in our country are homeless. But we must also understand that shelter is not only a roof over our heads. More important, it's also the feeling that one is being taken care of psychologically and emotionally, being cared for and cared about. It's loving friends, family, a shared history.

On May 25, 1991, I was watching the news on television and saw the exodus of the Ethiopian Jews en masse — some 14,000 being brought to Israel in one weekend. I was flooded with emotions and memories of my own life as a refugee. I was moved to do something about this extraordinary event, this wonderful act of courage. And so some friends and I began to raise money and eventually made a documentary film called *Surviving Salvation*. It tells the story of a people who left their 16th-century culture to enter the 20th century in a new land because that is where they felt they belonged. Today they are striving to feel emotionally and psychologically at home—sheltered, as we all must be.

5. Freedom, the Ultimate Necessity

If anything is more important than sex, it is freedom. It is being able to live where you want to, not to have to ask permission to do the kind of work you want to do, being able to practice your own religion. To be able to walk among your fellow human beings without bending your head to anyone.

In large part we have that in the United States, but there are still too many of us who are not truly free, who are not living fully according to the American ideal. But even with our racial turmoil, our problems with poverty, unemployment and so forth, none of us can forget we are free—we can make things better, if we use our enormous energy to help each other. I hope we will do that. ■

. . . and 10 Important Things You Should Know about Sex

Now that I have told you what I think could be more important than sex, please do not get the idea that I have forgotten sex. Here is some advice for us middle-aged people:

1. No matter what you think, you can do it. It may be a little different than it used to be, but it is still sex.

2. It is important to take your time. Don't rush into it. If you are feeling a little pooped by evening, don't think about doing it tonight—wait till morning, when you are refreshed.

3. If you were athletically inclined toward different positions when you were young, you need to ease up now and stick to the easier positions. Even if your head hasn't changed, your body has.

4. For men only: As you get older, simply thinking about sex may no longer make your blood run to where it should be. And sometimes even such things as looking at erotic pictures won't help. What will help is touching the penis. Either you do it, or your mate does it for you. Or you do it together—that kind of touching usually works.

5. Touching the whole body is important for both of you. If you never did it, do it now. Massage each other—not hard, but erotically, caressingly.

6. When you touch like that, you must do it *for* each other, not *to* each other. And I advise you not to do it for each other at the same time. Please him one day, for instance, and the next day please her.

7. Masturbation is all right both for relieving your frustration and for keeping your sexual organs healthy and active when you don't have access to sex with a partner.

8. Don't be embarrassed to use a vibrator to satisfy yourself or your partner. I know this is a delicate subject, but we do need to help ourselves sometimes.

9. Do not take your anger, disappointments and frustrations into the bedroom with you. To have good sex at any age, you need to feel good. And if you feel good, sex will make you feel even better.

10. Of course, to do anything well, we need to be healthy. So take care of yourself, physically and mentally.

—R.W.

TRUTH OR CONSEQUENCES

What happened when the author tried telling only the truth for 72 hours

By Jeremy Larner

I thought it would be easy: merely to tell the truth for three days. A breeze for a guy like myself, who at 56 has learned to say what he means, no longer trembling with the youthful need to impress or the belief that his secret truths, if unleashed, would shake loose tidal waves of embarrassment and retaliation. The danger, I thought, was the triviality of the truth telling required in my humdrum daily routine — Did you remember to mail the check? Talk to the dentist? Who let the dog in/left the water on/ate the ice cream? To raise the pressure, I chose three days toward the end of my vacation, when I knew that my wife and I would be a bit uptight at the thought of heading back to the world of desks and clocks, petty arrangements and responsibilities.

But first, what did I mean by truth? That, too, seemed simple enough. I'd take truth as the absence of lying, and lying as an attempt to mislead, even when one's words are literally true — or when one lies from good intentions ("Honey, you're the brightest and most beautiful person in the Grand Canyon").

So as August runs out on Martha's Vineyard, I blithely start Day One of the truth test. And start again. After five days, I'm beginning to realize how automatically one lies in response to daily rhetoric. "Don't you just love the heat?" "Doesn't Uncle Ralph make a great fish-organ stew?" "Are you sure you don't mind the kids coming through at night to use the bathroom?" Ever genial, I say sure, sure, and my daily record of consecutive truth telling snaps as irrevocably as a called third strike.

The truth is, there's too damn many friends and relatives sharing one old summer house. With thin walls and people in every room, we're too crowded to make waves, or even grouchy little wavelets. I'm afraid (and my wife, knowing me, is even more afraid) that if I permit myself to murmur that the kids are a trifle noisy, the teenage rap songs are inflaming my psoriasis, or the chewing gum in my laptop computer is somewhat inconvenient, I'll lose it totally and begin to rant and rave.

So I decide to start my three days on the afternoon we leave. But even then, as we dress and load the car, three little lies pop out of me in reply to three ordinary questions. "Did you remember that the garbage gets separated into five categories before you took it to the dump?" "Did my mother say to call back?" "Isn't it amazing that the president rode the sister of the same horse I rode three days before?"

It seems that all I'm accomplishing with my inner Truth Alert is to catch my lies after I tell them. I sound just like a kind of person who has always annoyed me — the guy who takes a ponderous pause before he answers anything. Is he considering how to tell the truth, how to lie, or simply how to control the slightest outbreak of spontaneity?

"Is something on your mind?" my wife asks, as I sit staring behind the wheel while a red light clicks to green. "No, Honey," I reply automatically. I have to install some automatic block, or my experiment will never get off the ground. So, by counting to 10 before answering any question, I manage to get through that night truthfully.

Twenty grim hours of the truth finds me driving down Interstate 95 to New York, desperate to collect some books and lock myself in my bathroom until the three days are up. Alas, a siren sounds, my adrenaline surges, and I begin to immerse myself in a role of rueful innocence that has not prevented a traffic ticket since 1958. But while the officer does his John Wayne stroll to my car, I collect myself. I'll give him an overwhelming dose of truthfulness.

COP: Got any idea how fast you were going?
JL: [in tones sad and subdued throughout] Yes, I do.
COP: Well?
JL: About 67 miles an hour.
COP: Right on! [getting angrier] So why the hell didn't you slow down?
JL: I was in a hurry.
COP: Were you now?
JL: Besides, I saw no need for it. The conditions were safe, I was in perfect control, and no other car was near me.

What do you say when your spouse asks you to list all her faults?

COP: Is that for you to judge?
JL: Who else?
COP: The speed law, the highway patrol and me! You got a problem with that?
JL: [with a miserable sigh] Yes.
WIFE: *Why are you talking like an idiot!*
JL: Because I'm an honest man.
WIFE: You broke the law.
JL: I know that.
WIFE: Then why in heaven's name are you arguing?
JL: I'm not arguing, just giving my truthful opinion.
COP: You're not showing up on the prior-felony screen.
JL: I'm just an honest man.
COP: What are you trying to pull, buddy?
JL: I'm wondering if truth pays.
COP: Oh, it does, it does . . .

And sure enough, after five long hours at a nearby courthouse, full of delay and gratuitous insult, the truth was directed to pay $500.

Following which, the local magistrate asked me what I was thinking, and I happened to be wondering just what bank account the fines went into. That piece of honest curiosity upped the payment.

As we were released into the free world of Traffic-trap, Connecticut, I was approached on the sidewalk by the type of authoritative panhandler who wouldn't dream of bothering to lie to you. "You have any change?" he growled at me.

"Yes," I said. I was able to tell the truth and walk away with my change jingling in my pocket. It was all I had left.

I continued my truth telling until late on the second night, when I lay, off-guard, reading in bed after a long day of nerve-racking inhibition. My wife suddenly asked, in a musing tone, what I considered her greatest weakness.

I hesitated. "You, my love, are a somewhat irrational person."

I had indeed told the truth (except for the "somewhat"), and to my relief, my wife laughed. Then she blew it.

"What are my other faults?"

"Offhand," I said, "I can't think of any."

We laughed, but I knew that I'd not been truthful.

The last day of truth, spent mostly at my desk, was a fiasco. Some fact-checking simpleton from a magazine of celebrity worship telephoned to confirm a story that a movie star I'd known in the '70s, when I wrote scripts in L.A., used to go one-on-one with me at basketball and beat me. I couldn't care less who beat whom in the distant past, but I knew what would ensue were I to be quoted contradicting the star's, shall we say, fantasy. I lied for expedience, bolstering the already perpetually bolstered ego, not from pride or pleasure but to avoid pain.

Next I got a call from an artist friend who has recently married a viciously humorless professor writing a "major reappraisal" on the use of hidden sadistic imagery in Wordsworth. He phoned to remind me of my promise to dine with them at the Hard Rock Cafe. I knew I could not submit to the falsehood of opinion masquerading as knowledge or the falsehood of noise masquerading as music. I couldn't have brought it off, even back in the days when I thought that there was an advantage to gain from it. So when my friend began to press me for an exact date, I reached down to a cool well of truth within myself and said I would prefer him to drop by my loft, alone, for a quiet cup of coffee. He then told me that I was insulting his wife because I was jealous of him and attracted to her. When I mildly but firmly disagreed, he asked me if I had not thought, for all these years, that his paintings were overrated and overpriced.

Later I tried to think how I might have answered that question truthfully. It would have taken a delicate discrimination between most of his work and some of it, but the result would have been the same. The question was the wrong question, susceptible of no useful answer, designed (intentionally or not) to end our friendship. Which it did.

Some people you just can't tell the truth to.

The truth is, people who can live without lies turn out to be people I don't know very well. Lies begin quarrels, but they also settle them. Without lies, storytellers cannot get at the truth. Kindly lies nurture true love, like the love between a trusting parent and a trusting child, each of whom is destined to lie to the other many times. Nevertheless, we know in the gut that those who lie without scruple have gone too far. In our own lies most of us search for truths we can hold to and are devastated should someone we love prove morally untrue. To have no truth at all is not a romantic stance but an empty pose; it means never having had a connection to the world that one can depend on.

You may think I'm wandering here to cover my miserable failure at the three-day truth test. So let's get it over with: My failure was massive and probably hopeless, and sprinkled with more lies, large and small, helpful and hurtful, intentional and accidental, than I have room to set down here, even if you could trust what I say. I began the experiment thinking myself one of nature's own truth tellers and came out a confirmed liar. Like Huck Finn in the book of the same name, I can't go free and easy down my own particular river without lying to the people on the banks who believe in slavery and who would stop me if they knew the freedom I enjoyed. But that's grandiose, isn't it, giving myself all the best of it? The truth is, I lie also for bad reasons or for no good reason, and I'm told there are times I don't even notice my lying. The only credit I might claim from this experiment is that when I concentrate, whether at the time or later, I seem to know when I am telling the truth and when I am lying.

But by the nature of our species, this can't be entirely sure, either for me or for you, dear reader. My guess is that you, too, incur your own difficulties and delights in this area. Am I way off base? Tell me the truth . . . if you feel like it, if you're up to it, and if you think we both can take it. ■

Jeremy Larner is the author of many books, screenplays and poems, including the best-seller Drive, He Said. *He won an Academy Award for best original screenplay for* The Candidate *(1972).*

HAVE MORE MORAL IMAGINATION!

Nobel Peace Prize winner Elie Wiesel sounds a cry for leadership that can bring victories of the soul and spirit.

By Harry Stein

The Background. When Elie Wiesel was awarded the Nobel Peace Prize in 1986, the chairman of the Nobel committee called him "one of the most important spiritual leaders and guides in an age when violence, repression and racism continue to challenge the world. . . . His message is one of peace, atonement and human dignity." In a characteristic response, Wiesel (pictured at right)) noted simply that the honor would perhaps allow him to "speak louder" and "reach more people."

Wiesel continues to speak out. In 1993, at the dedication of the new United States Holocaust Memorial Museum in Washington, D.C., Wiesel decried the brutal "ethnic cleansing" taking place in the former Yugoslavia. "We cannot tolerate the excruciating sights of this old new war," he said. Then he turned to confront the man standing by his side. "Mr. President," he told Bill Clinton, "this bloodshed must be stopped. It will not stop unless we stop it."

Wiesel knows all about the horrors of genocide, having

barely survived the Holocaust a half century ago. Born in 1928 in the northern Romanian town of Sighet, he was encouraged to become a rabbi by his mother, herself the daughter of a respected Hasidic scholar. But then pro-Axis Hungary annexed Sighet and the surrounding territories in 1940, and four years later Hitler implemented his "final solution to the Jewish question" in the area. Along with the 15,000 other Jews in his town and more than 400,000 throughout the country, 16-year-old Wiesel was deported to a concentration camp.

Over the next year, as a prisoner in Birkenau, Auschwitz, Buna and Buchenwald, he experienced the savage reality of the camps. He lost his mother and a sister to the ovens. He saw his father starving. Indeed, that time was so unspeakably horrifying that after his liberation, Wiesel made a vow to remain silent on the subject for 10 years.

Settling in France at the war's end, he studied literature, philosophy and psychology at the Sorbonne and embarked on a career as a journalist. Even then, Wiesel knew he had a profound responsibility to bear witness. The result was his first memoir, *Night*, published in France in 1958 and in the United States in 1960 (where he became a citizen in 1963). A book based on his experiences in the camps, it announced the arrival of a literary voice of immense power.

Over the years that followed, as he produced dozens of works of both fiction and nonfiction, that reputation continued to grow. But above all, it was his growing stature as a moral authority that increasingly seized the world's attention. For not only in his writing but on the lecture circuit and later in the classroom, Wiesel saw his role as resisting institutionalized evil and indifference wherever it arose. In recent years he has been as active against apartheid in South Africa as on behalf of Jews in the former Soviet Union; as committed to the fight against hunger and disease as to overcoming intolerance based on religion.

It is not enough, as Wiesel puts it, simply to dwell on the tragedy of the past: "We must go into the despair and go beyond it, by working and doing for somebody else, by using it for something else." But as he notes below, the first step to learning from the past is remembering it.

The Interview.

The underlying theme of my life's work is a commitment to memory. When I'm asked how I hope I'll be remembered 50 and 100 years from now, my answer is very simple: as someone who tried not to forget.

More than anything else, it is the way we talk about the past that matters. We mustn't seek to exploit it, using it simply to make whatever point we happen to want made. It must be respected, celebrated, explored on its own terms. When memory is respected, entering its gates leads us to other gates and other memories, and on and on in a true quest after our best selves.

The past is there for the same purpose as culture itself: to sensitize us. Because I read Shakespeare in a certain way, I'm sensitive to other people's pain. To cruelty. To jealousy. To avarice. To inequity. To the vast complexity of human feeling, to our frailties and the inherent contradictions in our lives. *Romeo and Juliet* is a story not only about love but about hatred; it's not just about bitterness but tenderness. Reading it, one cannot but care more about others.

Many people do not realize that I actually speak very little about the Holocaust. The subject is so sensitive that I'm constantly aware of the possibility of its being trivialized. Yes, of course, I carry within me the deep conviction that it is the most important subject; indeed, one thinks of the world in terms of Before and After—Before Auschwitz and After Auschwitz. I saw the SS at work. Their victims were my friends, my family, my people. Yet my task is not only to recapitulate that horror but to remember, to attach myself to the memory of all those who preceded me and speak for what they represented. I do not want the memory of preceding Jewish generations, whether in the fifteenth century or the first, to be wiped out. For if it is, then the Nazis will have succeeded.

Still, I will confess that in the contemporary world, the effort to honor the past often seems like an uphill battle. I feel it day after day, occasionally to the point that I'm threatened with paralysis. Why do it? I find myself wondering. Why add my words to all the other words that go unheeded? I look around me, and all I see is words being abused and misused, their content defiled.

That is among the unspoken tragedies of our age. Our century is the noisiest in human history. Never before has there been a time of such tumult—so many people talking, so much shouting—with so little being said and so little inclination to listen. In the midst of all the noise, it is a time of unprecedented isolation. You see people on the streets with their headphones on—to me, that's the ultimate. They don't even want to hear anything else. Can you imagine? I sometimes conjure up a nightmare vision of others calling to them for help—or warning them of danger to themselves—and their being oblivious. Such isolation becomes not only a sin but a punishment.

I'm certainly no media basher; I abhor censorship. But with its endless violence and foolishness, the media only add to the din—and also to the wildly distorted view of priorities. Over and over, the idea is put forth that if you are more violent—if you possess the greater physical strength—you will win. But that isn't the way it really is. There are victories of the soul and spirit. Sometimes, even if you lose, you win. Remember Bull Connor, the racist police chief in Alabama? He thought he won when he set the dogs on the civil rights demonstrators and threw them in jail. He didn't even know the definition of winning. In a different sense, often I'm afraid, neither do we.

Many who criticize democracy don't have a real conception of the alternative.

What we must struggle against, above all, is isolation, one from another, for by now we ought to have learned that its consequences are tragic. During the war, it would have been enough for a few people in the right places to have said no, and there would have been no Holocaust. Literally with a few words, Churchill or Roosevelt could have ordered the Allies to bomb the rail lines to the camps and thus save innumerable lives. If they had just felt that basic human connection. If they had simply proclaimed, "These people are human beings, and we will not stand for their murder!"

The fact that they failed to do so changed everything. It unleashed an entirely new magnitude of evil upon humankind, and it is affecting us still. It has become part of the air we breathe. A few years ago, when the Berlin Wall came down and communism collapsed, who could have believed the utter chaos that would follow? You go to Yugoslavia, and people tell you maybe it was better under Tito. In Russia you hear people say they'd prefer a "benevolent" Soviet leader. Anti-Semitism in Hungary is rampant. In Poland also.

And then there's Germany: That there, of all places, we would see a reemergence of racist violence is almost more than the imagination can grasp! In that place, every tree, every building, every cloud, every wall, every person in the street, ought to testify to the outcome of ethnic hatred.

As you can imagine, I am not well regarded in that part of the world because I try to remind them of their special responsibility.

Several years ago I gave a speech in Vienna—in fact, from the very balcony where the last speaker had been Hitler. I said, "I'm not convinced that history has a sense of justice, but it surely has a sense of humor. The previous speaker from this balcony was Adolf Hitler. His crowd was much larger—and far more enthusiastic than you."

Will Germany find its way to true democracy? I have faith in its youth. Many young Germans seek to cope with their nation's past. That is encouraging.

As for Eastern Europe, the situation there is disturbing. There are those who say the reason we're witnessing brutal upheavals in Yugoslavia, Georgia and elsewhere has to do with the nature of democracy itself, with its inherent instability.

I say most of those who criticize democracy just don't have any real conception of the alternative. Culture, memory itself, is a condition of freedom. Under totalitarianism, you have only pseudoculture: The entire country wears headphones, hearing only one voice. In a dictatorship, it is total isolation—intellectual, cultural, moral.

Yes, in a democracy there is conflict and strife. But of conflict is born vibrancy. You can't even make a decent play without conflict; all you'll have is a sermon.

One great problem today is a lack of moral direction. Even in America, there exists not one moral authority with influence over those who make the crucial decisions; someone with the kind of power that Albert Einstein once had, or even Edward R. Murrow.

My constant frustration is seeing vast pain and suffering, and knowing how readily it might be alleviated if only those in power would act. The allies sent more than 600,000 soldiers to the Persian Gulf. In Yugoslavia, all it would have taken is the major nations getting together to say "Stop it!" It would have changed everything. And what an example for young people!

I don't know—I don't like to accuse people who live their lives in public of being immoral. More often it's just a lack of imagination—moral imagination. I truly don't think they understand the yearning for morality among average people. Immediately after the Gulf War, when he had 80 percent support, why couldn't George Bush have announced, "We won a war, now let's start another against fanaticism, homelessness and bigotry." Can you imagine if he'd done that? Aside from everything else, he'd have saved his own political future.

Part of what leadership should be is finding new ways to look at the world.

But one keeps hoping. Imagine an assemblage at the White House of our most important spiritual and intellectual leaders—100 people for three days, with a mandate to reevaluate our society, our nation, the world. That's part of what leadership should be, finding new ways to look at the world.

For I truly do believe, as we come to the end of the century and the millennium, that we are nearing a historic turning point. Silent voices are saying, "Enough of the 20th century, let's start anew!" Millions of well-intentioned people feel it, too. "Don't burden us with the past," they say. "Give us a chance to start off fresh in a new century."

Already we see a concerted effort to eradicate the most documented tragedy in history. During my own Nobel ceremony, demonstrators from all over Europe were marching outside the hall, shouting that the Holocaust never occurred. These morally perturbed people have tremendous amounts of money and great devotion to their cause. If they can say this now, how much stronger will their voices be in coming years?

Fewer and fewer survivors remain to offer living proof to the contrary. Soon there will be none left at all. Then, then, will come the greatest test yet of both our memory and our moral will. ■

Harry Stein is author of Ethics and Other Liabilities, The Major Bullet *and* Infinity's Child *(Delacorte), and* Hooplah *(Dell).*

US? WEAK CONSUMERS?

You've gotta be kidding!

By Marcia Seligson

I can't speak for you, of course, but I loathe being considered irrelevant, insignificant and extraneous. I mention this because not long ago the *New York Times* ran a piece entitled "3 Networks Frantically Seek Fountain of Youth and Profits," the general theme of which was that, with the exception of CBS, the television networks are utterly uninterested in attracting, keeping or otherwise paying any attention to older viewers. ABC executives boldly confessed that they "do not sell one single dollar of advertising based on reaching viewers over the age of 49." Indeed, as the 45-year-old founding president of the Fox Broadcasting Company sniped, "We don't really need anyone over 50 years of age to succeed with our business plan." (He didn't return my four telephone calls, so I assume he has no need of journalists over 50, either.)

Well. These sentiments from the network giants betray some mind-numbing truths, not the least of which is that the sole and entire purpose of television is the selling of painkillers and toothpaste. The "vision thing" is not, as you might have assumed, about entertaining, educating, informing or provoking thought —and hawking diet soda to pay for these noble goals. On the contrary, I now begin to understand that television's only *raison d'être* is to be the vehicle for the marketing of diet soda. A network exec, who insisted on anonymity as adamantly as if he were confessing to Iraqgate, told me that "advertisers don't care about viewers, only consumers." And the masterminds believe that we over 50 are not valuable consumers/viewers to court in that single-minded mission.

Why not, for goodness' sake? Mean net worth is highest between ages 55 and 64 —$292,500 as contrasted with $148,300 in the 35–44 age group. Mean income in the 45–54 group is the highest of all ages. Only one out of every four Americans is over 50, but we control half of America's buying power as well as three-quarters of the country's assets. We represent $150 billion in yearly discretionary income. We are not, as the saying goes, chopped liver.

We also shop till we drop, if I am the slightest indication of American midlife buyers— I who consider a day spent at the Secaucus, New Jersey, factory-outlet stores to be as satisfying, probably as thrilling, as sex and certainly more long-lasting.

A friend invited me a while back to her house, where somebody was having a sort of Tupperware party—only instead of plastic containers, cashmere wonders from the Mideast were being sold. My friend, who is given to neither personal excess nor great wealth, sprang for three identical sweater-and-pants outfits in different colors. "Joyce," I gasped, astonished at her extravagance. "Forgive me, but do you really need all three of these?" She snarled at me uncharacteristically. "What does need have to do with it?" she protested. "We're talking greed." Eat your heart out, Mr. Fox Broadcasting. We have more money, time and worldly taste than your yuppy puppies.

Of all the mean-spirited abuses in the *New York Times* article, perhaps the deepest cut was the following curt explanation for the broadcasters' indifference to us: "What is behind this emphasis on youth is the conviction of advertising executives that only younger people are willing to try new products." I see. Once we have decided to purchase Tide or Tylenol or Oreos at a young age, we will never alter our habits, we will buy those brands forever, so why bother with us. We are terrified of new paper towels. "This is not some senior-citizen activist issue," said the young, defensive senior VP of research for ABC, Alan Wurtzel. "This is purely a marketing issue."

Aha. So we are stodgy, inflexible, "set in our ways" (as my mother used to say of any guy who was 35 and still unmarried). We are afraid of change, frightened of new experiences, rigid in our tastes and unwilling to experiment. That is the message behind this deadly invalidation. You cannot tell that to me. I am a person who has altered my hair color four times in the past six months, so please do not tell me about fearing change.

Since the age of 49—at which I became inconsequential to the world of broadcastingadvertising, which I guess is one word—I have changed my career, from being a full-time journalist to being a half-time journalist, half-time business entrepreneur; I have renovated my house, acquired a weekend retreat on the Venice, California, beach, sold my house, and in the process of all this change have bought seven couches; I have become an obsessed bike rider and taken six bike trips to different parts of Europe. It would not be too strong a statement to say that I live for change.

I like to vary the route I drive home and have been known to go blocks out of the way just to see some fresh sights. Seeing fresh sights seems to me to be one of the keys to staying jubilant, or at least curious, about life. I am not one of those people who go back to the same hotel on the same Hawaiian island at the same time every year because it's comfortable and familiar, when just beyond are all those mysterious Pacific islands. Well, you could argue that a palm tree is a palm tree, and isn't it lovely to have the waiter remember you from last year and always know precisely how you want your lamb chops cooked. But, at least for me, it's a yawn.

I am so ever-shifting that my husband, Tom, who is not quite 50 and therefore is more relevant than I, considers himself fortunate that I'm not compelled toward variety in the marriage department, turning him in for a new, better and different model. I do, however, consistently think about how to amuse us so life stays cheery. Occasionally, I will drag the poor guy to a flamenco nightclub for the 2 A.M. show.

Also, please do not ever accuse me of being a tiresome, predictable consumer. I was the first on my block to purchase an entire case of fat-free taco chips, when they were so new I had to get them shipped directly from the company in Austin, Texas. I also sprang for a case of oil-free, spicy pinto bean dip. (Do you have any idea how long it takes to use up a case of bean dip?) I was the one who turned my local health-food emporium on to these yummies, and now they're all over Los Angeles. Eat your heart out, Mr. Toothpaste. I could have done that for you, too.

Where did the myth come from, that as you get older you get more narrow-minded and intractable? When I was in my 20s, I had staunchly held opinions about everything—I mean every single thing—and I was right about all of them. I clung to my opinions like fingernails grasping onto a cliff edge for survival. I would say things like "I never buy anything made in Greece" or "I never eat Hungarian food" (something about the politics, I recall) or "Only nerds use Breck shampoo." I was extremely worried about what was hip and cool, and that determined most of my choices. I was not what you would call an openhearted or desirable consumer. But today I am.

Now, Tom is the ultimate dream of anybody who's selling anything. He is always looking for the perfect fill-in-the-blank. When we were dating, 12 years ago, he kept appearing with different little personal cassette players. I counted them one day, and there were over a dozen. To my eye, they did exactly the same thing, and why on earth did he need all of them, and, in fact, why did he continue to purchase more? He tried in vain to explain the distinctions of each to me until I was completely confused and utterly bored.

When I was in my 20s, what was hip determined my buying choices.

The truth is, my husband is an insatiable consumer, particularly—but not exclusively—of high-tech gadgets. He is the light in the life of Sony, NEC and Panasonic and always will be despite his inevitable march into the future. And he's clearly not alone in his excesses. Mr. Network, you are a jerk if you don't recognize the "Tom factor" in your aging viewers. I say "Mr." Network because if women ran that world, they would intuitively grasp that certain fires will never leave the belly.

Now hear this: You think I'm not willing to try new products, eh? Yes, I've used the same dishwasher detergent for years, but it has nothing to do with rigidity or even what they call Brand Loyalty. I use all the samples that appear periodically in my mailbox, and they are as fine with me as my good old standby. The germane factor here is that I don't care much about the whole subject, and I'm sure one brand is about the same as another, and I don't intend to waste a nanosecond thinking about it. Perhaps it's up to the geniuses who invent, package and market new dishwasher soap to be clever and creative enough to convince me to change brands. If I don't, it's your fault for producing uninspiring, tedious advertising and an undistinguishable product—not mine for being 50.

One final message to the network programmers who would so readily discard me: I'm mad as hell and I'm not going to watch *Doogie Howser* anymore. Furthermore, I'm going to do what all the kids do: When your commercials come on, I'm switching to MTV. Ha!

Marcia Seligson is a journalist and founder and producing artistic director of a new theater in Los Angeles.

Are You a Compulsive Shopper?

By Myrna Lewis

Do you frequently have a strong and irresistible urge to go shopping, even if it means spending more money than you actually have? If so, you may have a problem.

"Compulsive shopping usually develops earlier in life," explains Donald W. Black, M.D., associate professor of psychiatry at the University of Iowa College of Medicine, "but unlike some disorders, this one doesn't decrease with age. Men and women in their 60s and 70s can still be caught up in it."

For such people, Black notes, shopping begins as something exciting and fun—and then guilt sets in. "Shoppers often know they don't need an item but buy it anyway. Many end up stowing it away, unopened, in the closet with their many other past purchases. Over time, buying things may become more and more of a focus. If the problem is serious enough, it can cause financial crises, marital troubles—and even lead to check forgery and other legal difficulties."

If you worry that your buying habits may be getting out of hand, take our compulsive-shopping quiz. A scoring guide appears at right, along with Black's suggestions for handling the problem.

Indicate how often you do the following by marking the appropriate spaces with an X:

	VERY OFTEN	OFTEN	SOMETIMES	RARELY	NEVER
1. I buy things even when I know I can't afford them.					
2. I write checks when I don't have money in the bank to cover them.					
3. If I have any extra money after paying all my bills, I feel I have to spend it.					
4. I make only minimum payments on my credit cards.					
5. I feel anxious on the days I don't go shopping.					
6. I buy things to make myself feel better.					
7. I feel I have to hide my spending habits from other people.					

Scoring

For each answer of *Very Often*, score 5 points; *Often* equals 4; *Sometimes,* 3; *Rarely,* 2; and *Never,* 1. Add up your points. Scores between 7 and 21 indicate that your shopping habits are probably not of the compulsive kind. Totals over 21 should be considered a red flag, and scores between 28 and 35 put you in the danger zone.

"Fortunately, most compulsive shoppers can be helped by simple interventions geared to change the behavior," says Black. "I tell my clients to (1) go shopping with a friend or family member—a 'witness' whose presence is a deterrent to overspending; (2) leave the culprits at home—if you tend to write checks or use credit cards when you shop, don't take them along; and (3) remember that when you omit shopping from your life, you will be left with a big void. The challenge is to find something to fill that void, an activity that gives you as much satisfaction as your shopping habit once did. If these ploys don't work, professional counseling might be called for."

Quiz adapted from a compulsive-buying scale originally developed by Ronald J. Faber and Thomas C. O'Guinn and published in the Journal of Consumer Research.

The venerable former senator J. William Fulbright wishes Americans

USED THEIR BRAINS MORE!

By Harry Stein

The Background. Few figures of the Vietnam era aroused greater passion than J. William Fulbright, who served as Democratic senator from Arkansas from 1945 to 1974. To supporters of the war, the chairman of the Foreign Relations Committee was the ultimate turncoat, a onetime loyalist who became the sharpest thorn in President Lyndon B. Johnson's side. But for many still imbued with the idealism of the Kennedy years, he represented the real light at the end of the tunnel—the possibility that, in spite of everything, the United States government could be as open, generous and humane in practice as it was in theory.

By the time Fulbright (right) was elected to the Senate at age 39, he had already compiled a remarkable résumé: football star and student-body president at the University of Arkansas; Rhodes scholar; corporation CEO; professor of law; president of the University of Arkansas; congressman. But it is the 30 years that followed, from the closing days of World War II through the war in Vietnam, for which he is remembered. "There is no one else," columnist Walter Lippmann wrote at the height of Fulbright's Senate influence, "so powerful and so wise."

Fulbright's style, an odd mix of the professorial and the folksy, belied the hostility he sometimes caused. Following a Republican sweep of both houses of Congress in 1946, the junior senator semi-seriously suggested that President Truman follow the example of a former British prime minister who stepped aside in favor of an opposition leader. Truman was not amused. Noting that Fulbright had studied in England as a Rhodes scholar, he described him as "an overeducated Oxford S.O.B."

A few years later Fulbright became the first senator to

publicly attack Senator Joseph McCarthy and his methods. In the atmosphere of fear and repression, Fulbright was risking not only his political life but his physical safety.

It was his break with Lyndon Johnson over Vietnam that proved most fateful, both politically and personally. A longtime LBJ ally, Fulbright had introduced the 1964 Tonkin Gulf Resolution (giving the president authority to take military action without explicit congressional authority), which Johnson subsequently used to justify his dramatic expansion of the war. Less than six months later, Fulbright's questioning of Vietnam policy established him as the preeminent inside-Washington critic of the war. The damage was instant and irreparable. He provoked a backlash more powerful than any he'd known. It would lead to his defeat at the polls and his retirement from politics.

At 87, looking back on his public career, he preferred to dwell on the constructive legislation in which he had a hand—most notably, the Fulbright Act, a landmark program of academic exchange between nations. He remained acutely aware of a problem that the exchange program was in part intended to address—what he saw as an American tendency, individually and as a people, toward self-satisfied provincialism. Fulbright gave his views on such concerns during our conversation in his Washington law office, three years before his death.

The Interview.

We've all heard moaning and groaning in recent years about how much we Americans don't know. Hardly a day goes by that we don't run across some new statistic on the failure of our schools to teach math and science, or how many of our kids can't locate France or Russia on a globe—never mind speak French or Russian; how even our diplomats and top businesspeople tend to reflect our cultural blindness. Well, it's all too true, of course. And maybe it's finally begun to sink in how great an impact all of this is having on our ability to compete in the world.

But even that won't get to the root of the problem, which is that most of us just don't care how little we know. We're not embarrassed about it, and no one is embarrassed for us. Even if we hear talk about intellectual laziness or muddy thinking or cultural inferiority, it seems like someone else's problem. All of us, myself included, have the tendency to look at it that way. Which is precisely what makes such an attitude so insidious. I can tell you that this has been responsible for all the great mistakes I made in public life.

To put it plainly: There is nothing more important in life than knowing what you know—not only because it can prevent you from being foolish, nor even because it breeds humility. Knowledge simply makes life richer. There's so much out there that should pique our curiosity—about how people do things in other places, about our past, about how we ourselves tick. It's idiotic to think that we've got it made because we happen to have been born in this great land. We're not innately superior to anyone, and without the curiosity to look past the TV listings, we're half dead.

More than any other people I'm familiar with, we Americans tend to live entirely in the moment. What happened yesterday doesn't matter. There are good reasons for this: After all, most of our forebears came to this country to escape some awful things, so it's natural that we would regard the traditions we left behind as stodgy. But we've forgotten that there is deep solace in the long view. We're forever bending ourselves out of shape to make some kind of impact now, today—even if it's only noise.

You see that no more clearly than here in Washington, where so many of our worst tendencies thrive in exaggerated form. There's this desperation for attention, regardless of content.

I used to say that our smaller cities and towns were a refuge from the constant struggle in places like Washington. But that's not so much the case anymore. The media have influenced our values to such an extent that all of us must now make a conscious, daily effort to distinguish the meaningful from the trivial.

Just look at all the attention that's been paid lately to the personal lives of politicians.

Bill Clinton was nearly destroyed. I've known Clinton since he was a young man—he did work for the Foreign Relations Committee. And we have in common the fact that we were both Rhodes scholars from Arkansas. What happened to him during his first campaign was just disgraceful.

Yet we concentrate on sensational journalism and pay not the slightest attention to what such people have to say about our economic difficulties or anything else. With this tiny attention span of ours, we seem to be annoyed by the responsibilities of self-government. It's no exaggeration to say that this could lead to the moral deterioration of our democracy.

How serious can you claim to be about your country when you select a man as your leader because he was an attractive movie actor? Don't get me wrong—he's a nice movie actor, and it's not his fault. We're the ones who put him in charge of our country.

It's irrational. Would anyone pick a banker who's never stepped inside a bank before? Would someone choose to be defended by a lawyer who'd never been to law school? Or even go to a restaurant where the chef doesn't know his way around a kitchen?

What I'm saying is that we've got to be more demanding of ourselves. We've got to start placing a higher premium on brains—including our own. We've got to understand how vital it is to never cease trying to explore and grow.

I was lucky enough to have that understanding pounded into me early. My mother was appalled by incuriosity. Still, her learning never made her arrogant—quite the opposite. Though she achieved a great deal in her life—ended up running a newspaper and writing a regular column for it—she often said that she was never without the fear that she didn't know what she was talking about. Which strikes me as a good way of staying on top of things.

"We've been too parochial about our politics and culture," says the late Senator Fulbright.

Not that I grew up much less provincial than most young Americans. I was raised on a farm, and it wasn't until I went to Oxford at 20 that I'd been east of the Mississippi. But when I did, it was an eye-opener. To this day, I regard it as the most important experience of my life. Then, after three years in England, I spent another year in France and Austria—not doing very much, just spending a lot of time in cafés, learning enough French and German to get by.

Yet that, too, proved immensely valuable. Later on, when I was a member of the Senate, it was those experiences that led me to the conclusion that we needed a program to send our students abroad. And, to date, that program has affected more than 180,000 lives.

Of course, now that the Fulbright Scholarships enjoy such general approval, almost no one remembers that it was only through fantastic good luck that in 1945 the program was adopted at all. The fact is, those who would have opposed it were not aware of its existence until it was too late. As proposed, it did not require any outlay of money; it had been placed on a track reserved for noncontroversial legislation and it breezed through the Senate late one afternoon.

But not long afterward, old man [Kenneth] McKellar, the senior senator from Tennessee and chairman of the Appropriations Committee, collared me. "Young man," he said, "that bill that went through here the other day is a great shame. It's a terrible thing to be sending our young boys and girls abroad to be exposed to those foreign 'isms." He was quite adamant about it, and there is no question that he would have stopped it, if he could have.

It was exactly thinking like this that I hoped the Fulbright Scholarship program would counteract. Most of us in

Congress knew a lot more about our states than anything else. In those years, I myself was paying more attention to rice, cotton and cattle prices than to anything that was going on abroad — and if I hadn't had the Rhodes, I probably wouldn't have paid the rest of the world any notice at all. Why notice? After all, we were the seat of power, not them.

I'll never forget the evening in 1956 that I was invited by the Russian ambassador to attend the Washington premiere of the Bolshoi Ballet. This was a big deal, but we, the greatest country in the world, didn't have a space in our capital suitable for ballet. The ballet had to be held in an old movie palace downtown, and it was embarrassing to see that these wonderful dancers had no room in which to dance. Soon after that I launched the legislation that eventually led to the construction of the Kennedy Center.

By then, I'd been living in Washington for more than 10 years, and I'd never noticed this hole in our cultural life.

You get lazy. It's just so easy, living a comfortable life in a narrow world, and you're not even aware of the extent to which it leaves you incomplete. Asleep at the switch.

In a way, I suppose that's what happened to me in the early Vietnam period. By then, I had been chairman of the Foreign Relations Committee for a few years and had received more than my share of attention. I'd been suggested as Secretary of State — not something I wanted, but flattering nonetheless — and considered myself well versed in foreign policy. Yet in the summer of 1964, when Lyndon Johnson claimed we had been ruthlessly attacked in the Tonkin Gulf, I just accepted the administration's version of things. As chair of the committee, I allowed my name to be used as sponsor of the resolution.

There are reasons for that. The president was of my party, and he was in the midst of a campaign against Barry Goldwater, whom at the time I considered dangerous. My actions were natural, assuming that Johnson was telling the truth. Almost no one raised serious questions just then about our policies in Southeast Asia. Even Oregon's Wayne Morse, one of the two senators to oppose the resolution, only spoke against it for an hour — which was nothing for him.

I'm not proud of my actions. At that point, I didn't know a lot about Vietnam — not as much as I should have. I used to go over to the White House, and [Secretary of Defense] Robert McNamara and [Secretary of State] Dean Rusk would be there, and the message was always the same: One of them had just come back from Vietnam, and we were about to win; it was only a matter of time and commitment. I didn't know enough to be skeptical.

It wasn't till the following year, when my committee began holding hearings, that I began to fully grasp that it was a civil war — one that we had no business getting involved in. I had been thinking of not liking the idea of a big country imposing its will on a smaller one. Maybe it's because I'm from Arkansas and grew up with the idea of the Yankees imposing themselves on Southerners. Still, by the time I realized what the war in Vietnam was really about, the damage had been done.

I'll tell you something else: I wasn't the only one who stumbled into it with blinders on. Poor Lyndon — he didn't know anything about it.

Before our split over the war, we had been friends. I understood him — which is why I have never resented him, as so many others have come to. To my mind, his tragedy was the same as the country's. He was bighearted yet parochial. I don't think he'd ever been out of Texas until he came up to Washington. Here was a man who yearned to do right. He just didn't know enough to identify what right was.

I remember once when he was the Senate Majority Leader. We were in Paris together for an interparliamentary meeting. Aside from official business, he wouldn't leave his hotel. He even asked my wife to go shopping for his family. His discomfort with foreigners was clear; he did not want to meet those French!

I've thought about Lyndon Johnson in Paris many times since. In a sense, that was what got us into Vietnam. ■

TRUST SCIENCE NOT AUTHORITY

Noted astronomer Carl Sagan believed that democracy can thrive only if people think for themselves.

By Claudia Dreifus

The Background. There may be billions and billions of stars out in the universe, but when it comes to science teachers, America had a homegrown star in Carl Sagan (1934–96). In addition to his renown as a television personality, he was the author of more than 30 books, most recently *The Demon-Haunted World: Science as a Candle in the Dark* (Random House).

Sagan first garnered public attention in 1977 when he wrote *The Dragons of Eden: Speculations on the Evolution of Human Intelligence.* The book won a Pulitzer Prize and was a best-seller. Then Johnny Carson invited him to talk about the wonders of space on *The Tonight Show,* and Sagan became a media supernova.

The public seemed to adore watching this handsome young Cornell University professor enthuse about black holes and quarks. Sagan (right) became so popular that his 1980 *Cosmos* series on PBS drew an estimated 500 million viewers in 60 countries.

Sagan continued to exercise his unique talent for communicating the joys of scientific discovery. In *The Demon-Haunted World,* he argued that science does not just reveal to us the secrets of our universe; its very process—the relentless search for the truth—is a basic tool of democracy.

Science can also prolong life, a fact for which Sagan had a deeply personal appreciation: In 1994 he was diagnosed with a potentially fatal disorder called myelodysplasia, which affects the body's ability to produce healthy blood cells. His determined battle against the disease was a testament to Sagan's personal courage and the miracles of modern medicine.

Meeting with him at his home in upstate New York shortly before his death, it was obvious that Sagan retained his intellectual energy and infectious delight with all things in creation. His dining room was filled with books and drawings and photographs of his wife, Ann, daughter Sasha, 13, and son Sam, 5. As we sipped coffee, we looked out the window to see a noisy flock of geese fly by. "I love the idea that they talk to one another," Sagan said with a smile. "Wonder what they're saying."

The Interview.

I'm interested in the marriage between skepticism and wonder. Either of those two qualities alone won't get you far. You need to be open to all sorts of unusual, unexpected possibilities and at the same time run them through a rigorous, skeptical filter because a lot of appealing ideas are just wrong.

Most of us start out full of wonder. Then we learn from painful experience the need for skepticism. Certainly, that's been my situation.

It wasn't until I got to college that I understood how many belief systems — endorsed by famous scientists, politicians and religious leaders — had been fundamentally wrong: for instance, that we're at the center of the universe; that the universe was made for us; that we are unconnected with other animals; that we see by means of something coming out of the eye and bouncing off things, when, in fact, light bounces off things and comes into the eye. There's a huge list of similar examples. Once you realize this, the necessity of treating skeptically the pronouncements of leaders from all fields becomes very clear.

There's something quintessentially democratic about skepticism because it requires that citizens make their own judgments. And it's quintessentially scientific because arguments from authority are anathema in science; "authorities" make mistakes, too. One mistake is the stripping down of our educational system and the mediocre intellectual attainments expected of students. We're creating credulous citizens to whom it's easier for a political or religious charlatan to sell a bill of goods.

As it is, there's a huge number of television offerings about the supernatural and the paranormal that introduce hardly any tough questions. They don't present an equal number of skeptics to balance the believers in their presentations. The executives at the networks are thinking only about rating points and profits; irresponsible, I think, given the enormous influence of television. And what about publishers who publish books on these subjects without including any serious qualifications? And newspapers that don't preface their astrology columns with a warning, such as "for entertainment only"? These people are all promulgating pseudoscience.

The idea that true science is not a humanity, or that science is inhumane, seems to me very strange — in fact, almost suicidal.

The vast majority of people on Earth owe their very lives to science and technology. Look at the role of antibiotics and the full panoply of modern medicines, especially inoculation. Many of our loved ones would be dead if not for modern medical science. Look at agriculture: Without science and technology, all but about 10 million of us would have nothing to eat.

I have a vivid sense of the role of science in saving lives. My life was saved by a successful bone-marrow transplant. I'm one of the oldest persons to undergo such a procedure. It didn't exist 20 years ago. Many of the subsidiary medications I've taken and procedures I've undergone are only 5 or 10 years old.

Of course, scientists and physicians can make mistakes. To make sure that the advice you have been given is the best, you need to comparison-shop, to ask a number of experts and see if they agree with one another. That's a component of the scientific method.

There is a danger in thinking that understanding all the medical details is tantamount to controlling the disease. It is not. After a while, I decided that when the general direction was clear, I needed to ease up, let the physicians do what they thought best, ask a few key questions and not obsess over the details.

There's no question that a serious illness is a character-building experience. Your sense of the preciousness of life is enormously underscored, as is your sense of concern and compassion for others, of how vulnerable we humans are and of how capricious fate is. My illness enhanced my love and appreciation for my wife, Annie, who was amazing. We picked up and moved to Seattle for six months so I could get the medical care I needed. She did that with good cheer. And for two young children, that's a big change. They were wonderful.

Close relatives came and stayed with us. It was great getting together with the family. I received the bone-marrow transplant from my sister, who turned out to be a perfect match. If that weren't the case, my chances of survival would have been much less. I was very lucky.

I didn't have any religious experiences during this period, but many religious people prayed for me. I know that on Easter Sunday, 1995, 5,000 people at the Cathedral of St. John the Divine in New York City prayed for me. I was touched by that. A Hindu priest told me that he and his followers have been praying for me on the banks of the Ganges. So did an Islamic leader and countless Christians and Jews. There's something moving about all this compassion and good will. I wouldn't fight the contention that maybe these prayers helped me get better—the brain and the emotions have a powerful influence on the body. But it was scientific knowledge and the love of my family that saved my life.

"Studying other worlds helps us protect this one," says Sagan.

Facing a serious illness can be a profound, transforming experience, but studying the cosmos has also given me a sense of perspective. Studying other worlds gives deep insights into our own—especially what dumb things not to do.

If you study Venus, you find a surface temperature of 900° F that is due to a carbon-dioxide-based greenhouse effect. This provides an important cautionary tale for those of us who argue against pouring huge amounts of carbon dioxide into our atmosphere. It argues against the reactionaries who say that global warming is an invention of liberal college professors designed to embarrass industry.

Likewise, Mars is a planet with vast ozone depletion, where ultraviolet light from the sun is pouring down unimpeded. When you look at that ground, you see an antiseptic surface fried by ultraviolet light. This warns those who are still busy depleting our ozone layer, who still say that chlorofluorocarbons are not a problem.

Those are two examples where studying other worlds helps us protect this one. Generally, I would say that in studying the cosmos, I feel an increasing sense of our responsibility to leave a world better than the one we were given. We're far from doing that. The world is in much more fragile and dangerous shape now than it was 25 or 50 years ago.

I've spent a lot of time fighting the American and Russian nuclear-arms buildup, nuclear-weapons testing and the "Star Wars" program. I did it because I had some relevant expertise. But I also did so because, if the worst happens, I want to have an answer for my children and grandchildren if they ask me, "What did you do to try and prevent it?"

The older I get, the more profound I think is my responsibility to the young. They are an aperture into the future. ■

Claudia Dreifus is a contributing writer to the New York Times Sunday Magazine.

Signs Of the Times

By Erica Lansky

The boomers have shaped our culture in many ways. Countless trends and fads have come and gone, subject to this generation's whims . . . and some seem here to stay. Blame the boomers for Barbie. Their kids can take responsibility for Barney. *New Choices* compiled the following list of pop-culture landmarks, then and now. Is this progress, you may well ask? In some cases, even the boomers look back with nostalgia.

THEN	NOW
Love Story	***The Bridges of Madison County***
Peyton Place	***Melrose Place***
drive-in movies	**Blockbuster videos**
Dr. Kildare	***ER***
Cary Grant	**Hugh Grant**
game shows	**talk shows**
surfing	**surfing the NET**
G.I. Joe	**Power Rangers**
Mary Tyler Moore	**Demi Moore**
Twiggy	**Kate Moss**
James Stewart	**Tom Hanks**
Snoopy	**Snoop Doggy Dogg**
I Love Lucy	***Roseanne***
mod	**grunge**
Snap! Crackle! Pop!	**Snapple**
Car 54, Where Are You?	***NYPD Blue***
going braless	**the Wonderbra**
John Wayne	**John Wayne Bobbitt**
space travel	**cyberspace**
roller skates	**Rollerblades**
Julia Child	**Martha Stewart**
The Beverly Hillbillies	***Beverly Hills 90210***
fallout shelters	**homeless shelters**
the Cold War	**global warming**
long-distance calls	**e-mail**
Miltown	**Prozac**
Edward R. Murrow	**Geraldo Rivera**
Playtex 18-Hour Girdle	**liposuction**
love beads	**love handles**
GE College Bowl	***Dumb and Dumber***
Vitalis	**minoxidil**
Alice's Restaurant	**Hard Rock Cafe**
Star Trek	***Star Trek: The Next Generation***
Sonny and Cher	**Cher**
The Graduate	***Forrest Gump***
"Plastics."	**"Life is like a box of chocolates . . ."**
the Pill	**estrogen replacement therapy**
shopping centers	**Mall of America**
black pride	**gay pride**
Candid Camera	***America's Funniest Home Videos***
Jerry Lewis	**Jim Carrey**
VW vans	**minivans**
Mary Poppins	***Mrs. Doubtfire***
Richard Nixon on *Laugh-In*	**Bill Clinton on MTV**
social activism	**political correctness**
Butch Cassidy & the Sundance Kid	***Thelma & Louise***
doves/hawks	**pro-choicers/ anti-abortionists**
Sesame Street	***Barney***
The Flintstones	***The Simpsons***
Barbie	**Barbie**

ABOUT CONTRIBUTORS OF BOXED FEATURES

Eleanor Foa Dienstag writes the "Living Alone" column for *New Choices* magazine and is author of *In Good Company: 125 Years at the Heinz.*

Melody L. Kollath is a Certified Financial Planner (CFP) practitioner, chairman of the board of the Colorado Society of CFPs, and a member of the advisory board for *New Choices* magazine.

Erica Lansky was assistant editor for *New Choices* magazine.

Myrna Lewis, M.S.W., is a psychotherapist, gerontologist and assistant professor at the Mount Sinai School of Medicine in New York, and a contributing editor for *New Choices* magazine.

Deborah Mason is a contributing editor for *New Choices* magazine. She also contributes regularly as a writer for *The New York Times.*

Nissa Simon is senior health editor for *New Choices* magazine.

DATES OF FIRST PUBLICATION

ON AGE AND AGING:
New at Getting Old—3/94; Be Dependable, Live Longer—5/94; So Your Body and Mind Won't Let You Down—3/96; Do You Think Young—or Old?—10/95; Don't Grow Up: Charles Schulz—6/95; How We Deal with Growing Older—12/95; Who Age Better, Men or Women?—9/96; Male Menopause—8/94; Your Thoughts and Longevity—7/94; Sudden Personality Changes—6/94; Women Surge On!—3/94; Crankier or More Tolerant?—4/96; How to Deal with Midlife Regrets—5/95; Ageism—9/96; Age and Boredom—11/94

ON MARRIAGE:
Learning the New Intimacy—4/96; Making Your Intimate Conversations Better—5/94; Be a Better Spouse or Companion—10/95; Trapped in Marriage?—5/95; Top 5 Topics to Discuss Before Remarrying—11/94; A Husband May Not Be Good for Your Health—11/95; Why Women Over 50 Have Affairs—11/94; Sex, Marriage, Self-Image—11/94; To Feel Connected—2/93; Pet Names Can Enhance Your Marriage—9/94

ON PARENTS & CHILDREN:
What Keeps Us from Chaos: Arthur Miller—10/94; Building a Stronger Mother–Daughter Bond—9/96; Inevitable Family Rifts—11/95; The Power of Memories—4/95; How to Communicate Better with Your Adult Children—2/96; Voluntary Associations —12/92; Family-Reunion Jitters—6/96; "Mom and Dad, I'm Gay"—9/94; Grandparenting in the '90s—5/94; How to Be a Better Grandparent—9/96; Overcoming Fear of Grandparenting—3/94; Better Bedtime Stories—9/93; Reinventing the American Grandparent—3/96; Good-bye, Dad . . . and Thanks—4/94

ON FRIENDS & LOVERS:
With You I Am Not Alone—10/92; Ways to Make—and Keep—Friends—7/95; He Was the Perfect Catch, But —9/96; Young Friends Are a Must—7/94; Call Your Old Friends Now—7/95; The Greenpoint Girls—4/93; Are You Too Lonely?—3/96; Singles Dating —3/95; Can Sexuality Be "Used Up?"—7/96; Turning Former Lovers Into Friends—9/95; Seeking Mr. Right—11/93; Six Ways to Update Your Lovemaking—10/95; Friends Forever? Not Always—9/96; Men Need Hugs Too—6/95; When They Had Given Up on Love—9/92

ON WORK & NEW CHALLENGES:
The Truth About After 50—3/96; Confessions of a Boomer—3/96; Meeting the Challenges of Leaving the Workforce—3/96; National Survey: Boomers Happiness Index—2/96; Past 50 and Taking New Risks—9/93; Psyching Yourself for a Job Search—7/96; Just Imagine—7/96; The Single Life: Freedom to Choose —2/96; Changing Channels at 50—3/95; Job Market Hiring Practices—12/93; Get Sly—And Live Better—7/93; New Career at 50?—12/93; Are You Stress-Resistant—12/93

ON VALUES:
Rosy Dreams vs. Harsh Truths—11/92; How Do Your Family Values Measure Up?—4/96; What We Believe—9/92; Do You Make a Difference in Your Community—7/96; More Important Than Sex—11/92; 10 Important Things You Should Know About Sex—11/92; Truth or Consequences—12/93; Have More Moral Imagination: Elie Wiesel—12/93; Us? Weak Consumers?—3/93; Are You a Compulsive Shopper? —2/95; J. William Fulbright Wishes Americans Used Their Brains More! —11/92; Trust Science Not Authority: Carl Sagan—9/96; Signs of the Times—3/96

ART AND PHOTOGRAPHY CREDITS

13 Courtesy Roy Blount, Jr., 14 PhotoDisc, 16 Danuta Jarecka, 21 Douglas Kirkland, 24 Danuta Jarecka, 28 Danuta Jarecka, 31 Carolyn Taylor, 32 Luciana Pampalone, 40 Danuta Jarecka, 43 Danuta Jarecka, 45 PhotoDisc, 47 Danuta Jarecka, 51 Danuta Jarecka, 54 Andrea Baruffi, 57 Carolyn Taylor, 58 Danuta Jarecka, 64 John English, 68 Yousuf Karsh/Woodfin Camp, 71 Comstock, 73 Danuta Jarecka, 76 Danuta Jarecka, 79 Comstock, 80 Red Morgan, 85 Danuta Jarecka, 88 Theo Westenberger/Gamma-Liaison, 93 Courtesy William Kennedy, 95 Comstock, 96 Danuta Jarecka, 100 Danuta Jarecka, 103 Susan Stillman, 105 Michael Foreman, 108 Courtesy Laurence I. Barrett, 112 George Whipple III, 117 Danuta Jarecka, 124 Courtesy Pearl Rosenberg, 128 Trix Rosen, 132 Olivier Martel/Matrix, 135 Danuta Jarecka, 140-143 Michael David Brown, 144 Danuta Jarecka, 148 Robert Hunt, 151 Robert Hunt, 152 NBC News, 154 Alex Bee, 156 Danuta Jarecka, 158 Michael Ventura, 162 Krasner/Trebitz Photography, 167 Teresa Fasolino, 171 Eric Rasmussen, 176 Reuters/Corbis-Bettmann 181 Carolyn Taylor, 183 Carolyn Taylor, 184 UPI/Corbis-Bettmann, 188 Andy Freeberg.